From The Library Of
WILBURN M. POTTER

Battle of Despair

Battle of Despair

Bentonville and the North Carolina Campaign

Robert P. Broadwater

Mercer University Press
Macon, Georgia

ISBN 0-86554-821-8
MUP/H624

1400 Coleman Avenue
Macon, Georgia 31207

First Edition.

∞The paper used in this publication meets the minimum requirements of American National Standard for Information Sciences—Permanence of Paper for Printed Library Materials, ANSI Z39.48-1992.

Library of Congress Cataloging-in-Publication Data

Broadwater, Robert P., 1958-
Battle of despair : Bentonville and the North Carolina campaign / Robert P. Broadwater.-- 1st ed.
p. cm.
Includes bibliographical references and index.
ISBN 0-86554-821-8 (hardback : alk. paper)
1. Bentonville, Battle of, Bentonville, N.C., 1865. 2. North Carolina—History—Civil War, 1861–1865--Campaigns. 3. United States—History—Civil War, 1861–1865—Campaigns. I. Title.
E477.7.B76 2004
973.7'38--dc22

2004003009

This book is dedicated to Dixie. To dreams that make our spirits soar, lost causes that test our souls, and love that endures, no matter what.

Table of Contents

ACKNOWLEDGMENTS

I would like to express my appreciation to a number of people whose assistance, support, and encouragement made the writing of this manuscript possible:

Thanks to Jeffrey D. Wert for all the words of wisdom, and for the encouragement given at precisely the right moment.

Thanks also to John Michael Priest for sharing his knowledge of the writing game and for his support.

To the helpful staffs working in the manuscript sections of the Chicago Public Library, Perkins Library of Duke University, University of Georgia Archives, Illinois State Historical Society, Indiana Historical Society, Iowa State Historical Archives, Library of Congress, Bentley Historical Library of the University of Michigan, Military History Institute at Carlisle Barracks, Minnesota historical Society, Southern Historical Collection of the University of North Carolina, Ohio Historical Society, and the State historical Society of Wisconsin. Your assistance is greatly appreciated.

Special thanks to Nancy Dearing Rossbacher for her editorial work on the manuscript, and for her suggestions and corrections to my all-too-numerous grammatical and structural mistakes. I fear I may have made you work too hard, though I really appreciate all you have done.

General Joseph E. Johnston. Assigned as commander of the newly designated Army of the South, Johnston was charged with stopping the Union army under William T. Sherman. Given the shortages in men and materials that he faced, it is amazing that he came as close as he did to delivering the Union army a serious check at Bentonville.

Major General William T. Sherman. Flushed with victory from his March to the Sea, Sherman seems to have been caught somewhat unaware by Joe Johnston at Bentonville. Sherman's army had met such token resistance thus far in the Carolina Campaign that he may have felt the Confederacy was not able to field an army capable of facing him.

Confederate General Braxton Bragg. He was unable to deliver the Federals a check at the battle of Kinston, and his indecisive actions on the field of Bentonville contributed to the Confederate victory on the first day being less than anticipated.

Major General William T. Sherman and several of his leading officers. Sherman is seated in the middle. Major General Henry W. Slocum, one of the wing commanders, is seated to Sherman's left, and Major General Oliver O. Howard, the other wing commander is standing at Sherman's far right. Photo credit to: Massachusetts Commandery Military Order of the Loyal Legion and the US Army Military History Institute.

Major General Judson Kilpatrick. Sherman's cavalry chief during the campaign. Thoutely saved his reputation.

Confederate General Pierre G.T. Beauregard. With the Army of the South being so overloaded in top generals, Beauregard was assigned to serve as Johnston's second in command.

Contemporary sketch of the battle of Kinston. Note the dense undergrowth around the swamp.

Period artist's depiction of the battle of Kinston. Differs greatly from the contemporary soldier's sketch in that there is little or no undergrowth to be seen.

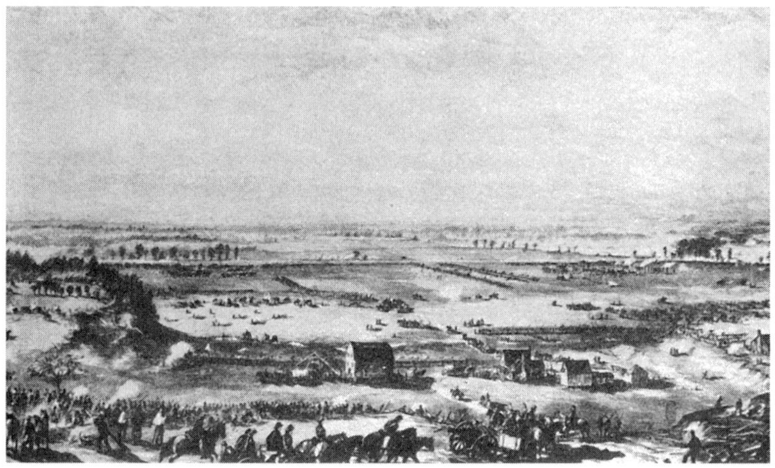

Panoramic view of the battle of Bentonville. Artists conception, showing the Confederate assault in the distance, and the Union reinforcements forming on the ridge.

Confederate President Jefferson Davis. To the very end, Davis refused to accept the realities of the military situation. Though Johnston had been defeated, and had no hope of being able to prevent Sherman's army from going where ever it pleased, Davis refused to contemplate surrendering that army.

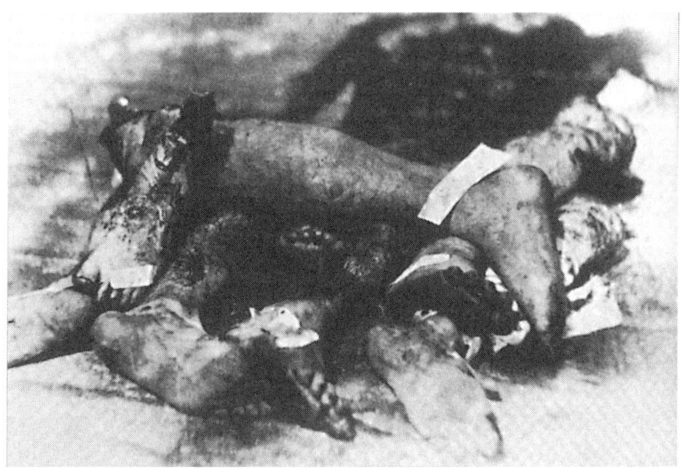

A pile of amputated arms and legs. Scenes like this had become all too common by the end of the war, prompting one Union soldier to look at such a pile after the battle and try to determine whether the legs belonged to cavalrymen or infantrymen, the legs of the infantrymen being much more muscular due to the marching.

Lieutenant General Ulysses S. Grant. His intervention following the receipt of the first draft of Sherman's surrender terms to Johnston probably saved that general's career.

Major General Robert Hoke. His veterans from the Army of Northern Virginia saw bitter fighting as they attempted to sweep the last regiments of Union infantry from the field on the first day's fighting.

Major General Alfred Terry. The Union forces under his, and General Schofield's command, moving in from the coast, provided Sherman with numerical superiority that Johnston could not hope to battle against.

Brigadier General William P. Carlin. His were among the first Federal troops to receive the Confederate onslaught. When his men retreated, Carlin found himself virtually surrounded by Confederates, and barely escaped capture.

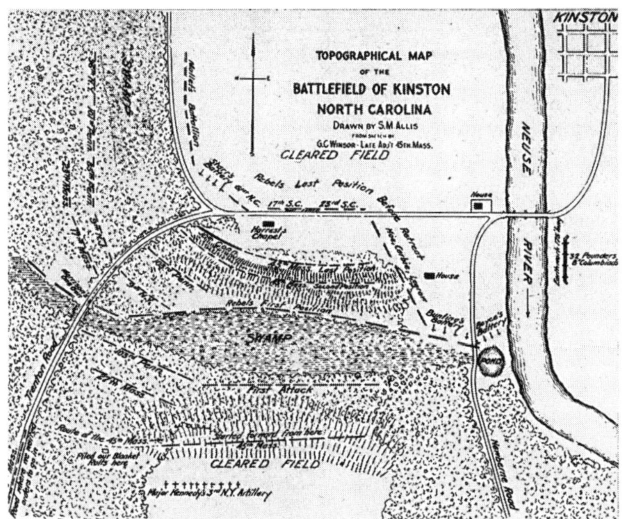

Topographical map of the battle of Kinston drawn by a member of the 45th Massachusetts Infantry, from memory. Note that his drawing shows the area to be heavily forested.

Major General Jefferson C. Davis. His division was roughly handled during the first day, but he used his reserves judiciously, and in the end, they were able to hold their ground against the Confederate attacks.

Brigadier General William B. Hazen. His was the first brigade to come to the assistance of Slocum's wing, following the Confederate attack.

Brigadier General Horatio Van Cleve. The men of his brigade fought from both sides of their hastily constructed works, as they fought off Confederate attacks from both front and rear.

Artist's conception of the surrender negotiations between Sherman and Johnston. Obviously, the artist had never seen Bennett Place. The setting in the meeting room is far too lavish for the simple log cabin occupied by the Bennett's.

The Bennett house, where Sherman and Johnston met to discuss terms for the surrender of the Confederate army. Photo credit to: Massachusetts Commandery Military Order of the Loyal Legion and the US Army Military History Institute.

INTRODUCTION

The battle of Bentonville, North Carolina, has never attained the stature of historical merit enjoyed by other more well-known fields of conflict. In fact, very little has ever been written about the battle. This fact is curious considering the importance it held in determining the outcome of the war and the large number of troops engaged. Casualty figures for both sides place the battle far ahead of engagements that have become familiar to students of the war through the writings and lectures of period historians. Bentonville was the last-gasp effort of the Confederate western armies to stop the relentless drive of General William T. Sherman's legions and prevent the total destruction of the South's last remaining supply sources. The battle served as a picture of the war itself, on a smaller scale, as the Southern leaders counted on the valor of the soldiers in gray to overcome the superior numbers of the Union army. Success and hope for Southern arms were the result of the first day's conflict with a determined stalemate marking the second day. By the third day, the concentration of the Union armies had created a disparity of numbers that compelled the Confederates to withdraw from the field before the army could be captured or destroyed. Indeed, the battle had mirrored the life of the Confederacy. The dash and daring of the early years that had been the architect of numerous victories had given way to the pluck and determination of a country that refused to acknowledge the inevitability of its ultimate defeat.

In terms of size, the Battle of Bentonville was witness to greater losses than Wilson's Creek, Cross Keys, Cedar Mountain, Chickasaw Bayou, Fort Pillow, Kennesaw Mountain, and New Market, to name but a few.[1] The combined forces on the field numbered over 70,000 men and the fighting was as severe as any seen in the war. Why then has this battle been so long neglected by historians? Possibly it is because of the fact that it was a battle between the western armies. Throughout the course of the war, the public mind was focused upon the operations of the Eastern Theater and the battles fought in Virginia, Maryland, and Pennsylvania. With the seat of government for both nations being in this area, the heightened importance attached to the region and military forces operating within it is understandable, and from beginning to end, the public focused on Washington and Richmond. Western battles would momentarily capture the imagination of the civilian population of both sides, but would invariably return to events in the east. Historians largely continued to spotlight the eastern battles in the post-war years, relegating the western theater to a backstage level of importance. Recent years have seen a shift in this thinking, as a new emphasis on the western campaigns has taken hold in the literary offerings of Civil War authors.

Another possible explanation for the lack of information on the battle could be found in the time of its occurrence. As close to the end of the war as it was, it became overshadowed by the momentous events that followed in rapid succession following its conclusion. The battles around Richmond and Petersburg that broke the Confederate lines, compelling the evacuation of the Southern army, the surrender at Appomattox and the assassination of President Lincoln, all served to diminish the importance of the great battle when viewed in comparison with the other great events that followed it. Journalists had many more timely stories to write about as they sensed the end approaching.

Also, the war had exacted such a terrible price by the time of Bentonville that the battle simply may not have stirred the emotions of a public made numb by four years of casualty rolls. Had the battle taken place in the early years of the war, it would have been

---

[1] William H. Price, *The Civil War Centennial Handbook* (Arlington VA: Prince Lithographic Company, 1961) 67.

considered one of the great struggles of the conflict. When viewed after the bloodbaths of Shiloh, Antietam, Gettysburg, and Chickamauga, it was taken by the public to be little more than a large skirmish. This perception was reinforced by the huge losses the Army of the Potomac had sustained from spring 1864 till the conclusion of operations around the Richmond and Petersburg lines. Subsequent to the siege operations around the Confederate capital, Grant's overland campaign had inflicted a greater number of casualties on the two contending armies than the aggregate total of the forces involved in the Battle of Bentonville.[2]

Casualty lists of varying length had become almost a daily feature in newspapers North and South, and the constant exposure to these reminders of the war's tremendous costs served to harden the populace. They were no longer shaken by battles whose losses were calculated in numbers less than tens of thousands, and Bentonville did not produce the carnage necessary to shock the public.

Last, there is the popular notion that Sherman's forces had been left to their own devices once Lieutenant General John Bell Hood embarked on his tragic invasion of Tennessee. Sherman's March to the Sea and the Campaign of the Carolinas that followed were accompanied by few battles and very low casualty rates, and this only added to the emphasis placed on the eastern theater. Sherman seemed to be going where he wanted and doing as he pleased and the whole campaign added to the perception that the real fighting was being done in Virginia and the western army was merely out on a lark. The fact that Sherman had faced little opposition during the march north from Savannah was due to the Confederacy's inability to field a force sufficient to deal with him the absence of Hood's Army of Tennessee. This knowledge was general throughout the North and was the foundation for the belief that the Union Army had not faced much of a challenge from their adversary at Bentonville.

It was felt that the Confederate Army had been made up of "cradle and grave" enlistments: those well under and over standard military age. While there were examples of this in Johnston's army, it

---

[2] Ibid.

accounted for only a small portion of his available force. The vast majority were men who were veteran soldiers, having faced the fire of muskets or warships on many occasions. They were a proud, determined group of men who had proved their valor on battlefields throughout the land. Though their numbers had been painfully diminished through the four long years of war, they were ready, willing, and able to prove that they were still a dangerous opponent, that there was still bite in the old dog. Outmanned and outgunned, they came ever so close to achieving the success that Johnston had envisioned when he drew up plans for the battle. It was a desperate gamble taken by a general out of good options and it nearly worked.

In the following chapters, the story of this last battle of the western armies will unfold through the eyes of the men who fought it. Their words will bring life to this long-neglected chapter of Civil War history and will, it is hoped, create further interest in this important conflict, bringing it on par with some of the more widely-known battles.

It is the story of men whose pride and courage could not be diminished by the overpowering odds they faced; of men whose valor and determination would not allow them to settle for anything short of complete victory. In all, it is the story of the war in miniature and the brave men who saw it through to its final conclusion.

1

THE GATHERING

The winter of 1864–1865 had been a period of continual reverses for the Confederates in the Southern seaboard states. With General John Bell Hood and the Army of Tennessee marching off toward the state that gave them their name for a campaign they hoped would compel Sherman to follow, the seaboard had been left with no organized defense against Union forces. What was left were separated commands, mostly detailed for coastal defense. These units, spread between Charleston, South Carolina, and Wilmington, North Carolina, faced the prospect of being defeated or destroyed in detail if they lay in the path of the Federal juggernaut. The most they could hope to accomplish were limited holding actions as they withdrew from their assigned stations. One by one they fell. Charleston, Savannah, Wilmington, Columbia; all were surrendered to the overpowering force of the men in blue. But this very action of giving up Southern territory directly facilitated that which the Confederacy needed most: a concentration of its available forces. The separated commands were being driven together by the Union march and were actually adding to their numbers with each new retreat. Each step north made by Sherman's men compressed the Confederates together, recreating an army.

With Hood's disaster at Nashville in December 1864 and his subsequent removal from command, the shattered remnants of the Army of Tennessee were falling back toward the seaboard states once more. Though their ranks had been almost decimated in the fighting at Atlanta, Franklin, and Nashville, they were hard fighters who would help to stiffen any resistance against Sherman. Lieutenant General Alexander Peter Stewart commanded the army now and he began resting and refitting his troops, preparatory to the march east.

On 9 February 1865, Robert E. Lee was officially given command of all the Confederate armies as General in Chief. Among his primary concerns was creating a unified command in the Carolinas that could stop Sherman before he was able to link up with General U. S. Grant's Army of the Potomac to overwhelm Lee and his fellow besieged defenders. On 23 February 1865, he took a giant step in that direction with the appointment of General Joseph E. Johnston as commander of the newly designated Army of the South.[1] Lee had already detached all that he could spare from the Army of Northern Virginia in the form of General Robert Hoke's division, and he had sent Wade Hampton south to assume command of the available cavalry. No more could be taken from his lines, already stretched dangerously thin. Johnston was left to gather all the manpower he could find in his department.

Johnston's immediate pools of men consisted of General Braxton Bragg and the men of the Cape Fear defenses, including Hoke's division; Lieutenant General William J. Hardee with the coastal garrisons from Charleston and Savannah; and Lieutenant General Wade Hampton's cavalry, which was compose of the divisions of General Joe Wheeler and General Marion C. Butler. All told, these commands amounted to no more than 18,000 men,[2] and according to General Hampton, "It would scarcely have been possible to disperse a force more effectually than was done in our case."[3] Added to this total would be the 3,900 men from the Army of Tennessee who had already arrived in the Carolinas, and it was hoped that more men from that army could be forwarded as soon as they could be organized. Though this pitifully small remainder bore little resemblance to the grand army that had begun the campaign with full ranks just a year

---

[1] Craig L. Symonds, *Joseph E. Johnston: A Civil War Biography* (New York: W. W. Norton & Co., 1992) 344–47.

[2] Ibid.

[3] Robert Underwood Johnson and Clarence Clough Buel, *Battles and Leaders of the Civil War*, 4 vols. (New York: The Century Company, 1884–1888) 4:701.

ago, Johnston welcomed their coming. He was especially grateful for the leadership the little army possessed. "The value of the latter was much increased by the comparatively great number of distinguished officers serving among them, who had long been the pride and ornament of that army," he later wrote.[4]

In this last confrontation between the western armies, the issue would be decided by men who had faced each other in battle and who had become professional soldiers in the process. General Sherman's army was likewise filled with veterans, with 78 percent of the men in his command having originally enlisted in 1861 or 1862. His proportion of officers was even greater, with 98 percent of the noncommissioned officers and 99 percent of the company level officers having also enlisted during the 1861–1862 period. Many of his men were serving in their second tour of duty, and while the rate of re-enlistment in the Union army was about 6.5 percent Sherman's army realized reenlistment of almost 50 percent.[5]

These were men who were still in the army because they chose to be. The encumbrance of the huge numbers of draftees and bounty men that had so decreased the effectiveness of numbers in the Army of the Potomac was not evident here. The majority of the men under Sherman were fighting for their convictions, not because the government was forcing them to or because of monetary considerations. They exuded a pride that can only come from veteran soldiers who have met the test of battle head on and come away from the experience with the knowledge that they could be trusted to do their duty whenever their commander required it. The March to the Sea had furthered this pride. They had done what no other army had ever attempted, having conducted an entire campaign in enemy country, all the while isolated from supplies or support from their own army. They had lived off of the land, marched and done as they

---

[4] Gen. Joseph E. Johnston, *Narrative of Military Operations Directed During the Late War Between the States by Joseph E. Johnston, General, C.S.A.* (New York: D. Appleton and Co., 1874) 384.

[5] Joseph T. Glatthaar, *The March to the Sea and Beyond: Sherman*'s *Troops in the Savannah and Carolina Campaigns* (New York: New York University Press, 1986) 187.

pleased, and by the time they reached Savannah, the average private in the ranks knew as well as his commanders the magnitude of their accomplishment. The march had been demoralizing to the Confederacy, as no battlefield losses could have been. The South was viewed as being no longer able to defend herself when an enemy army could operate virtually unopposed in the heart of the nation. These Union veterans knew that they had made history by being part of this march, that they would ever be able to point to the event with self-respect.

They were more than battle hardened: they were battle smart. Four years of in the field training had taught them all the lessons of soldiers. They did not need to be led as in the past; rather, they merely needed to be told what was expected of them. Whatever their pre-war vocations had been, they were now professionals in a new occupation, graduates of the school of war.

These men in blue, these hardy, self-reliant souls were largely from the Midwest, where the pioneer spirit thrived. Overcoming adversities was a normal part of everyday life; in fact, it was life. This self-reliance, this ability to persevere through any obstacle, infused a spirit of individualism in the western army that set it apart from the other military forces of the Union.[6] The March to the Sea had only intensified that spirit.

Westerners were known for an ability to adapt to their environment, a sense of resourcefulness in all situations, and the Federal soldiers lived up to this reputation in their campaign through the Carolinas. The elements themselves had seemed to conspire against them in their march north from Savannah, as the incessant winter rains of the South made roads nearly impassable and caused the numerous streams and creeks along their route to spill over their banks. But roads were corduroyed and streams bridged with a rapidity that amazed even the men who were doing the work. The march north was becoming a marvel of military mobility, unequaled in the annals of war.

---

[6] See appendix A.

Though flushed with victory, these old vets fully realized that their opponents were not yet defeated. More fighting would take place and more lives would be lost before they could go home. Thousands tried to assure their survival in the upcoming battles by purchasing repeating rifles for their own use. For the sum of $48, approximately four month's pay, a soldier could arm himself with any one of a variety or repeaters. Among the most popular with the Union soldiers was the Spencer. Its seven-shot magazine provided the owner with a firepower not dreamed of with standard-issue weapons, especially the outdated issues with which the western army had been force to fight much of the war. Until after the fall of Vicksburg, in summer 1863, most of the arms in the western army consisted of early smoothbore patterns, predominantly the Model 1842 Springfield. With the fall of Vicksburg, many Union units were re-equipped with captured Southern Enfields and were given the opportunity for the first time in the war to fight with modern weapons.[7] The Enfields improved the firing capacity of the men in the ranks, and this fact was not lost upon them when the chance to gain more modern and deadly armament presented itself. Four months pay was a small amount to spend for the advantages a repeater could give its owner.

Needless to say, the Confederates held a different opinion of the repeaters. As one Indiana soldier put it, "I think the Johnny's are getting rattled; they are afraid of our repeating rifles. They say we are not fair, that we have guns we load up on Sunday and shoot all the rest of the week."[8] The War Department had shied away from this new technology because it feared soldiers would not take deliberate aim if they knew they had multiple shots and would expend ammunition uselessly. Maybe that would have been a logical assessment for new recruits, but not for the old campaigners with Sherman who knew the value of each shot.

---

[7] William B. Edwards, *Civil War Guns* (Secaucus NJ: Castle Books, 1962) 92.

[8] D. R Lucas, *History of the 99th Indiana Infantry* (Lafayette IN: Rossert Spring, 1985) 99.

A list of the general officers in the armies opposing Sherman would read like a who's who of the war. Like their men, these generals had served since the beginning, most of them in the capacity they now held. They too had learned to be professionals during their on-the-job training. These captains and majors of the old army, these lawyers and politicians, they were the survivors of the war's battlefield tests. Gone were the incompetent from their ranks, their commissions lost along with their reputations. Those who remained had not only learned the art of war, they had written their own new chapters on the subject for later generations to study.

General Joe Johnston was among the leading generals in the Confederacy, his popularity with his troops only slightly less pronounced than that enjoyed by General Robert E. Lee. He had served in Virginia in the early days of the war, when his timely arrival with his army on the field of Manassas had won the first major battle of the war for the South. He had, however, become embroiled in a personal quarrel with President Davis after that victory that would effect the balance of his military career as he served the remainder of the war under the cloud of bitterness that existed between he and his commander in chief.

Johnston's wounding at the Battle of Seven Pines in spring 1862 necessitated his removal from command of the principal Confederate army in Virginia. The mantle was passed to the able hands of Robert E. Lee. For Johnston, already a national hero, the next command post would take him to Mississippi where he was to coordinate the defense of Vicksburg. Though Johnston was the ranking officer available at the time to send to the department, Davis still did not trust Johnston's judgment, and he therefore directed a great many personal orders to the general in command of the city's garrison, Lieutenant General John C. Pemberton. What resulted was a confusing duplicity of command structures that impeded any concerted effort on the city's behalf.

With the fall of Vicksburg, Johnston found himself without a major command again. His next appointment to army command would come when he was placed in charge of the Army of Tennessee, replacing General Braxton Bragg after the disaster at Missionary

Ridge. In this position, he would eclipse his early war fame and finally emerge as one of the great generals of the Confederacy. He was able to revitalize the army after its demoralizing defeat, infusing it with a restored sense of pride. In the Atlanta Campaign, he proved to be a master of maneuver, orchestrating the movements of his army with all the skill of a conductor. The entire campaign is a textbook study of how large armies should be handled in the field. His Federal counterpart during the campaign was William T. Sherman, a consummate conductor in his own right, and the two generals parried and sparred across northwest Georgia, each looking for an opportunity to strike a crippling blow. As the two armies maneuvered ever closer to Atlanta, President Davis became impatient over what he considered to be Johnston's reluctance to engage the foe. He could not understand the cat and mouse game the two commanding generals were playing and watched daily for news that the Confederates were driving the Federals out of Georgia. Johnston instead was drawing the Union forces ever deeper into Georgia and away from their base of supplies. He was keeping his own army well in hand, waiting for the proper time to launch the counteroffensive. The retrograde movements he was making proved to be more than Davis was willing to stand, however, and Johnston was relieved of the command at the outskirts of Atlanta. Lieutenant General John Bell Hood took charge of the army there and finally provided Davis with the long-awaited offensive thrusts. In a series of battles around the city, Hood threw his men against the Federals with savage ferocity. But Hood was a fighting general, not a particularly good strategist, and his reckless charges played right into Sherman's hands. The Army of Tennessee was nearly broken during these engagements, suffering casualty rates that reduced its numbers to a level below that which was needed to contend with Sherman's host. From Atlanta, Hood led the army into Tennessee, where it was effectively destroyed in the battles of Franklin and Nashville.

Johnston was once more without a command. His next opportunity would come when Robert E. Lee was given overall control of the Confederate armies. Lee recognized Johnston's talent and leadership ability, but the fortunes of the Confederacy had changed dramatically since the days of the Atlanta Campaign. In 1864, the South still thought it could win the war. Now it was faced with the reality that winning was a remote possibility and that survival was the primary objective. Johnston was not taking command of a vast army as he had in the past; he would be trying to collect one from the fragmented parts that were still in the field.

Johnston would be ably assisted in his mission, for he had under his command many of the most famous military leaders in the Confederacy. Wade Hampton would be in charge of his cavalry, having been detached from the Army of Northern Virginia for service in the Carolinas. He had learned his trade under the tutelage of the immortal J. E. B. Stuart and had briefly commanded the cavalry of that army when Stuart was killed. A large portion of his troopers would be led by another officer who had exercised independent cavalry command during the war, Major General Joeseph Wheeler. With these two men in the top spots of his mounted force, Johnston could rest assured that this wing would be capably led.

This same level of command experience was prominent among the general officers who would lead Johnston's infantry. Including the newly-appointed commanding general, there would be three of the Confederacy's eight full general connected with the Army of the South. The first of these was General Pierre G. T. Beauregard, the dashing Creole from Louisiana. He had become the first war hero of the South when he ordered the bombardment of Fort Sumter in Charleston Harbor almost four years before. He had also commanded, along with Johnston at First Manassas, and the victory had earned both men the rank they now held. Like Johnston, he had seen service in varied theaters during the war, and it was fitting that the two generals who had been responsible for the first major victory of the eastern Confederate army should fight together again in the last major battle of the western army.

The third full general who would serve with the Army of the South was Braxton Bragg. Like his two counterparts, he had also served in a variety of posts during the conflict, including a period of time as the commander of the Army of Tennessee. Bragg had led that army through the Chattanooga Campaign and had been in charge during the battles of Chickamauga and Missionary Ridge. The general's latest assignment had been the defense of the Cape Fear River and the port of Wilmington, North Carolina. This city had been the last major port open to the Confederate shipping outside the Trans-Mississippi Department and was a vital supply source in the Southern war effort. The capture of Fort Fisher, located at the mouth of the Cape Fear, by a combined Union naval and military expedition on 15 January 1865 had sealed off the port and led to the evacuation of the city itself. Bragg possessed a checkered military record during the war and was well known for disputes with his fellow officers. In fact, one such dispute had led to his removal from command of the Army of Tennessee after Missionary Ridge. He was a great organizer and a competent strategist, but left something to be desired in his tactical abilities and his dealings with subordinate officers. No one could question his devotion to the Confederate cause or his willingness to sacrifice his all in its support, but he had a tendency to alienate those under his command and found himself one of the least respected generals in the Confederacy by the end of the war.

Bragg had managed to maintain the devotion of one highly placed official throughout the conflict: Jefferson Davis. The two men shared a mutual friendship and admiration that had sustained the general. Davis was extremely rigid and inflexible in his personal deportment. For him, personal feelings counted as heavily in his government decisions as any other motivation. He was as stalwart in his support of Bragg, despite his military shortcomings, as he was in his castigation of Joe Johnston, regardless of that officer's abilities or success. As the old saying goes, "My enemy's friend is my enemy also," and Bragg and Johnston would have a strained relationship throughout the upcoming campaign.

William J. Hardee would command one of the corps of the new army, which was composed mainly of garrison troops from Charleston. He is considered by many historians to be one of the three best corps commanders to fight for the South, the other two being Thomas "Stonewall" Jackson and James P. Longstreet. Most of his combat experience had come with the Army of Tennessee, where he had earned the nickname "Old Reliable." He had been offered command of the Army of Tennessee in recognition of his leadership ability following Bragg's removal, but had decline the honor, feeling himself undeserving. In this decision he would form a consensus of one however, for his talent in battlefield command was without question and he enjoyed widespread support to accept the position. His refusal came after the Confederate defeat at Missionary Ridge, when Bragg was replaced, and resulted in President Davis having to make an alternate selection, Joe Johnston. Hardee served with the army throughout Johnston's tenure and under Hood in the battles around Atlanta. He requested reassignment after the battle of Jonesboro, Georgia because he disagreed with the way John Bell Hood had handled the army. Upon taking his leave from the Army of Tennessee, he made it known that his earlier refusal to accept top command would be reversed should the offer be made again. However, Hood was supported by President Davis, and Hardee was transferred to South Carolina, where he took charge of the Charleston defenses. The men he was bringing north from that city now had withstood numerous Federal attempts to take the port but they had never been engaged in a large infantry battle. They would constitute over a third of Johnston's available force, and though they were largely untested for the duty they were about to perform, their commander could be counted on to produce maximum results with them.

Among the other prominent general officers Johnston would have under his charge were Lieutenant General Daniel Harvey Hill and Major Generals Stephen D. Lee, Benjamin Franklin Cheatham, Patton Anderson, William W. Loring, John C. Brown, Edward C. Walthall, and Robert F. Hoke. A. P. Stewart, the recently promoted lieutenant general, would command the remaining fragment of the Army of Tennessee. Beauregard would serve as Johnston's second in command, just as he had done at Manassas once Johnston arrived on that field. This wealth of talent and experience would pose one of Johnston's initial problems with the new army: his new command simply had too many divisional and corps grade officers for the amount of men in the ranks. Conditions necessitated that men who had led armies must now lead corps and that men who had led corps must be reduced to divisional command. In no other campaign of the war had a

Confederate army found itself so top heavy in command. Many of the generals had never worked together before, and that would only intensify the awkward situations that would occur when they found themselves leading another officer's troops or serving in an unaccustomed subordinate position, but if Johnston could effectively guard against dissension or having too many chiefs, he would have the material at hand to mold a first-rate command structure.

Union General William T. Sherman did not suffer from the same problems that faced Johnston. His army was already intact, some 60,000 strong, and the troops were every bit the equal of the Confederates in combat experience. Sherman had led this force since the beginning of the Atlanta campaign and he was well known to his men. He gained their respect and admiration through both his command ability and his approachable, easy manner with the ranks. In fact, "Uncle Billy" was the name most commonly used by the privates in referring to him.

Fame and respect had not always been associated with Sherman during the war. He had fought at the Battle of First Manassas as an unknown brigade commander, where he found it difficult at times to keep his men in line. During the march from Washington, his men were constantly falling out to appropriate chickens and pigs from the farms they passed. Sherman tried to end this pilfering, but to no avail. "Tell Colonel Sherman we will get all the water, pigs and chickens we want" was the common reply from the ranks.[9] Despite their liberal foraging on the way to the battle, his men fought as credibly as any on the Union side during the daylong struggle. After it was over, Sherman found himself promoted to the rank of brigadier general and assigned to the hot spot of Kentucky.

While he was stationed here, Sherman suffered what many historians believe to have been a nervous breakdown. He had analyzed how the war was shaping up and had correctly estimated that the cost to see it through to completion would be far above the popular opinion of the day. His anxiety, caused by what he felt to be a critical

---

[9] William C. Davis, *Battle at Bull Run: A History of the First Major Campaign of the Civil War* (Baton Rouge: Louisiana State University Press, 1977) 96.

shortage of manpower in his department, convince many of his superiors that he was unstable and led to his being relieved in Kentucky.

Sherman's next major role in the war would come as a division commander under Grant at Shiloh, where he and his men performed superbly, their stubborn resistance buying Grant time to reform his battered army and preventing the Confederates from driving them off the field. Under Grant, Sherman would enjoy a steady rise in position and fame. He became that general's most trusted subordinate, emulating in large degree the professional bond that had earlier been created between Robert E. Lee and "Stonewall" Jackson. Each new victory for Grant also won laurels for Sherman, as the two became the one-two punch of the western army.

With Grant's victory at Missionary Ridge came his promotion to general in chief of all the Union armies, and the obvious successor to his vacated spot was Sherman. He was comfortable with the men and knew that he could be relied on to carry out any strategic plans in an efficient and timely manner. Grant would personally go east to operate with the Army of the Potomac, and the one-two punch of Sherman and himself would rain down on the two main theaters of the war.

Sherman's capture of Atlanta and the subsequent March to the Sea had not only justified Grant's confidence in him and solidified his claim to being one of the top field generals produced by the Union during the war; it had also been a major factor in sustaining President Lincoln in office and assuring that the Federal armies would decide the outcome of the war on the battlefield.

The Overland Campaign of the Army of the Potomac in Virginia in the summer of 1864 had been as costly as any fought during the war. Lee had fended off all of Grant's efforts to crush the Army of Northern Virginia, and after months of bloodletting the campaign had settled into a siege of Richmond and Petersburg. In the west, Johnston was successfully keeping his army positioned between Sherman and Atlanta and was foiling Union attempts to capture that position. Public opinion saw the war as being deadlocked. The folks back home felt it was no closer to a conclusion that when the spring campaign had begun and felt that it was time to consider a negotiated peace with the Confederacy. With 1864 being an election year, the Democratic Party capitalized upon the issue of war weariness. The party's assertions that enough blood had been spilled for a war that could not be won struck home with voters in the North, and its promise to end the fighting at all costs became a rallying cry. Former commander of the Army of the Potomac, Major General George B. McClellan, was selected as the party's presidential candidate, and summer polls showed him ahead of Lincoln. Re-election seemed a remote possibility for the president, and he went so far as to meet with McClellan to discuss how the two might work together in the time between the election and inauguration to win the war before the Democrats took office.

If Lee could keep Grant out of Richmond and if Johnston could prevent Sherman from entering Atlanta, the Confederacy could gain its separation from the United States without defeating the Union armies. They did not have to win any major battles; rather, they had just to ensure that none were lost. At this critical juncture, President Davis chose to replace Joe Johnston with John Bell Hood in front of Atlanta. The change in leadership resulted in a change of strategy as well, with Hood giving battle on Sherman's terms. After several bloody assaults on the Union army, Hood was forced to evacuate the city and leave it in Sherman's hands. At last, the major Northern victory of the year had been achieved: Atlanta had fallen. Finally, the folks back North could see a light at the end of the tunnel. Sherman's victory had been important strategically, but it was absolutely pivotal politically. Support that had shifted from Lincoln began to return and enabled the president to carry a closely contested fall election.

With the March to the Sea, Sherman had proved beyond any doubt that the Confederacy was near its end. His unimpeded trek through the heart of Georgia had even convinced many Confederates of this fact. It had made him the most talked about general in the North, and his fame rivaled that of Grant himself. Now, he was setting a course through the Carolinas for a climactic meeting with his old nemesis. The war had changed since those early days at Manassas. Codes of civilized warfare had been rewritten, largely by Sherman, as the civilian population of the South was forced to share the privations of their military. In Sherman's first campaign of the war, he had tried to stop his men from looting the country through which they passed. Now they were encouraged to do so and were organized for the purpose. By visiting the terrors of war upon Southern civilians, Sherman hoped to be able to destroy their will to resist and bring the conflict to a more rapid conclusion. His men took to the project with a vengeance, but they saved their most terrible destruction and pilfering for South Carolina, feeling that state had borne the largest share of responsibility for starting the war in the first place.

Sherman, like Johnston, would be assisted by a battery of capable general officers. He had divided his army into two wings, each commanded by an officer who won his reputation with the Army of the Potomac. Major General Oliver O. Howard would lead the right wing and Major General Henry W. Slocum commanded the left. Each wing would be composed of approximately 30,333 men, more than Johnston could hope to gather in time to meet their combined numbers.

Both wing commanders had been conspicuous in their wartime service to date, having participate in many of the greatest battles of the war, including Antietam, Chancellorsville, and Gettysburg. They were accustomed to desperate struggles, however, there was an underlying animosity between these two generals that both attempted to set aside. A slight rift first occurred during the Gettysburg Campaign when Howard accused Slocum of being dilatory in bringing his corps to the assistance of Howard's hard-pressed men. The resentment, thus fostered, evidenced itself in the fact that from that time forward, he was referred to by Howard's staff as "Slow Come." Then, when Sherman had organized his army into the wing formation that he used in his March to the Sea and through the Carolinas, he had opted to name Howard as his second in command, giving a slight to Slocum who outranked Howard.[10]

---

[10] Mark L. Bradley, *Last Stand in the Carolinas: The Battle of Bentonville* (Campbell CA: Savas Publishing Company, 1996) 10, 341–42.

O. O. Howard had also begun his war service as a brigade commander at First Manassas, and remained with the Army of the Potomac till fall 1863, fighting in all the major engagements in the east. He had lost his right arm from a wound received at Fair Oaks, but returned to the army a mere eighty days later to resume his duties.[11] At Chancellorsville, he commanded the XI Corps, on the right of the Union army, and was criticized for failing to protect his flank and allowing "Stonewall" Jackson's assault to take the army by surprise. After the death of Major General Reynolds at Gettysburg on the first day of the fighting, Howard temporarily assumed command of all Union forces on the field and was voted the thanks of Congress for selecting their position on Cemetery Ridge.

When Major General Joseph Hooker was sent to the relief of General William Rosencrans's army after the battle of Chickamauga, Howard and his XI Corps, along with the XII Corps, made up the relieving force. From that point on, his service had been with the western army, and he had taken part in every engagement from the battles at Chattanooga onward. He had been assigned command of the IV Corps when Major General James B. McPherson was killed in the fighting around Atlanta, and had risen to command of the Union Army of the Tennessee during the now famous March. His force would constitute the right wing of Sherman's army through the Carolinas.

General Henry W. Slocum, an officer whose war service closely paralleled that of Howards, also commanded a Federal brigade at First Manassas. Slocum became the second youngest major general in the Union army when he was commissioned to that rank on 25 July 1862.[12] He led a division from the Peninsula Campaign through the Battle of Antietam and was put in charge of the XII Corps after the latter. He participated in the Battle of Chancellorsville with his corps, where he became embroiled in a quarrel with the army commander, Joe Hooker, over official criticisms he had made concerning that

---

[11] Ezra J. Warner, *Generals in Blue; Lives of the Union Commanders* (Baton Rouge: Louisiana State University Press, 1960) 238.

[12] Ibid., 452.

general's handling of the army in the engagement. At Gettysburg, the XII Corps held the right of the Union line and was responsible for fending off the numerous assaults of the Confederates against Culp's Hill.

His corps was included in the force sent to Rosecrans in fall 1863, and when Slocum learned that it was to be commanded by Joe Hooker, he submitted his resignation to the War Department. The request was refused by Secretary of War Edward Stanton, but a compromise was worked out so that Slocum, with a division of his corps, could operate independent of Hooker's command. Slocum and this division would be charged with the protection of the Nashville and Chattanooga Railroad, while the remainder of his corps served under Hooker.

Just before the beginning of the Atlanta Campaign, Slocum was transferred to the Vicksburg District, where he served until August 1864. In the meantime, his corps had been consolidated with XI Corps into the newly created XX Corps, under Hooker's command. When Howard was promoted to head the Army of the Tennessee, Hooker took offense to being passed over for the spot and promptly tendered his resignation, which was accepted in Washington. Slocum was called east to assume Hooker's vacated position in time to accompany the corps as the first Union forces to enter the city of Atlanta on 2 September 1864. During the March he was given charge of the XIV Corps as well, with these two units making up the left wing.

In addition to Howard and Slocum, Sherman would be assisted by other hard-fighting generals, Major Generals John A. Logan, Frank P. Blair, Jr., Jefferson C. Davis, Joseph A. Mower, John W. Geary, James D. Morgan, and William P. Carlin, to name a few. His cavalry would be under the direction of Major General Judson Kilpatrick, another transfer from the Army of the Potomac. Kilpatrick had not graduated from West Point until May 1861, but he managed to receive a volunteer commission as captain of the 5th New York Infantry in time to see action at the skirmish of Big Behel, Virginia, where he earned the distinction of being the first regular officer to be wounded in action.[13] In September of that same year, he became colonel of the 2nd New York Cavalry, serving in that branch in all of the engagements of the army through Gettysburg. In February 1864 he had led a raid to Richmond with his cavalry division for the purpose of releasing Union prisoners held in the city. The mission was an absolute failure and resulted in claims from the Confederate government that its object had been the assassination of President Davis and other high-ranking officials. In April 1864 General Grant sent Kilpatrick south to take command of a division of Sherman's cavalry, and he was severely wounded at Resaca during the initial stages of the Atlanta Campaign.

Known for his recklessness and headlong thrusts, Sherman nevertheless gave him command of his cavalry wing with the comment, "I know that Kilpatrick is a hell of a damned fool, but I want just that sort of man to command my cavalry in this expedition."[14] The general felt Kilpatrick's aggressive style would pay dividends in the overland marches that lay ahead.

Joe Johnston would indeed have his hands full assembling an army capable of contending with this Federal force. To add to his discomfiture, he would have to cope with two additional Union armies in his theater of operations, Major General Jacob Cox's force at New Berne and Major General John Schofield's at Wilmington. While trying to impeded Sherman's advance to prevent his uniting with Grant's army, Johnston would also have to guard against the joining of these three forces. Their combined numbers would be too overwhelming for him to even contemplate risking a general engagement.

Schofield, following his participation in the battles of Franklin and Nashville, was sent east with his XXIII Corps to Wilmington. He also assumed command of Major General Alfred Terry's army, portions of the XXIV and XXV Corps, which had been victorious in the expedition to capture Fort Fisher. Using Wilmington as a base of supplies, he was to advance his force, about 20,000 strong, inland

---

[13] Ibid., 266.
[14] Ibid., 267.

from the port city to effect a juncture with Sherman's army advancing up the coast. It would be the first time since leaving Savannah that Sherman's men would be supplied by the Federal government.

General Jacob Cox was detached from the XXIII Corps by Schofield and sent to New Berne for the purpose of raising a provisional corps there. He would have approximately 13,000 men in his command, and was to move forward, in conjunction with Schofield, toward the rendezvous point with Sherman at Goldsboro.

With the Virginia theater and Grant's army in his rear, Sherman's army in his front, and Schofield's forces on his left, Joe Johnston was indeed in an unenviable position. It would take all of the skills he possessed to keep his army in hand in the face of these overwhelming odds, while at the same time looking for an opportunity to strike a crippling blow against one of the forces before all could be united. Lee had restored Johnston's reputation as a general by reinstating him to command, but the difficulties involved in operating that command would test his abilities to the limit.

2

ENGAGEMENT AT KINSTON

Joe Johnston officially assumed command of his new army on 25 February 1865 at Charlotte, North Carolina. Hardee and his force of some 7,500 men was over 50 miles away at Cheraw, just south of the North Carolina border. He was doing what he could to slow the Federal advance, but Sherman's blue waves rolled on relentlessly. General Bragg and his command were located in the vicinity of Goldsboro, some 150 miles northeast of Hardee's men. He had withdrawn to this spot following the capture of Wilmington, which occurred on the very day that Johnston was given command of the department. The Army of Tennessee, such as it was, could be arriving on the scene at any time, but they would be forwarded piecemeal, and by mid-March only 4,000 to 5,000 would be in North Carolina with the Army of the South. The cavalry force, under Hampton, was operating with Hardee, and with the addition of Joe Wheeler's mounted men were harassing the Federal columns at every opportunity.

Johnston's first concern was to select a point to consolidate his scattered fragments into an army before they could be eliminated individually. Once this merging was accomplished, he would have an aggregate of just over 20,000 men, not nearly enough to contend with all the Federals in his department but possibly enough to do good service against a portion of them.

Fayetteville was selected as the rendezvous point, but the speed of Sherman's advance necessitated that another site be selected, as the Union army would be in possession of the place before the Confederates could arrive. Lee had ordered the general to position himself so that he could defend the area around Raleigh, the last source of supplies for both armies. His next selection was the town of Smithfield, located along the North Carolina Central Railroad, just north of Bentonville. Anxious over his ability to mass an army capable of doing battle with Sherman, he sent a message to Lee shortly after arriving in Charlotte, stating, "It is too late to expect met to concentrate troops capable of driving back Sherman." Three days late he sent another message to Lee, which further stressed his fears. "Your order…implies that you regard these forces as adequate to the object… In my opinion these troops form an army too weak to cope with Sherman." The general in chief was aware of the limitations Johnston would have to work under and he advised the latter to do the best he could with the resources at hand, emphasizing that "nothing can be sent from here to your assistance."[1]

When Lee stated that nothing could be sent for Johnston's assistance he was referring to more than just manpower. It was discovered that enough rations to subsist 60,000 men for over four months had been collected at depots along the North Carolina Railroad. Johnston's men would be in dire need of these rations once they were collected together, and the general sought permission to utilize a portion of them to offset his own supply problems. This request was summarily refused by both Lee and Secretary of War John Breckinridge, who informed Johnston that the rations in question were the property of the Army of Northern Virginia and could not be drawn by his forces.[2] Though apprehensive about his chances of success in the mission, Johnston remained inspired by the confidence Lee had shown in him. In a letter to Confederate Senator Louis Trezevant Wigfall of Texas, he wrote, "Be assured that a Knight of old never fought under his king more loyally than I'll serve under Gen. Lee."[3]

---

[1] Craig L. Symonds, *Joseph E. Johnston: A Civil War Biography* (New York: W. W. Norton & Co., 1992) 344.

[2] Mark L. Bradley, *Last Stand in the Carolinas: The Battle of Bentonville* (Campbell CA: Savas Publishing Company, 1996) 77.

[3] Symonds, *Joseph E. Johnston*, 344.

His first order of business was to get the men ready to fight both materially and emotionally. Still looking to the provisioning of his men, Johnston received information that a large quantity of coffee, sugar, and alcohol was in the possession of the navy at Charlotte, at the Confederate Navy Yard. He asked Secretary of War John C. Breckinridge for permission to seize the supplies since the Confederate navy had all but ceased to exist and further requested that four months back pay be forwarded for distribution among the men. Breckinridge replied that he had permission to take any supplies he needed from the naval stores, but the request for money would have to be denied for the present. The government was broke and, as the secretary put it, was "almost universally paralyzed for want of means." Regarding future supply needs, the general was advised to provision the army "by collecting subsistence through the country."[4]

With the army still widely separated and far from being organized, Johnston received a request from General Braxton Bragg for reinforcement to enable him to strike the Union forces under General Jacob Dolson Cox that were advancing from New Berne. The Federal contingent, some 13,000 strong, was advancing along the line of the Atlantic & North Carolina Railroad toward Goldsboro. Cox had been sent to New Berne with a division of the XXIII Corps because of a lack of rolling stock on the Wilmington and Weldon Railroad. He was to take command of the Union garrison already in the city and with his combined force was to coordinate his movements with those of General Schofield. The two wings would converge on Goldsboro from the east and southeast, making themselves ready to open communications with Sherman. Cox was still several miles east of Kinston when Bragg made his request for additional men. His advance was being somewhat delayed by the necessity of repairing the tracks as he moved inland to ensure a constant source of supplies from New Bern. Bragg, then at Goldsboro with his command, was not hampered by this constraint of movement. He had sufficient rolling stock to convey his men to the point of battle and the tracks lying within control of the Confederates were still in working order. With

---

[4] Ibid., 346.

Johnston's approval, he would transport his troops to the vicinity of Kinston and deliver a blow to Cox's men before they could either reach Goldsboro or unite with Schofield.

Johnston consented to provide Bragg with what forces he had in the immediate area hoping that Cox could be turned back at Kinston, thus leaving him less encumbered to concentrate against Sherman. It is possible that he also sought to show Bragg that no ill feelings were being harbored over the incident the previous summer when Bragg had declined to send reinforcements to Johnston at Dalton, Georgia.

The general had moved his headquarters to Fayetteville on 4 March, halfway between Hardee and Bragg, and the only forces he had within supporting range of the proposed movement against Kinston were the recently arrived fragments of the Army of Tennessee at Smithfield, temporarily under the command of General Daniel Harvey Hill. They consisted of Hill's own division, commanded by Colonel J. G. Coltart, General Edmund W. Pettus's Brigade of Carter L. Stevenson's division, and General Henry D. Clayton's division of Lee's corps, in all about 2,000 men.

Hill was opposed to making the movement, not from a military standpoint, but from personal reasons stemming from a previous incident with General Bragg. That general had made accusations about Hill's conduct following the battle of Chickamauga, damaging Hill's reputation, and Hill was loath to finding himself once again under Bragg's command. Johnston tried to smooth over this rift between his commanders as best he could. Though he ordered Hill to advance his men to Bragg's aid, his tone was very conciliatory toward the former. "I beg you to forget the past for this emergency," he implored. Hill obeyed with the request: "I hope that it may be possible & consistent with [the] intents of the service to give me another commander than General Bragg. He has made me the scapegoat once & would do it again."[5]

Orders were received at Smithfield on 7 March and according to Hill, the men "were at once placed upon the cars and encamped that

[5] Ibid., 346.

night beyond the Neuse and below Kinston."[6] Shortly before daylight on the morning of 8 March, Hill's men were directed to relieve General Robert Frederick Hoke's division, then in trenches along Southwest Creek, so that division could make a flank movement to the Federal left. General Clayton's division had followed Hill and the main body and did not arrive on the field until about 8:00 A.M., at which time they were directed to accompany Hoke. General Johnson Hagood's Brigade and the North Carolina Reserves were detached from his command and added to Hill's.

The Federals were positioned approximately 3 miles southeast of Kinston. To their rear was Dover Swamp, a morass of swamps and bogs both surrounded by and laced with streams and creeks. The swamp ground encompassed an area of about 20 square miles and served as a natural barrier for any military operations. The line of the Atlantic and North Carolina Railroad bisected it a little north of center and ran in a northwesterly direction to Kinston. The Lower Trent Road skirted the southern and western edges of the swamp and connected the town of Trenton with Kinston by way of the Neuse Road, which followed the contours of the Neuse River in a southwest to northwest loop into the city. The only other way through the swamp was the Dover Road, which ran in a southwesterly direction through the upper half of the slough till it crossed the Lower Trent Road at Wise's Forks at the westernmost terminus of the swamp. It then curved in a northwesterly direction till it also joined the Neuse Road. The other main roads in the area were the British Road, an offshoot of the Neuse Road, which ran in a southwesterly direction and crossed the railroad as well as the Dover and Lower Trent Roads. Continuing for a little over 3 miles, it crossed Upper Trent Road before joining the Wilmington Road south of Kinston. The two latter roads both joined the Neuse Road just south of Kinston and ran in a southerly and southeasterly direction respectively. With the exception of British Road, all of the routes crossed over Southwest

---

[6] *The War of the Rebellion: A Compilation of the Official Records of the Union and Confederate Armies* (Washington, DC: Government Printing Office, 1895) ser. 1, vol. 47, pt. 1, 1087

Creek, a tributary of the Neuse that emptied into that river at a point about 2 miles east of Kinston and snaked its way back through the country to a position a little over 2 miles south of the city.

Cox's men had advanced as far as Wise's Forks by 7 March, where information was received that Hoke's forces were in the area. The Union commander showed little concern over this report though, for he felt fully capable of fending off any effort Hoke might be able to mount with the limited means under his command. Nevertheless, he ordered that all of his forces be concentrated on the dry ground on the western side of the swamp along Southwest Creek. Since repairs on the tracks had not progressed that far, Cox's men would be 10 miles ahead of their railroad supply line with but few wagons to connect the two points. The transportation situation posed a potential problem for the Union forces should the Confederates take the offensive, and while Cox was confident he could deal with Hoke, he was also "sure that we should be short of supplies."[7]

General Schofield arrived on the scene on the morning of 8 March for a meeting with Cox, coming to Kinston area by way of Beaufort. They met at nine o'clock and after discussing the possibility of securing a crossing of the Southwest Creek at the railroad bridge to facilitate the repair of that structure, they mounted to ride to Brigadier General Innis Palmer's headquarters. A message came in from Brigadier General Samuel Carter at Wise's Forks that he had been informed by a Negro that a large force of Confederates had crossed Southwest Creek at the Wilmington Road in the early morning hours.[8]

Cox dismissed the report at first. He had his cavalry picketed at the bridge on the Upper Trent Road with instructions to patrol beyond the Wilmington Road. If the Confederates had indeed crossed there, he was sure that his own troops would have observed it. Just to be safe, he ordered the cavalry to check out the story and directed

---

[7] Gen. Jacob Dolson Cox, *Military Reminiscences of the Civil War* (New York: Charles Scribner's Sons, 1900) 434.

[8] Ibid., 435.

General Samuel P. Carter to provide a brigade of infantry from his division to support the reconnaissance.[9]

Before the orders could be carried forward, another message arrived from the front reporting that a heavy force of the Confederates had attacked Upham's Brigade and had succeeded in effecting a lodgment between it and the rest of the division. Almost simultaneously came news from the cavalry that their pickets had been driven from the bridge at the upper Trent Road and it was now in Confederate hands. The cavalry picket had been located 2 miles from the left of Upham's Brigade on the British Road, and Cox noted that "it was too evident that the duty of the horsemen had not been well done." He ordered General Thomas Ruger, whose 1st Division XXIII Corps was in the rear of the advance, to march immediately to the front. This done, he and Schofield galloped to Wise's Forks to assess the situation in person.[10]

This initial attack had been delivered by Hoke's command with the intention of seizing the Lower Trent and Dover Roads at Wise's Forks. General Hill had been directed to cross the Southwest Creek downstream from Hoke's position and to seize the British and Neuse Roads. When he heard Hoke's attack begin, he was to advance his own forces and cut off the retreat of the Federals. At the sound of Hoke's guns, Hill threw forward his skirmish line of the 50th Alabama under the command of Captain E. B. Vaughan, followed by the North Carolina Reserves under Brigadier General Lawrence S. Baker in line of battle. "The North Carolina Reserves advanced very handsomely for a time, but at length one regiment (the First, I think) broke, and the rest lay down and could not be got forward."[11]

But Hoke's advance was not progressing as scheduled. After crossing the river, he gained the British Road and pushed north toward its intersection with Dover Road, where he made contact with Upham's Brigade. Thinking he was on the flank of the Federal line, he advanced against Upham, thus partially exposing his own flank and

---

[9] Ibid., 435.
[10] Ibid., 435.
[11] *OR*, ser. 1, vol. 47, pt. 1, 1087.

rear to the remainder of Carter's division, which was positioned to the left. With the first appearance of the Confederates, Upham had hurried the 17th Massachusetts to the British Road, about a quarter mile south of the Dover Road, where they deployed with a section of artillery. The Bay State men found the position untenable, being far outflanked on either end, and they were soon put to rout. All of the horses for one of the field pieces were killed and an attempt to haul off the gun by hand proved futile. Upham's other regiment, the 15th Connecticut, was ordered to have its left battalion change front to the south to face the impending assailment by the Rebs. The departure of the 17th Massachusetts had exposed their flank, and the Connecticut boys were being prepared to meet a charge in both front and flank.[12]

General Hill was supposed to be in position on the right flank of Upham's Brigade but the advance of the North Carolina Reserves had encountered a swamp. Leaving Baker's men at the spot where they had stopped, he took the rest of his force, consisting of the brigades of Generals Johnson Hagood and Edmund Pettus, as well as that of Colonel John Coltart, on a circuitous route around the marshy ground. When Hoke's attack was under way, he turned his line in the direction of the firing and found himself directly on the flank of the right battalion of the 15th Connecticut. Hill's movement was "completely successful," and "the Yankees ran in the wildest confusion." So complete was the initial rout on this front that Captain Vaughan and forty-five of his skirmishers from the 50th Alabama were able to capture about 300 prisoners themselves. As the regiment fell back before Hill's lines toward the left of the battalion, the realization that they were trapped between Hoke an Hill caused most of the regiment to surrender to the former. The 15th Connecticut was out of the fight and had all but ceased to exist as a unit.[13]

The attention of the Confederates, being momentarily focused upon the Connecticut regiment, allowed Upham and the majority of the 17th Massachusetts to retire to the portion of the main line held by Carter's division. Carter held the left of the Union line, with

---

[12] Cox, *Military Reminiscences*, 435–36.

[13] Ibid., 436 and *OR*, ser. 1, vol. 47, pt. 1, 1087.

General Innis Palmer's division holding the right. A large gap existed between the two commands, and Cox ordered Ruger's division to fill the hole and present a continuous line when his units were on the field. Before that division could be gotten up, Cox directed that the cavalry, which had attached itself to the left flank of Carter's division, be rushed to the center to form a dismounted skirmish line. The 15th Connecticut had borne the brunt of the Confederate attack thus far and had seen a tremendous number of its members forced to surrender, but their losses were buying Ruger the time he needed to get his division in line and close the gap. Much of the ground being fought over was forested or marshy, and dictated that the Confederate movement would be delayed from a continual need to stop and redress their lines. By the time the 15th Connecticut boys had given up the fight, Ruger's men were in line and the opportunity to cut the Union forces in half had passed.[14]

General Cox arrived at the front after the attack had begun. Seeking the whereabouts of General Carter, he was informed that the general had taken a regiment forward on the Dover Road to try to reopen communication with Upham. Cox continued forward in search of Carter and caught up with him, still on the Dover Road trying to make his way toward the sound of the fighting. Firing indicated that the Confederates were in close proximity to the lightly defended Union center, and Cox ordered the general to strengthen his main line in front of Wise's Forks as much as possible and position his artillery at that spot, near to the Dover Road, The advance regiment was to restrict its action to providing a bold skirmish front, falling back to the main position as the enemy line of battle advanced.[15]

General Hill was very satisfied with the action thus far and felt that several thousand Federals could have been capture with little loss to his own men. This belief on the part of Hill substantiates the statement of Captain Vaughan's that the "Yankee rout was more complete than he had ever seen before," for Hill had only 2,000 men under his command with which he could capture these "several

[14] Cox, *Military Reminiscences*, 436.
[15] Ibid., 437.

thousand" prisoners. At this critical juncture, Major Parker, General Bragg's adjutant general, arrived with orders for Hill. According to Bragg, Hoke had suggested that Hill's force be redirected to enter the British Road by way of the Neuse Road. The message further stated that this movement should result in a large number of captures and Bragg ordered it to be carried out at once.[16]

Owing to the swamp that had impeded Hill's earlier movements, he was now forced to make a circuitous march back to the left to reach the assigned location. "I pushed on rapidly," Hill would write, "and threw a picket across to the British Road, and went to it in person, but saw no enemy." It was now 4:30 P.M. and the firing heard in the distance convinced Hill that General Hoke's men were not driving the Federals as anticipated. Upon consulting with his officers, it was decided that the proper place to have positioned the division should have been on the Dover Road where it crossed the railroad, but with the exception of General Baker, all felt it too late and too hazardous to begin the 3–4 mile march back to that spot. Besides, his men were already skirmishing with a Federal line well protected by field works. Bragg solved the indecision with a second message, delivered shortly after the consultation of Hill's officers. In it he directed the general to recross the Southwest Creek and proceed down the Dover Road for a juncture with Hoke if it was, in his opinion, now too late to carry out the earlier order. Hill responded to the latest instructions at once and began his retrograde movement. The march was hampered by the terrain, as had been all the Confederate movements during the day, and the column did not make contact with Hoke's command until midnight. Hill's men, weary from a full day of fighting, marching, and countermarching were finally allowed rest.[17]

Hill did not realize that he faced little real danger from the Union forces his men were skirmishing with in the afternoon. Cox had learned of the presence of some units from the Army of Tennessee earlier that afternoon, and the news had caused him to adopt a very defensive posture. The Union commander could not be sure how

---

[16] *OR*, ser. 1, vol. 47, pt. 1, 1087.
[17] Ibid., 1087.

heavily Hoke had been reinforced, but this revelation that men from the western army were in his front caused him to exercise caution in his movement. His defensive posture was intensified by Hill's countermarch to the British Road, as Cox thought it was new column of Confederates just arriving on the field. Unsure of the numbers in his front, the general was not about to take the offensive against Hill's command.[18]

The inability of Hoke to drive the Federals had been due to his misconception of the exact position of their flank. As previously stated, he believed that he was assaulting the end of the Union line when he launched the attack on Upham. As his advance exposed his own flank and rear to fire from Carter's division, he was compelled to about face and engage this threat. He pressed back the advance regiment of Carter's division, which Cox had ordered to be used as skirmishers, to the main line at Wise's Forks, where his men were greeted with fire from massed artillery and musketry that checked their advance. Though Hoke reformed his lines and attempted to carry the position several more times, he was easlily repulsed at each occasion. The fighting was then confined to heavy skirmishes along Carter and Ruger's fronts until darkness ended the battle.[19]

The Confederates had not accomplished all that they had hoped for in the day's fighting but their results were impressive nonetheless. Bragg was able to send the following report of his success to Johnston from his headquarters in Kinston:

> We attacked the enemy today about four miles in front of Kinston, and drove him from his position. He disputed the ground obstinately, and now confronts us about three miles from his original line. We captured three pieces of artillery and several hundred prisoners. The number of his dead and wounded left on the field is large. Our own loss, under Providence, is comparatively small. Major-Generals Hill and

---

[18] Cox, *Military Reminiscences*, 439.

[19] Ibid., 437–38.

> Hoke have exhibited their usual zeal, energy and gallantry in achieving this result. Our troops behaved most handsomely.
>
> Schofield is not in our front. Major-General Cox, from West Virginia, is reported by prisoners to be in command, with three divisions.[20]

Bragg forwarded copies of the dispatch, minus the second paragraph, to General Lee in Petersburg and to Colonel Sale, the assistant adjutant general of the Department of North Carolina in Goldsboro.

The morning of 9 March found both armies fully entrenched and ready for the events of the day. General Hill's line was formed in an "L" configuration, with his right being parallel to British Road and his left perpendicular to it, covering the railroad to Southwest Creek. General Hoke and his men were directed to make a movement against the Federal right flank, with Hill providing a diversion by advancing his skirmish line along the British Road. Captain Vaughn, as corps officer of the day, was once again given command of the skirmishers, and he advanced and seized the skirmish line of the Federals, but was forced to abandon it in short order, being pressed by a heavy line of battle.

The Federals had made good use of their time on the preceding night and their works had been strengthened by the placement of abatis and slashed timber in their front. Cox had refused both of his flanks and removed a brigade from Ruger's line to act as a reserve should the Confederates resume the attack. The length of the line coupled with the removal of this front line brigade caused the works to be thinly held in places, but Cox was sure he could hold against the still unknown enemy force in his front. His faith was bolstered by the fact that two divisions of the XXIII Corps were advancing from Wilmington to his assistance. Schofield had returned to New Bern to issue orders for the reinforcements to come to Kinston with all possible haste, and Cox was sure that with their addition he could hold

---

[20] Don C. Seitz, *Braxton Bragg: General of the Confederacy* (Columbia: The State Company, 1924) 514.

against anything the Confederates could throw his way. His major concern was a shortage of ammunition in his ranks. Though work on the railroad was being pushed forward at a hurried rate, the tracks were still far short of Cox's position and roads through the swamp, muddied by recent rains, were all but impassable. Orders were issued to remain on the defensive and to conserve all available ammunition as much as possible.[21]

About 10:00 A.M., General Palmer reported sighting Hoke's division moving toward the Neuse Road. The Confederates were retracing their steps along much the same route that Hill's men had the previous afternoon. He had advance to Palmer's flank only to find it firmly entrenched behind good works, and had decided that an assault against them was out of the question. After demonstrating for a while in front of the Federal line, he had withdrawn for the purpose of recrossing the Southwest Creek and once more joining with Hill. Hoke's action was contrary to Bragg's order that "Success must be achieved," but Hoke felt that it was the only options he had under the circumstances.[22]

With Hoke's return to the main Confederate line, the action for the remainder of the day became that of skirmishing only. General Bragg was content to allow the situation to become static, as he had been informed that more troops were already on the way toward his position and would probably arrive sometime that day. This new force was a part of Lieutenant General Ambrose P. Stewart's corps and was under the command of Major General Edward Walthall. With the added strength their numbers would give him, Bragg reasoned that he would be strong enough to finally accomplish his objective and plans were formed to launch a final attack on Friday, 10 March.[23]

The skirmishing was kept up all along the front throughout the night of 9 March and the early morning hours of 10 March, reminding many of the participants of the days they had faced each other during the Atlanta Campaign. Bragg had ordered Walthall's men

---

[21] Cox, *Military Reminiscences*, 440.
[22] Ibid., 440.
[23] Cox, *Military Reminiscences*, 441.

to replace those of Hoke in the line so that the latter could make a movement around the left of the Federal position. The destination of the maneuver would be the Lower Trent Road, from which place it was judged that the Confederates would be able to take Carter's division in reverse. Strong skirmishing was to be kept up all along the front to mask Hoke's movements, and this was to be escalated into demonstrations by Hill's and Walthall's commands when firing was heard from the direction from whence Hoke had gone.[24]

A frontal assault against the Federal line would be out of the question. Hill's officers had informed him that the men were shy of entrenchment after their experience in attacking them in Hood's Tennessee Campaign. The memories of the slaughter at Franklin and Nashville were still too vivid in their minds for these soldiers to even contemplate such a headlong rush. General Hill notified Bragg as to this reluctance in the ranks, and the commander instructed him to advance a double line of skirmishers when Hoke's firing was heard. The idea of being in skirmish line rather than battle line was wholly acceptable to the men.[25]

By 11:00 A.M., Hoke was in position and ready to hit the flank, but Cox had learned of his movements and had strengthened the Union left with two additional brigades from Ruger's division. He also shifted one of Palmer's brigades from the right to the center to bolster Ruger's now depleted line. The artillery of both Carter and Ruger was concentrated on the left, and when Hoke got under way around 11:30 A.M., his men ran straight into a hailstorm of cannon and muskets. Though initially stunned by this rough reception, Hoke rallied his line and threw them forward again. The result was a fierce little fight that raged for about an hour in front of the Union flank. Hoke's line had lapped so far over the Lower Trent Road that it was threatening to cut off the use of the Dover Road to the Federals. Cox was particularly concerned over this circumstance because General Schofield was returning from New Bern to the front and might find himself in danger of being captured. Palmer was directed to have a

---

[24] *OR*, ser. 1, vol. 47, pt. 1, 1088.
[25] Ibid.

message signaled down the track telling the commander to stay with the trains until he received further news from the front.[26]

Artillery fire was playing havoc with Hoke's line, and after sixty minutes of fighting, the impetus was waning from his assault. Cox sensed that the Confederates were about played out and he chose that time to go on the offensive himself, advancing Colonel John C. McQuiston's Brigade from his left against Hoke's right flank, breaking the Confederate line and driving it from the field.

Cox did not have long to savor his victory for he found that his weakened center was now in danger as Hill's double line of skirmishers moving against it. There was to have been coordination between the two movements, but Hill had been delayed by the forested terrain. The failure to coordinate the assaults had afforded General Cox the opportunity to mass his forces against Hoke and defeat that threat before he was hotly engaged with Hill.

The Confederate skirmish lines drove their opposing numbers back upon their main line, thus capturing the first line of Federal rifle pits. Cox reacted by shifting the brigades he had detached from Ruger back to center, calling off the pursuit of Hoke's force. The collective artillery of Carter and Ruger was also sent to the center to be massed in front of Hill. News of Hoke's repulse soon reached Hill and he could see, by the wave of blue collecting in his front, that the Federals were preparing to greet him with all they had. Union numbers and the formidable works they were defending caused Hill to report the current state of affairs to Bragg and request further instructions. With the situation as it was, there was nothing for the Confederate chieftain to do but order Hill to fall back.[27]

Bragg still had hopes of being able to resume the offensive, but as the day wore on, he learned of the approach of Federal reinforcements from Wilmington, the two divisions of the XXIII Corps that Schofield had fetched from New Bern. This news threw him into indecision. At one time he urged additional men be sent to him so that the offensive could be undertaken again, and at others he

---

[26] Cox, *Military Reminiscences*, 442.

[27] *OR*, ser. 1, vol. 47, pt. 1 1088.

suggested that the forces at his front were too formidable to consider attacking and that he should withdraw to form a junction with the rest of the army near Raleigh. From the information Johnston had available, he decided that no further good could come from pressing the issue at Kinston, and the withdrawal toward Raleigh was ordered. Bragg's main concern now was for some 200,000 rations that were stored at Kinston. He desperately desired to prevent their falling into the Federal hands, and at 6:00 P.M. he wired Johnston: "There is no doubt about the movement of a heavy column from Wilmington in this direction. Will you have any means of delaying Sherman so as to enable me to save supplies, or must the junction be immediate?"[28]

Johnston wanted to consolidate his forces as soon as possible, but the order to withdraw was not immediate. Bragg would have some time to try and save what he could of the badly needed supplies. His army had crossed the Neuse River at nightfall and set up a hasty camp near the city, and by 11:15 P.M., Bragg was able to wire that he had transportation present for 10,000 men, as well as for the supplies. He informed the commander of his instructions to forward all supplies not needed by the army in North Carolina to Lee in Virginia.[29]

General Hoke was detailed to serve as the rear guard for the army, but Cox was not disposed to pursue. He was still not sure exactly how many men the Confederates had at his front, and the arrival of men of A. P. Stewart's corps under General Walthall the previous day had only intensified his defensive posture. The possibility that there were two entire corps from the Army of Tennessee acting with Hoke's force caused him to be extremely cautious. Defending his position behind strong works was one thing, but taking the offensive against an enemy of unknown size was quite another. Once he was certain that the Confederates had withdrawn from his front, Cox began to make plans for a retrograde movement of his own, back to the end of his rail line where he could be sure of rectifying his supply shortage.

---

[28] Seitz, *Braxton Bragg,* 514–15.

[29] *OR*, ser. 1, vol. 47, pt. 1, 1088 and Seitz, *Braxton Bragg*, 515.

The fighting at Kinston thus ended with both sides retiring from the contested ground. It had not been a large affair, comparatively speaking, and was in fact, considered little more than a large skirmish by this stage of the war. Both sides claimed victory in the encounter, but the battle must be considered a Union triumph based on the fact that the Confederates were unable to accomplish their goal of destroying Cox's force. True, causalities were greatly in favor of the Confederates with losses of only a little over 200 versus 1,337 total losses inflicted on the Federals. Around 900 of the Union casualties were captured, most of those numbers coming from the 15th Connecticut during Hill and Hoke's attack on 8 March. Still, the Federals had a force on the field of some 12,000 men, with two fresh divisions on the way. Against that number Bragg could only muster 8,000. He had done well considering the disparity in size of his army compared with the Federals, especially since his men were the ones doing the attacking, but the goal of destroying Cox had never been a realistic one. Nevertheless, he claimed the victory by measure of the losses he had inflicted on the enemy in his officials reports to Johnston and President Davis, leading one Union officer to state, "It is a query whether Bragg lies to Davis officially, or whether these dispatches are only intended for the people, 'to fire the Southern heart.'"[30]

Bragg's attempt to relieve the pressure on the Army of the South was a failure. Cox and Schofield were still in the field, ready to join with Sherman's northward moving columns. If the Confederates were to buy time to allow their army to refit and reform it would have to come from another quarter. The battle of Kinston would prove to be Braxton Bragg's last opportunity to exercise independent field command. For the remainder of the war, he would be acting in the role of a corps commander under Johnston.

---

[30] Thomas Osburn, *The Fiery Trail: A Union Officer's Account of Sherman's Last Campaign* (Knoxville: University of Tennessee Press, 1986) 186.

3

"OLD RELIABLE" AT AVERASBORO

Joe Johnston had been forced to abandon further attempts to subdue Cox at Kinston, in part because of the rapid pace Sherman's army in its march towards the heart of the state. Any entanglements with Cox now might prevent him from being able to consolidate his forces in front of Sherman and would result in his plan working in reverse, with the Confederates being isolated and defeated in detail.

Since leaving Savannah on 19 January, the Union army had had to endure not only the harassing tactics of the Rebels, but they had also had to endure some of the worst winter weather seen in the region in years. In almost two months of marching, it had rained all but three days. The constant deluge had turned the numerous streams and creeks along their path into raging torrents and had created seas of mud where there had once been roads. For much of the march, the problems of transportation were more severe than those presented by the Confederate military. Roads had to be corduroyed almost every foot of the way, and the streams, creeks and rivers had to bridged for any crossing. A winter campaign in such terrible weather should have provided the Confederates with a degree of breathing space, sticking the Union army in the mud, but that respite was not to come. Sherman's men were not mired in the muck. In fact, they were hardly slowed at all by the inclement conditions and had become so adept at overcoming obstacles that the march was turning into a marvel of military engineering.

On 11 March 1865, the day after the fighting at Kinston ended, Sherman's legions took possession of Fayetteville, North Carolina,

Johnston's original selection as a concentration point for his army. The city was spared the destruction that had been visited upon so many other towns along the Union line of march, with the exception of the old Federal armory which was completely destroyed under the supervision of Colonel Orlando Poe, Sherman's chief engineer.[1] Some of Sherman's own soldiers were growing tired of the destruction of the army by this time. The fires of South Carolina had quenched their thirst for vengeance sufficiently to allow these mean to take pity on the civilians unlucky enough to live within their path.

Some men, like Charles S. Brown of the 21st Michigan, were thankful that the war was "in the south" and reflected on how they themselves would have acted if the destruction had taken place in the North. "You can never imagine a pillaged house," Brown wrote home, "never unless an army passes through your town & if this thing had been in the north I would *Bushwack* untill [sic] every man was either dead or I was. If such scenes should be enacted through Mich. I would never live as long as one of the invading army did. I do not blame the south & shall not if they do go to Guerrilla Warfare." Brown seemed comforted by the fact that the destruction in North Carolina was greatly reduced from that in South Carolina, writing that, "the men seem by instinct to treat N.C. as well as possible."[2]

The occupation of Fayetteville provided the men with an opportunity for a short rest and to once again be in contact with their own government. With the city being on the Cape Fear River, ships were sent from Wilmington to deliver supplies and the first mail and money the men had been issued for months. As far as supplies were concerned, the troops had managed quite well in obtaining sustenance from the Southern countryside, but they were not always provided with an abundant larder. Private Robert B. Hoadley wrote to his cousin that "[s]ome of the time it was very poor country, their [sic] was a few days that I could of [sic] eat a dog if he had been half

---

[1] Nathaniel Cheairs Hughes, Jr., *Bentonville: The Final Battle of Sherman & Johnston* (Chapel Hill: University of North Carolina Press, 1996) 77.

[2] Charles S. Brown to Etta, 25 April 1865, Charles S. Brown Papers, Perkins Library, Duke University, Durham NC.

cooked."[3] Now there would be hardtack and salt pork and a return to "normal" army fare.

But food was not the item of supply most urgently needed by the Union army, clothing and shoes were. The wear and tear of the long campaign, combined with the almost constant saturation caused by the rains, had reduced the uniforms of the men to mere tatters. At first glance, they appeared to be more of an assemblage of vagabonds and ruffians than an army. The ragged façade belied the spirit and confidence these men possessed, however, and just as the people of Frederick, Maryland, had noted an inexplicable military grandeur to be evident in Robert E. Lee's tattered Confederates during the Antietam Campaign, the residents of Fayetteville could tell that these Yankees were fighting men, regardless of their dress.

Shoes were a precious commodity by the time the army reached Fayetteville, with thousands upon thousands of the Federal infantrymen plodding along barefooted in the ranks. One veteran soldier from Illinois recorded in his dairy: "I have had to march barefoot again today and my feet keep getting worse. If I do not get in camp soon I will have to give up."[4] After so long being without shoes, their acquisition did not always provide the desired effect. In another journal entry this soldier continues, "This morning I realized a new pair of boots and I was anxious in the morning to start so I could experience the pleasure which I anticipated but my hopes and anticipations were cast asunder when I had traveled about five miles for they raised about a dozen blisters on my feet."[5]

Clothing consisted of a heterogeneous mixture of tattered uniforms and civilian dress. Most of the men's trousers were missing one or both legs below the knees, as these had been used to patch other areas more important to keep covered. Coats suffered from the same usage, and bare arms could be seen in almost every formation. Some of the men had appropriated civilian clothes to replace their

---

[3] Robert Bruce Hoadley to Cousin, 8 April 1865, Robert Bruce Hoadley Papers, Perkins Library, Duke University, Durham NC.

[4] John E. Risedorph Diary, 19 March 1865, Minnesota Historical Society, St. Paul MN.

[5] Ibid.

worn-out uniforms, and some had even donned parts of captured Confederate uniforms. Headgear was a model of diversity. Though some soldiers had their issued hats still in one piece, they were a small minority. Far more common were the men who wore a brimless hat or the brim alone, as a sort of visor. As with the other clothing, a wide variety of civilian headgear peppered the ranks. Though the officers were, by and large, well dressed, the men "looked more like Falstaff's ragged regiment than soldiers of the United States."[6]

Unfortunately, the supply ships coming up the Cape Fear from Wilmington did not contain any appreciable quantities of clothing, and the Union troops, for one of the rare times in the war, would go into battle looking more like the Rebels than the Confederates themselves did. The mail, the pay, and the rations were most welcome, though, as was the chance to take a few days break from the constant marching.

The story of how the supply ships got there at all is one of daring and resourcefulness. Sherman had known of the expedition against Fort Fisher and the port of Wilmington, but having no communication with the government since Savannah, he was not aware of how the operation had gone. Therefore, he sent a scout ahead, when still 150 miles distant from the city, with instructions to make arrangements for the supply ships that were now steaming into Fayetteville. In order to ensure the success of the mission, Sherman directed General O. O. Howard to select another man to be sent with the same message. Howard actually chose two men: Sergeant Myron J. Amick and Private Quimby, both of the 36th Illinois. The men were both given Confederate uniforms and were possessed of a passable Southern drawl, so their prospects of passing through Southern lines were excellent. The message from Sherman had been written on as small a piece of paper as possible and was then hidden in the end of a plug of tobacco, so that it could be easily disposed of in case of

---

[6] John Richard Boyle, *Soldiers True: The Story of the One Hundred and Eleventh Regiment Pennsylvania Veteran Volunteers* (New York Eaton & Sons, 1903) 287 and Julian Hinkley, *Service With the Third Wisconsin Infantry* (Madison: Wisconsin History Committee, 1912) 171.

capture. Amick and Quimby set out for Wilmington a full nine hours behind Sherman's scout, and the probability was that they would arrive in the city with a message that had already been presented. The two had a difficult time crossing over into Confederate lines, but once inside, their uniforms and accent allayed any suspicions, and they were even escorted for a part of their journey by some of Wade Hampton's Cavalry. One morning when they stopped for breakfast at a private home, they were asked many questions regarding the war by the lady of the house. "Where do you suppose Sherman will go next?" was one of her inquiries. Amick, for a moment, forgot himself and answered, "We never know until we get there." Quimby caught his attention before he could get in any deeper, and the private's facial expression caused Amick to realize his mistake. The scouts had taken their leave of the lady and had ridden about 10 miles down the road, where they were negotiating for a fresh horse, when they noticed a Confederate captain and two men approaching them from the direction they had come. The captain's demeanor and questions soon convinced Amick that the officer had been told of the slip by the Southern lady and quick thinking would be necessary. Taking his revolver from its holster, Amick leveled it at the Rebel captain and said, "I believe youans are Yankee spies; so surrender! If my suspicions are correct, youans will hang as sure as fate; so prove yourselves clar." This move took the captain totally by surprise and he took great pains to prove his loyalty to the uniform he wore. Amick apologized for doubting the officer and the two scouts were allowed to pass by unmolested. The way was clear until they reached the outskirts of Wilmington, where they once more had to evade the Southern pickets by making use of the local swamps. Once safely inside the Union lines, they called on General Terry to deliver the message, two days ahead of Sherman's own man. For his service on this mission, Sherman rewarded Amick with a lieutenant's commission.[7]

---

[7] L. G. Bennett and W. M. Haigh, *History of the Thirty-Sixth Regiment Illinois Volunteers, During the War of the Rebellion* (Aurora IL: Knickerbocker & Hodder, Printers and Binders, 1876) 788–89.

Northern newspapers that came with mail provided the first glimpse the soldiers had had in months about how the folks back home were viewing their march. One *New York Tribune* article professed a fear that the Confederates would "do in" Sherman's boys while they were struggling through the swamps of North Carolina. Theodore Upson of the 100th Indiana took offense to the article, stating, "What a lot of faint hearts they must be down there in New York! I wish they would get all of the Johnny's together; we can handle them if Grant will only hold Lee and his Army—don't worry about us, Mr. 'Tribune'; you just cheer up your boys around Richmond and after we get through with our job here we will go and help them and finish things in a rush."[8]

Little did Upson realize that Joe Johnston was even then trying to "get all the Johnny's together" to accommodate him. When General Bragg was ordered to withdraw from Kinston, his instructions were to regroup his command at Goldsboro and await the concentration of the rest of the army there. But Bragg suggested that a more appropriate location would be the town of Smithfield, situated along the Atlantic and North Carolina Railroad in a position central to both Goldsboro and Raleigh. He informed Johnston that he would stop all troops at that place to hold them in readiness unless contrary to the commander's wishes.[9]

Generals Hardee and Hampton had been keeping their forces posted in front of Sherman and were being driven toward the point of concentration as the Federals advanced. No fight had been made to deny Fayetteville to the invaders, only the daily skirmishing that had become such a part of the campaign. In fact, Union cavalry under Kilpatrick surprised the Confederates on reaching the town and almost captured General Hampton in the process. One of Joe Wheeler's troopers was not so lucky as Hampton. He stood in the road and fired at the Union advance as it entered the town, staying

---

[8] Oscar Osburn Winther, *With Sherman to the Sea: The Civil War Letters Diaries & Reminiscences of Theodore Upson* (Baton Rouge: Louisiana State University Press, 1943) 156–57.

[9] Don C. Seitz, *Braxon Bragg: General of the Confederacy* (Columbia: The State Company, 1924) 515.

too long in the spot to make good his escape. The prisoner was "brought before Kilpatrick who asked him if he had done so. He acknowledged it. Kill turned around to his boys & pointed to one of the handsome shade trees of the town remarked, 'Boys; do you see that limb,' was answered 'yes, aye-aye, of course', ect. & added 'Well then; string him up,' and rode on about his business. The poor fellow in less than 5 minutes was going heavenward."[10]

As Hardee evacuated the town, the headlong rush of the advanced cavalry might have indicated that the Federals were preparing to attack him in force, and "Old Reliable" made the proper dispositions for such an event. He could not know that Sherman intended to stay in Fayetteville for a few days for a much-needed rest. The delay here would give Johnston a little while longer to bring troops in from the Army of Tennessee, but time was not the only consideration in receiving men from the western army. The commander had assigned General Pierre Gustave Toutant Beauregard to the defense of the railroad running from Greensboro and Charlotte to Chester, South Carolina, as one of his first official acts as commander of the Army of the South when he took charge in Charlotte. Johnston had been embarrassed over replacing Beauregard in the top position and had sought to ease the situation as much as possible by assigning that general to a post where he could still exercise a degree of independent command. Unfortunately, the Creole took the independent command portion of his assignment too much to heart, creating his own separate command within Johnston's department. Many of the men who were coming east from the Army of Tennessee were diverted from their march to join Johnston to become part of Beauregard's command. Two full divisions of Cheatham's corps, at least two brigades of Stewart's corps, and several other units were held by Beauregard at Greensboro, Raleigh, Charlotte, Danville, and other points. It is estimated that between the first week of March and the first week of April, Beauregard controlled between 6,000 and 8,000 men, spread from Danville, Virginia, to upper South Carolina. It is a

---

[10] Charles S. Brown to Etta, 26 April 1865, Charles S. Brown Papers, Perkins Library, Duke University, Durham NC.

mystery why Johnston did not pressure Beauregard to forward these much-needed reinforcements to his army. The only possible explanations are that he was still trying to help Beauregard save face in an embarrassing situation and he wished to keep the line of communication through Danville to General Lee open.[11]

General Benjamin Franklin Cheatham could not understand the reasoning and he was perplexed at the situation. That officer was leading his men to join Johnston when they experienced a one-week delay at Salisbury, North Carolina. He was eager to reach the remainder of the army, and his patience finally gave way when the men had been loaded on cars for transportation to the front and another interruption occurred. It seems that another train was blocking the track, and when Cheatham went to inquire of its conductor why it was not moving, he received the smart reply that the conductor was "running that part of the business, sir." The exasperated general was done talking. He landed a right to the head of the conductor, knocking him down into the mud. As one of his veterans later remembered, the conductor "was up and had his train moving before he took time to shake off the mud." Cheatham and his men would not reach Johnston in time to participate in the army's final battles, but it was certainly through no lack of effort on his part.[12]

Cheatham would not be the only high ranking officer from the western army who would not be able to join Johnston before the battle with Sherman. General Stephen D. Lee was still recovering from a wound received during the Nashville Campaign, but he was given command of a rendezvous camp in Augusta, Georgia, with orders to collect and forward to North Carolina all stragglers, returning wounded, and soldiers back from furlough he could. By 18 March, Lee had gathered a force of 5,000 men, which he had temporarily assigned to nonpermanent brigades, and he started north to join Johnston. But

---

[11] Thomas Lawrence Connelly, *Autumn of Glory: The Army of Tennessee, 1861–1865* (Baton Rouge: Louisiana State University Press, 1971) 524–25.

[12] Christopher Losson, *Tennessee's Forgotten Warriors: Frank Cheatham and His Confederate Division* (Knoxville: University of Tennessee Press, 1989) 246.

these old veterans had already fought their last battle. They would arrive in North Carolina in time for some skirmishing before the surrender, but their numbers would not be available for the final battle.[13]

Johnston would also be minus all of the artillery from the Army of Tennessee for the upcoming campaign. Following the defeat at Nashville, about half of the ordnance had been sent to Mobile, Alabama, with the remainder earmarked for Johnston, but the batteries were in such desperate need of refitting and so destitute in terms of transportations that only one of them ever reached North Carolina, and that was not till 12 April. The artillery was not a real problem for Johnston, as he already had more than he could logistically support. Of the thirty light batteries he had with the army, he would eventually consolidate them into ten good ones.[14]

With the inability of so many sorely needed men to connect with the army, the Confederates hopes to amass a suitable force to contend with Sherman were gloomy indeed. Sherman reported 57,676 men present with his army on 1 March 1865. By 17 March, Johnston had in his immediate control only 14,685 with which to oppose them.[15] The only other sizable additions he could count on arriving were General Hardee and his men from Sherman's front, as they fell back toward Smithfield. Other than the obvious disparity in size that the Confederates would be working under, the two principle problems they faced would be getting an idea whether Sherman was marching on Goldsboro or Raleigh, and trying to figure out how they could induce the Federals into leaving a portion of their force exposed and vulnerable.

General Johnston knew Sherman to be a master of maneuver, a general who could be counted on to keep his army firmly in hand, and he felt the chances of him leaving himself open for any attack were

---

[13] Herman Hattaway, *General Stephen D. Lee* (Jackson: University Press of Mississippi, 1976) 153.

[14] Larry J. Daniel, *Cannoneers in Gray: The Field Artillery of the Army of Tennessee, 1861–1865* (Tuscaloosa: University of Alabama Press, 1984) 184.

[15] Robert Underwood Johnson and Clarence Clough Buel, *Battles and Leaders of the Civil War*, 4 vols. (New York: The Century Company, 1884–1888) 4:698, 700.

remote. For this reason, he once more contacted General Lee to urge that the two armies be united against one of the Federal threats, be it in North Carolina or Virginia. Lee vetoed the proposal on the grounds that he could not extricate himself from the siege lines, and he still held the belief that the Army of the South could deal Sherman a setback and retake the initiative in the campaign.

General Hardee had withdrawn his force to Smith's Mills, a small hamlet near Averasboro, along the Black River. He had been instructed to remain vigilant for any indications the Federals might give regarding their intended objective. General Beauregard had wired Johnston on 14 March with his conviction that the Yankees would be turning toward Goldsboro and join with General Schofield's troops, but Johnston was still not entirely convinced. On 15 March, Judson Kilpatrick's cavalry pressed toward Hardee's Confederates, followed by the left wing, composed of the XX and XIV Corps. The Federals had concluded their rest in Fayetteville and were ready to make the final push for Virginia. Weather conditions were as miserable as ever. Continued rainfall had turned the roads into rivers of mud, and both armies were traveling with great difficulty. The Federals were relying, as always, on corduroying the road as they went. On the Confederate side, Hardee was facing a dilemma with his transportation. The Black River had become much swollen by the recent rains and he was unable to get his wagon train across. He would be forced to either abandon the train or to turn and fight the Yankees, and perhaps, hold them long enough for his wagons to be able to cross.[16]

Hardee deployed his men at once, and skirmishing with the Federal cavalry broke out. The old phrase from the Atlanta Campaign, "they don't push worth a damn," came back into usage. But Hardee was unsure how to place his army against the Federal forces and form a defense, as he now had fewer than 6,000 men under his command. Desertions and casualties had somewhat reduced his numbers since entering North Carolina, but the most significant reduction to the ranks had been caused by the withdrawal of Major General Ambrose R. Wright's South Carolina Brigade at the North

---

[16] Hinkley, *Service with the Third Wisconsin Infantry*, 171–72.

Carolina border. Governor A. G. Magrath felt that the needed to detain a portion of this state forces for home defense, and he ordered Wright to remain in South Carolina for that purpose, further reducing the number of available men that Johnston would be able to count as part of his army. Hardee's force was just slightly over half the number it had been two months ago in South Carolina, and including Wheeler's two brigades of cavalry, which had been assigned to him, he could muster only a total of 8,000 of all arms. Slocum was advancing with four divisions of his two corps, a total of just over 15,000 men. In addition, he had available one division from each corps that had been assigned to guard the trains of the left wing.[17]

The disparity in numbers, combined with the fact that most of his men were garrison troops who had never participated in an infantry battle, caused Hardee to adopt a defensive strategy that would maximize his resources. He settled upon a plan that had been proven successful in the Carolinas once before when General Daniel Morgan, in the Revolution, had faced the similar circumstances of being in command of mostly green troops who were outnumbered by the British. Morgan had developed his position in a series of defensive lines, one behind the other, and had placed his greenest men in the front lines and his most seasoned veterans in the rear. This strategy gave the green troops the security of being able to fall back to another prepared position when they became overpowered instead of being driven from the field, and it ensured that the defensive force would become stronger and more compact as it was pushed back, while the attackers would become strung out and disorganized. The plan had worked to perfection at the Battle of Cowpens, and Hardee virtually duplicated it in his orders for troop placement at Averasboro. In all, he would have five lines of works, including the cavalry and infantry skirmish lines, placed one behind the other, and covering a depth of 1 mile. All of the lines would be placed across the Fayetteville-Raleigh Road, which bisected the battlefield. Hardee formed his first main line in the rear of Oak Grove, the home of John Smith, of the family for

[17] Nathaniel Cheairs Hughes, Jr., *General William J. Hardee: Old Reliable* (Baton Rouge: Louisiana State University Press, 1965) 282.

which Smithfield was named.[18] Into this line he ordered the brigade of Colonel Alfred M. Rhett, with instructions to advance a skirmish line 200 yards ahead into the open field that fronted Rhett's position. Though the men of Rhett's command were part of the small number of "regulars" in the Confederate army, they had spent the war in the coastal forts in Charleston and were not battle tried.

Their introduction to infantry combat would be all the more difficult due to the fact that they would have to face their baptism minus their brigade commander. As Hardee was perfecting his defensive alignment on 15 March, Rhett, in his forward position, mistook a party of Yankee cavalry for his own troops and was taken prisoner. A few of Kilpatrick's troopers had ridden into the Confederate skirmish line as Rhett was supervising its progress. The colonel upbraided the men for their action, and was threatening to report them when one of the troopers leveled a pistol at his head and demanded his surrender stating that "if he didn't come along he'd make a hole through him."[19] Rhett was a Charleston blueblood and a member of one of the first families of South Carolina. He had served part of his duty during the war as commander at Fort Sumter, a fact he seemed disposed to communicate with his captors. Rhett's aristocratic status and his affiliation with Fort Sumter made him a target for the pent-up hostilities of his captors, and his acquired speech and manners, though consistent with the code of honor of Southern aristocracy, did little to defuse the animosity towards him.

With Rhett gone, Hardee assigned Colonel William Butler of the 1st South Carolina Regulars to serve as brigade commander. Two hundred yards to the rear of Butler's advanced line was the brigade of Brigadier General Stephen Elliot, both lines being under the direct supervision of division commander General William Taliaferro. Six hundred yard behind Elliott Hardee built his main line of works, occupied by the four veteran brigades of Major General Lafayette

---

[18] Jessie S. Smith, "On the Battlefield of Averasboro, N.C.," *Confederate Veteran Magazine* 34/1(1926): 49.

[19] Maj. George Ward Nichols, *The Story of the Great March, From the Diary of a Staff Officer* (New York: Harper & Bros. Publishers, 1865) 254.

McLaws's division. The left of the main line rested on a large swamp close to the Black River, and the right was extended, by means of a skirmish line, to the Cape Fear River. In the rear was a juncture of the Smithfield and the Averasboro roads that would allow the army to travel either to Raleigh or Goldsboro, whichever the case demanded. It was a formidable position, and the collapsible nature of the defensive lines ensured that it would be able to deliver maximum firepower when it was pushed back to the final line.[20]

The night of 15 March saw only scattered picket fire after the arrival of Brigadier General Joseph Hawley's brigade, and according to others, the Federal infantry did not press an attack. At dawn on 15 March, Kilpatrick and Hawley advanced to test the strength of Hardee's defenses, driving Butler's pickets back to the first battle line. Once he had developed the Confederate line and determined that Hardee was there in force, Kilpatrick sent back word that additional men would be needed. Major General Alpheus Williams, XX Corps commander, then sent up the divisions of General Nathaniel Jackson and General William Ward. The two Union divisions arrived on the field at 10:00 P.M., just as a line of Confederate skirmishers was pushing Kilpatrick's dismounted troopers back.

By this time, the John Smith home had become a Confederate hospital, all of its rooms being eventually filled with the Southern wounded. Smith had two brothers who lived just down the road toward Fayetteville, but the location of the armies placed their homes behind Union lines. William Smith's home saw the same usage as John's as the Federals occupied it for a hospital, performing surgery on top of a piano located in the parlor. The third brother, Farquhard, saw his home become headquarters for General Slocum. When the general arrived, he asked to meet the ladies of the house, as Mrs. Smith was a northern lady, and he believed they were related. Mr. Smith denied the request, stating, "When you cross the Mason and Dixon line, all ties of blood are lost." His animosity toward the Federals can be understood by the fact that he had sent all eight of his sons to serve in the Confederate army. The last, a boy of just sixteen years, had

---

[20] Hughes, *General William J. Hardee*, 282–83.

enlisted as a courier on General Hardee's staff only a few days before.[21]

When Williams's Union divisions arrived at the place, Kilpatrick's dismounted troopers were about to be swept from the field. They were almost out of ammunition and their right flank was being turned by Taliaferro's men. Major John A. Reynolds, chief of artillery, XX Corps, immediately positioned three batteries in a commanding position and opened fire on the advancing Rebels. The work of the cannoneers was well done, and the vigorous fire they maintained allowed the fresh brigades of the XX Corps to assume the offense.[22] Colonel Daniel Dustin's Second Brigade of Ward's division had the advance in the march to the battlefield. His men could hear the escalating sounds of battle as they neared the field, "and when about two miles out we heard the roar of a cannon ahead and concluded that Kilpatrick was getting a row ready for us to settle."[23]

Ward's division relieved the cavalry, and Kilpatrick moved his troopers off to the right to extend the infantry flank. General Jackson's 1st Division then came up and formed on the left of Ward's position. Colonel Henry Case's First Brigade of Ward's division was sent to the extreme left of the Union line in an effort to turn the Confederate right, and as they moved into position, the artillery continued to rain shells upon Butler's works preparatory to the Union assault from flank and front.

Private D. M. Tedder of the 1st South Carolina Regulars was not cowed by the Federal barrage. In fact, he was excited about being in the front line of works, "witch [sic] place we went all anxious for the fight."[24] They prepared to meet the Yankees who were forming to their front, unaware that Case's column was moving on their flank. Confederate artillery dueled with the Federals across the open field

---

[21] Smith, "On the Battlefield of Averasboro, N.C.," 48–49.

[22] John G. Barrett, *The Civil War in North Carolina* (Chapel Hill: University of North Carolina Press, 1963) 322.

[23] Ezra Button Diary, 16 March 1865, John B. Tripp Papers, State Historical Society of Wisconsin, Madison WI.

[24] Daniel Miles Tedder Diary, 13, Daniel Miles Tedder Papers, Southern Historical Collection, University of North Carolina, Chapel Hill NC.

and the Rebel infantry behind the works waited to add the crack of musketry to the heavy roar of shot and shell.

Sergeant C. H. Dickinson of Company E, 22nd Wisconsin, Dustin's Brigade, was directly across the field from the Confederate works. The 22nd had been detailed to support a section of artillery while they waited for Case's Brigade to get in position. Dickinson observed that "our gunners were making it quite interesting and lively, by throwing solid shot, and shells at the rebel guns we noticed after one of our shells had exploded in their camp, a great commotion, and that particular gun was silenced."[25]

"Then the order came to charge" upon Case's reaching his assigned spot,

> and with huzzas that fully equaled the rebel yell, we started on the run across that field for the rebel guns; and fully expecting to meet a charge of grape and canister; but nothing came but a volley of musketry from the rifle pits, and fortunately for us, they were so excited, that the bullets nearly all went over.
>
> As we mounted their works, we could see what caused the stampede, there was our flanking column coming up from their rear, thay [sic] had been hidden from us, by formation of the ground, and the rebel works; and that accounted for their wild shooting, that [sic] were getting between two fires, and it made them nervous.[26]

The whole affair was over "in an hour,"[27] and the Federals were in possession of the works. Private Tedder felt that the Confederates "cood of [sic] held them trough [sic] the fight if the 20th Corps had not Flanked us, but tha [sic] came completely on our Right flank an [sic] give us a Cross fire." Colonel Butler "give orders for every man

---

[25] Charles S. Dickinson Diary, 165, Charles H. Dickinson Papers, State Historical Society of Wisconsin, Madison WI.

[26] Ibid.

[27] Ezra Button Diary, 16 March 1865, John B. Tripp Papers, State Historical Society of Wisconsin, Madison WI.

to save himself that cood [sic]. We left at double quick, leaving 300 of our wounded at the works who wair [sic] unable to get off."[28]

> [Sergeant Dickinson]went over the works, just to the right of the gun we were aiming for, [where he found] a wounded rebel in the mud, in the bottom of the ditch; he had been hit by a cannon ball from one of our guns, which had gone through at least six feet of earth works, it had torn off the whole right side of his body, and he begged of our men to shot him, to put him out of misery and pain; but he lived only a few minutes; on looking around, we discovered what caused the commotion in their camp, when our gunners were treating them to a dose of shell.
>
> It was evident from appearances that a shell had exploded in their limber chest, it had wrecked the limber, tearing off the wheels, and of the chest, there was nothing to show that it ever existed.
>
> There lay six white horses, dead, and horribly mangled, which had evidently belonged to, and been hitched to the limber, the gunners, and drivers, were laying about, what was left of them, mangled by the exploding shells, past recognition; it was no wonder that gun was silenced; for the explosion of their own shells had killed every one in the vicinity of the limber.
>
> On inquiring of a prisoner about the battery, we learned that thay [sic] called themselves the South Carolina Tigers; thay [sic] had been in Forts in Charleston, since the commencement of the war; and when Sherman's army captured the City, had taken a light field battery.[29]

---

[28] Daniel Miles Tedder Diary, 14, Daniel Miles Tedder Papers, Southern Historical Collection, University of North Carolina, Chapel Hill NC.

[29] Charles S. Dickinson Diary, 164–65, Charles H. Dickinson Papers, State Historical Society of Wisconsin, Madison WI.

Following up on their initial success, the 1st and 3rd Divisions of the XX Corps advanced against the second line of Confederate works under General Elliott. General John Mitchell's 2nd Brigade, 2nd Division, was the advance of the XIV Corps and reached the field immediately following the capture of Butler's works. His brigade was formed on the left of the Union line, while Kilpatrick was ordered to pull back his cavalry on the extreme right and feel for the Goldsboro Road.

Butler's Brigade withdrew to the second line, where his men were reformed in the rear of Elliott's Brigade, with the exception of twenty men of the 1st South Carolina Regulars, who were detailed as sharpshooters and sent to the front.[30] The Confederates had lost over 300 men and two cannon at the first line, but they were prepared to meet the next Federal thrust.

General Kilpatrick assumed the immediate direction of the cavalry on the right, and his scouts soon reported the existence of a road leading off to the right, which circled around the rear of the Confederate position. With this information, the 9th Ohio Cavalry was ordered to proceed up the road in hopes of cutting off Elliott's line. They had advanced but a short distance when they were attacked by Colonel G. P. Harrison's Brigade of General McLaws's division. The Confederates had moved unseen through dense underbrush until they were within a few yards of the unsuspecting Yankees. The first clue the troopers had about the presence of the Rebels was a volley fired into their ranks. The Union cavalry was thrown back in confusion, closely followed by Harrison's Confederates. With the sound of firing in their front, the 9th Pennsylvania Cavalry, the next regiment in line, quickly deployed for action.

The 9th Ohio was driven back 200 yards where it met the Pennsylvanians, who, "as the Ninth Ohio passed through its intervals, opened so hot a fire upon the charging line that it fell back in confusion." It was now about 2:00 P.M., and the troopers had been fighting for almost eight hours. As Colonel Jordan of the 9th

---

[30] Daniel Miles Tedder Diary, 14, Daniel Miles Tedder Papers, Southern Historical Collection, University of North Carolina, Chapel Hill NC.

Pennsylvania related, "My command, having been in action from 6 a.m. till 2 p.m. almost without intermission, and having less than five rounds of ammunition to the man left, I was ordered to retire to the rear, to dismount the men, and allow my command to rest."[31]

By this time, Federal infantry had come up to relieve the cavalry, and Kilpatrick's whole command was given a rest. With mounting pressure on his front and the possibility of having his line flanked, Taliaferro evacuated his line and fell back in an orderly withdrawal on McLaws's main position. Taliaferro formed his division in the center of the Confederate line, across the road. On his left was McLaws's division, which extended to the bank of Black River, and on his right was Wheeler's dismounted cavalry to which had been added General John Kennedy's Brigade of McLaws's division. The Federal attack on the main line commenced at 3:00 P.M. and was led by General James Morgan's 2nd Division of the XIV Corps, which had recently arrived on the field. Morgan was dispatched to the Federal left, where he was to work his way around and flank the Confederate right, just as had been done earlier in the day at Butler's first line. Morgan found the going much more difficult than Case had, however. The rain had begun again and added to the difficulty in moving his men over the creeks, ravines, and muddy ground he had to cross to get into position. When he finally succeeded in getting his division to their assigned spot, Morgan found Wheeler and Kennedy entrenched behind a ravine in imposing works. The Confederates met Morgan with a "heavy and destructive fire" that stalled his advance. It was evident that the works were held in strength, and "It would have been worse than folly to have attempted a further advance."[32]

Ward and Jackson's divisions of the XX Corps were once more advancing against the front of the Rebel works. The troops had not been pushed forward very hard since taking the first line of Confederate entrenchments. In fact, the 22nd Wisconsin stopped at

---

[31] John W. Rowell, *Yankee Cavalrymen: Through the Civil War with the Ninth Pennsylvania Cavalry* (Knoxville: University of Tennessee Press, 1971) 240.

[32] McLaws Letter Book Journal, March 16, 1865, General Lafayette McLaws Papers. Southern Historical Collection, University of North Carolina, Chapel Hill NC.

the first line: "a short distance from the scattered remains of the South Carolina Tigers, we built fires, made coffee, and after a hearty dinner, moved on about one mile to their second line of works."[33]

The assaults of the XX Corps divisions were repulsed several times by Taliaferro and McLaws in the center, but as dusk was gathering on the horizon, Jackson's Union division made a movement by the Federal right in an attempt to turn the left flank of the Confederates. Hardee shifted Colonel Butler's Brigade from the center to the left to aide McLaws in repulsing this new threat at about 4:30 P.M. Both sides settled into their lines, and only intermittent skirmishing was continued until 8:00 P.M.[34]

At the time that Jackson launched the final Union assault of the day, General Hardee was sending word to Joe Johnston that his line had held firm and had resisted all attempts to break it, but that he planned to withdraw from it during the night. He had received intelligence from Wade Hampton that General Howard, with the right wing of the Union army, had crossed the Black River and could soon be in a position to cut off his line of retreat and crush him. Furthermore, he was probably influenced by General McLaws that the current lines had withstood all the pressure they could. McLaws was sure that the Yankees could have succeeded in turning his left if there had been but a little more daylight remaining. The next day would undoubtedly bring about a resumption of the pressure on his flank, and Mclaws did not feel it would hold.[35]

While the days fighting at Averasboro could hardly be considered a battle by the standards used in the fourth year of the war, it was also too large to be categorized as a skirmish. Union commanders reported their casualties as 682, and the XX Corps bore the bunt of the fighting with a loss of 485 men. Some Union estimates place the Confederate loss at Averasboro as high as 1,100, but the 500 casualties claimed by

---

[33] Charles S. Dickinson Diary, 165–66, Charles H. Dickinson Papers, State Historical Society of Wisconsin, Madison WI.

[34] McLaws Letter Book Journal, March 16, 1865, General Lafayette McLaws Papers. Southern Historical Collection, University of North Carolina, Chapel Hill NC.

[35] Hughes, *General William J. Hardee*, 284.

the Rebel commanders in their after-battle reports seems to be a more reasonable number, as they had fought the entire engagement from behind works with the Federals forced into the attacking role. By far the largest portion of the Confederate losses had been suffered during the initial charge on Butler's Brigade, with 300 of the total representing only those members of his unit that were captured.

Averasboro served little purpose to either side when viewed as a single event. Losses were relatively even for the two sides, with neither gaining a clear advantage on the field. Hardee had extricated his supply wagons, which had been among is primary concerns when deciding to offer battle to the Federals, but the check he gave to Sherman's forces was inconsequential and had only slowed the left wing by a day—it had not stopped it. When observed as a part of the larger campaign Averasboro must be considered as at least a moral victory to the Confederates, and it also provided them with the information needed to plan their next strategic move. After four months of setbacks, it provided the first positive results that had been attained against Sherman or a portion of his army. The men in the ranks were given to the opinion that they had administered a serious repulse to the Yankees and that they had inflicted serious casualties on the enemy. General Hardee added to this impression when he commended his command on their "giving the enemy the first serious check he has received since leaving Atlanta." He continued in his praise by stating, "The lieutenant-general augurs happily of the future service and reputation of troops who have signalize the opening of the campaign by admirable steadiness, endurance, and courage."[36] Greater even than the confidence it gave his men was the hard evidence the battle provided concerning the true direction of Sherman's March. Hampton's earlier report had been substantiated and there was no longer any doubt that the Federals were heading for Goldsboro. Johnston would now be free to concentrate on the defense of that place instead of having to divide his attention between there

[36] *The War of the Rebellion: A Compilation of the Official Records of the Union and Confederate Armies* (Washington, DC: Government Printing Office, 1895) ser. 1, vol. 47, pt. 1, 1411.

and Raleigh. Hardee's engagement would prove to be a greater accomplishment than was first thought a few days later at Bentonville. It had inadvertently caused a separation between Sherman's two wings, and would serve to give Johnston the opportunity he sought to strike a blow against an isolated part of the Union army. Without the engagement at Averasboro the Battle of Bentonville would not have been likely.

During the night of 16 March, Hardee evacuated his lines as per his earlier communication with Johnston. D. M. Tedder was serving on picket duty when "the picket line of my Brigade was unfortunately captured, the army left the brest [sic] works Completely to our Surprise [sic]. We was then taken to Gen. Sherman's headquarters, which place I stade [sic] one day only."[37] The war was over for Tedder, and he would spend its remaining days in a prison camp in New York. Hardee's army was heading toward Elevation, where he would still be able to cover the roads to Smithfield and to Raleigh. If Sherman turned to Goldsboro, he would join Johnston at Smithfield, and if he continued toward Raleigh, he would keep his army in front of the Federals until Johnston could join him. Joe Wheeler provided the definitive information Hardee was seeking on the afternoon of 17 March, and when the news was relayed to Johnston, he ordered Hardee to march at once for Bentonville.

Slocum found himself unexpectedly in possession of the battlefield on the morning of 17 March. His actions on 16 March had comprised a series of limited attacks and strong skirmish actions. A general assault had been planned for 17 March with all four of the divisions he had at hand. Undoubtedly, this attack would have been successful and would have seriously damaged Hardee's force. At the first light of day, Slocum ordered his divisions forward to "the line of rebel works which were found to be empty. After waiting here a while the bugle sounded the march and we [the 22nd Wisconsin Infantry] were away. Four miles over wretched road brought us to Averysboro [sic] where we went into camp but were told we might not stay over

---

[37] Daniel Miles Tedder Diary, 14–15, Daniel Miles Tedder Papers, Southern Historical Collection, University of North Carolina, Chapel Hill NC.

night. Our foragers have been skirmishing with the rebels all the a.m. Broken wagons, ambulances and artillery carriages are strung along the road promiscuously. Quite a number of wounded rebs were found at this place but no inhabitants and not room for many."[38]

The Federals did not have to wonder about someone finding their wounded. All of their casualties were being transported, along with the army, to prevent them falling into enemy hands, though it would have been more humane to have left the more severely injured behind and not have subjected them to the miseries of being bounced and banged along in the army wagons and ambulances. The Federals who had died at the William Stitch House were buried in the family garden before the army moved on, but were later moved to a National Cemetery in Raleigh.[39]

Colonel Alfred Rhett was accompanying his Northern captors on their march to Goldsboro. His rank and personality had caused him to bear the brunt of an act of General Kilpatrick in retaliation for an incident involving a Union officer. It seems that Captain Duncan of the 36th Illinois had been among the rear guard of the retreating Confederates when they were withdrawing from Fayetteville and were captured. He made good his escape some days later, but when he once more reached his own lines he was without shoes, coat, or hat, having only a handkerchief tied over his head. When asked how he came to be in such a condition, Duncan related that Wade Hampton's men had made him "get out of his hat, coat and shoes," which articles they promptly confiscated for their own use. The captain alleged that he petitioned Wade Hampton personally for protection normally afforded to an officer, but was answered only by a curse. When General Kilpatrick heard Duncan's story he was so angered that he took retribution against Colonel Rhett in like manner. He compelled Rhett to march on foot like an enlisted man and allowed his troopers

---

[38] Ezra Button Diary, 67, John B. Tripp Papers, State Historical Society of Wisconsin, Madison WI.

[39] Smith, "On the Battlefield of Averasboro, N.C.," 49.

to relieve the colonel of personal belongings, including the beautifully stitched jackboots, which were swapped for a pair of brogans.[40]

While the left wing had been engaged at Averasboro, the right wing of the army, under General Howard, had continued along on its daily marching schedule. The XV and XVII Corps, along with the trains of both wings, had crossed the Black River and South Creek on 16 March, using all parallel roads they could find to the Smithfield Road the left wing would be using. Wade Hampton, with Butler's cavalry, was harassing their movements but could do little to slow them down. He had tried to destroy the bridge across the Black River on 16 March, but his men were driven off before it could be fully fired. The Federals extinguished the flames and tried to cross, but they found it too weak to support the heavy carriages. A swamp extended for some 200 yard on either side of the river at this point, and the river had been corduroyed years before. This too gave way under the weight of the wagons. Though some of the infantry made it across, the march was halted at 10:00 A.M. and repair work was begun which took twelve hours to complete. Colonel Oscar Jackson of the 63rd Ohio had been one of the soldiers to cross over the bridge but the rest of his regiment was stranded on the opposite bank while repairs were underway. The colonel had ample time to study his surroundings and he was less than impressed by what he saw. "This river is as ugly a looking stream as I ever saw. When looked at in a body the water is as black as ink and at present there is quite a current. One poor rebel was wounded on the main bridge in the skirmish this morning and dropping into the water sank to rise no more, and the officer we lost, Captain Woodberry of the 10th Illinois Mounted Infantry, was drowned in the swamp after being wounded, before he could be helped."[41]

Most of the infantry got over the bridge that night, but the wagons waited for more bracing and reinforcement to be done. The

---

[40] Bennett and Haigh, *Thirty-Sixth Illinois Volunteers,* 789–90.

[41] David P. Jackson, *The Colonels Diary: Journals Kept before and during the Civil War by the Late Colonel Oscar L. Jackson of New Castle, Pennsylvania, Sometimes Commander of the 63rd Regiment O.V.I.* (Sharon PA: self published, 1922) 197.

bridge was not sufficiently strong for the trains to cross until 1:00 A.M. on the morning of the 17 March. At 6:00 A.M. the march was resumed up the Clinton Road, and after the trouble the army had been having crossing the swollen streams and rivers in the region, the prospect of just having to deal with the mud must have looked promising. One Union soldier, while wading waist-deep across a swollen stream was heard to remark, "I guess Uncle Billy has struck this stream endwise."[42]

General Howard was aware that the left wing had been engaged on 16 March, but he had received little information on how the battle had gone. Therefore, he decided to slow up his march a little on 17 March, covering a distance of only 6 miles before going into camp. Word reached him of the Confederate withdrawal from Slocum's front later in the day, and the march was planned to resume at full speed the next morning.

---

[42] Barrett, *Civil War in North Carolina*, 325.

4

JOHNSTON PLANS AN AMBUSH

General Hardee arrived at Elevation around noon on 17 March, and finding that there was to be no pursuit on the part of the Federals, he allowed his men to make camp and take a well-deserved rest. The cavalry forces under Wheeler and Hampton continued to harass the Yankees throughout the day, but there was no action of consequence before either wing of Sherman's army. At daybreak on 18 March, General Hampton reported information to Johnston regarding the disposition of the Federals columns that was to set in motion events which would culminate in the largest battle of the Carolinas Campaign. "According to the reports of our cavalry," General Johnston later wrote, "the Federal right wing was about half a day's march in advance of the left; so that there was probably an interval of a day's march between the heads of the two columns."[1]

This development was precisely the opening the Confederate commander had been hoping for. Hardee's delaying action at Averasboro had created a gap between the wings of the Union army, and if he could concentrate his forces against an exposed wing in time, he might defeat it before the rest of the army could come to it assistance. Hampton's intelligence reports made the choice of which wing to attack an easy one. The left wing was advancing on the road from Averasboro to Goldsboro, and the right wing was taking a more direct route on the road from Fayetteville. The left wing "was more

---

[1] Gen. Joseph E. Johnston, *Narrative of Military Operations Directed During the Late War Between the States by Joseph E. Johnston, General, C.S.A.* (New York: D. Appleton and Co., 1874) 384–85.

than a day's march from the point in its route opposite to the hamlet of Bentonville, where the two roads [that the wings were marching on] according to the map of North Carolina, were ten or twelve miles apart."[2]

The hamlet of Bentonville was 2 miles north of the road, and 16 miles southeast of Smithfield. General Hampton had examined the ground near the road and had found it to be a favorable position from which the Confederate army could launch an attack. He advised Johnston of the strong defensive nature of the ground and proposed that the army be united to fight the coming battle at that position.

While Johnston was laying plans for the decisive battle of the campaign, his virtues as a commander were being extolled on the floor of the Confederate Congress by Senator L. T. Wigfall, chairman of the Committee on Military Affairs. "What infused 'spirit and confidence' into the Army of Tennessee?" Senator Wigfall asked.

> Was it the consciousness that it, at last had a commander who, careless of his own life, was careful of that of his men, who knew when to take them under fire, and how to bring them out, and whose thorough soldiership would save them from ever being uselessly slaughtered by being led to battle except when some good purpose was to be accomplished, or some brilliant victory achieved?
>
> The complaint against Johnston cannot be that he would not fight, for he fought almost every day, killing or wounding 45,000 of the enemy, and losing 10,000 himself [during the Atlanta Campaign].
>
> Is it that he did not stake the cause of his country on a single cast of the dice—that he would not risk all on the issue of a single battle?"[3]

---

[2] Ibid., 384.

[3] Lt. Col. Wesley Thurman Leeper, *Rebels Valiant: Second Arkansas Mounted Rifles (Dismounted)* (Little Rock: Pioneer Press, 1964) 275.

Senator Wigfall could not know that Johnston proposed to do precisely that—to risk all on the outcome of a single engagement—on the morning after this speech. Even as the senator addressed his associates in the chamber, the general was making preparations for a "cast of the dice."

But Johnston could not know that he was in possession of inaccurate information as he made his arrangements for battle. The maps of North Carolina that were being used by both armies had been drawn many years before the war, none of them bearing a date later than 1854.[4] They were faulty in that they did not include roads that had been built in the last ten years, and they also were imprecise regarding actual distances between given points. From his maps, Johnston supposed the two wings of the Federal army to be separated by a day's march, from head of column to head of column, when in fact the positions of the XV and XVII Corps were located only "five to ten miles south of the road on which the left wing was advancing."[5]

Similarly, the distance between Bentonville and General Hardee's camp at Elevation was in error, but in the opposite manner. Elevation appeared to be an easy day's march away from Johnston's main force, according to the maps. In fact, the distance was greater than shown, meaning that all of the Union forces were closer to Bentonville than Hardee was. On the night of 18 March, the Federal left wing made camp 4–5 miles from Bentonville, "nearer, by several miles, than Hardee's bivouac."[6] "Old Reliable" had stopped for the night at Snead's House, some 5 miles northwest of Bentonville and 7 miles from the battle site.[7] He had been hampered in his advance not only by the pitiful condition of the rain-soaked roads, but also by the fact that the road Johnston had specified as his route of march did not

---

[4] Maj. George Ward Nichols, *The Story of the Great March, From the Diary of a Staff Officer* (New York: Harper & Bros. Publishers, 1865) 262.

[5] Alexander C. McClurg, *The Last Chance of the Confederacy* (Chicago: The Military Order of the Loyal Legion of the United States, Illinois; A. C. McClurg and Co., 1891) 372.

[6] Johnston, *Johnston's Narrative*, 385.

[7] Nathaniel Cheairs Hughes, Jr., *Bentonville: The Final Battle of Sherman & Johnston* (Chapel Hill: University of North Carolina Press, 1996) 31.

appear on the maps. Though his men were exhausted from the fighting at Averasboro and had not had anything to eat since the evening of 15 March, Hardee had sent a message to his commander that his force was on the march at 8:00 A.M. on 18 March.

The Confederate soldiers under Hardee were suffering the privations of a hard campaign, but so was their commander. Hardee was still much weakened from a bout of typhoid fever contracted at the beginning of the march north that had actually caused him to turn command of his army over to General McLaws for a period of time.[8]

The Federal troops, under Slocum, were ignorant of the Rebel concentration taking place in their front. General Sherman had discounted any possibility of a Confederate offensive, and his subordinate officers readily adopted their chieftain's opinion, despite growing signs to the contrary. In his autobiography, Sherman wrote, "All signs induced me to believe that the enemy would make no farther opposition to our progress, and would not attempt to strike us in the flank while in motion."[9] But the general was blinded by the success he had already achieved and could not see the situation unfolding before him. Several reports had already come in to headquarters stating that the Confederates were up to something and that there were rumors of a concentration. General Carlin had himself been the recipient of such information when he stopped for supper at the house of a local farmer. The head of the household was concerned about the Confederate activity in the area and expressed his fears that a battle would be fought on his farm the next day. Carlin, whose division of the XIV Corps was in the front of the left wing, repeated the conversation to General Jefferson Davis, who in turn advised Sherman of this intelligence. "No Jeff, there is nothing there but...cavalry," the commander replied. "Brush them out of the way in the morning."[10] Major Belknap of the foragers had forwarded a

---

[8] Jay Luvaas, *The Battle of Bentonville March 19–20–21, 1865* (Smithfield NC: Bentonville United Daughters of the Confederacy, n.d.) 5.

[9] McClurg, *Last Chance of the Confederacy*, 371.

[10] Gen. William P. Carlin, *The Battle of Bentonville*, vol. 3 (Cincinnati: Military Order of the Loyal Legion of the United States, Ohio; Robert Clark and Co., 1884) 235.

similar report concerning Rebel activity that he had gained from talking with civilians and wounded Confederate prisoners, but Sherman discounted it as well.[11] Though Confederate cavalry had been in their front both mornings since the battle of Averasboro, the general commanding saw no reason to change his assumptions. They had contended with Rebel cavalry almost every day since leaving Savannah, and there was no concrete evidence to support the contention that this was not a continuation of the Confederates harassing tactics. The army would resume its course for Goldsboro in the morning, convinced that there was no Confederate force of any consequence blocking its path.

The overconfidence held by the Yankees was in large measure due to the excellent work of screening done by General Wade Hampton and his cavalry. As soon as he had received confirmation from Johnston regarding the selected site of the battle, Hampton had placed his command in front of the Union column and retarded their movements throughout the day. Skirmishing began in the morning and continued into the afternoon, when the Confederates were pushed back by superior numbers. The troopers were forced back to the edge of a field belonging to the Cole family, the position Hampton had selected for the Confederate infantry. If there was to be a battle the next day, he would have to hold his ground and prevent the Federals from "brushing him aside." Hampton stated that he "dismounted all my men, placing them along the edge of the woods, and at great risk of losing my guns, I put my artillery some distance to the right of the road, where, though exposed, it had a commanding position. I knew that if a serious attack was made on me the guns would be lost, but I determined to run this risk in the hope of checking the Federal advance." The gravity of the situation and the nature of Hampton's gamble was not lost on the troopers in his command. After he had placed the artillery in its assigned position, a private in the ranks was

---

[11] C. E. Belknap, *Bentonville: "What a Bummer Knows About It,"* vol. 12 (Washington, DC: The Military Order of the Loyal Legion of the United States, District of Columbia, 1887) 6.

to remark: "Old Hampton is playing a bluff game, and if he don't mind Sherman will call him."[12]

The ruse worked. When the Federals finally got around to making an effort to take the cavalry's works it was almost sunset. Hampton had used the time allotted to materially strengthen his position, and his works presented a formidable sight to the Yankees who advanced against them in the twilight. Not knowing how many men were behind the fortifications, the attack was postponed till the next morning when there would be more daylight for the operation. Hampton had held. In the morning, a line of infantry would be in position along the opposite edge of the Cole field.

Johnston and the main body arrived at Bentonville after dark on 18 March, where Hampton briefed him on the day's proceedings. Without the opportunity to survey the ground himself, the commander was compelled to rely on the judgment of his cavalry chief for the deployment of his troops. The road on which the Federals were marching cut through a pine forest and ascended to a slight crest overlooking the open field of the Cole farm, where the cavalry had held them during the day. This open space continued past the Cole house for a distance of a little under a mile, where the ground was once more forested. Hampton proposed to set an ambush for the Yankees in the second stand of trees, behind the Cole house, where the Confederate line could be concealed from the Federals till the last possible moment. Johnston agreed with these preliminary conclusions and settled upon a battle plan that he had tried to use against Sherman a year before at Cassville, Georgia.

In the earlier engagement, General Leodius Polk was to have blocked the Federals in front while Hood's men were in line directly on the Union flank. Once the head of Sherman's column struck Polk's line, Hood was to advance to the attack. The plan had been a failure at Cassville due to the fact that General Hood had declined to attack once Polk was engaged, but Johnston was sure that it would be successful this time if everyone performed their assigned tasks. The

---

[12] Robert Underwood Johnson and Clarence Clough Buel, *Battles and Leaders of the Civil War*, 4 vols. (New York: The Century Company, 1884–1888) 4:702.

configuration of his line would resemble a sickle, with General Bragg occupying the handle portion that Polk had held a year before. On Bragg's right, forming the blade of the sickle, would be the commands of Stewart and Hardee. Once the Federal infantry was engaged with Bragg, the crushing blow was to be administered against their left flank and rear.[13] Hampton would have to continue his ruse for a little longer in the morning while the army marched the 2 miles from Bentonville and got into line. Then he was to fall back through Bragg's line and assume a position on the far right, extending Hardee's line. Everything was going according to schedule. Johnston had managed to get Bragg's and Stewart's men into Bentonville by nightfall of 18 March, and Hardee was on his way, having stopped for only a short time during the night and getting his men back on the road at 4:00 A.M. on the morning of 19 March. His tired and hungry men made a supreme effort to reach their objective, but the general must have been concerned about the condition they would be in when battle commenced.

Sunday, 19 March, dawned bright and beautiful in the Union camps. "The early spring morning was soft and balmy," wrote one Union veteran, "and the trees were covered with the delicate verdure which does not appear until May in the States north of the Ohio River."[14] The strains of the familiar anthem "Old Hundred" played by a regimental band awoke another soldier and caused him to remember that it was the Sabbath. As the band played, he thought that the song "never sounded to me more sweetly solemn than then, for with its strains came thoughts of home and dear ones there."[15]

But the blue-clad soldiers would not have much time to enjoy the lovely spring day or revel in the fact that for once it was not raining. They would soon be locked in mortal combat with an old enemy, and thoughts of home and loved ones had to be postponed. For many of them it would be the last time they would ever hear the old anthem

---

[13] Craig L. Symonds, *Joseph E. Johnston: A Civil War Biography* (New York: W. W. Norton & Co., 1992) 348.

[14] McClurg, *Last Chance of the Confederacy*, 369.

[15] Nichols, *Story of the Great March*, 261.

played. This day, beginning so peaceful and promising, would witness the end of many a young life.

The opposing cavalry had been skirmishing since before dawn as Hampton continued to screen the movements of the infantry while they got into position. The first shot of the battle was fired by W. H. Dowling of Butler's Cavalry. Dowling had been on picket duty when he saw a squad of men in blue coming down the road. He fired the opening shot of the battle, then fell back toward Johnston's main line.[16] At 7:00 A.M., General Carlin's division formed and moved down the road in the lead of the XIV Corps. As the regiments filed out of camp, Sherman, Slocum, and Davis held an impromptu meeting at a crossroads near the bivouac area of the previous night. Sherman had spent the last few days with the left wing and was preparing to leave and join Howard's wing for a while. All three were mounted, and as they discussed routes of march and other details of the final leg of the journey to Goldsboro, the sounds of the skirmishing to the front gave General Davis an instinctive feeling that something was amiss. Sherman held fast to the conviction he had voiced the previous night that the Confederates would not fight: "No Jeff, there is nothing there but Dibbrell's cavalry. Brush them out of the way. Good morning. I'll meet you tomorrow morning at Cox's Bridge." With that he rode away with his staff toward Howard.[17]

Colonel Harrison Hobart's 1st Brigade was in the lead of Carlin's division, followed by the 2nd Brigade under Colonel George P. Buell and the 3rd under Colonel David Miles, with all division wagons and pack mules to the rear. After a march of about 3 miles, Hobart came to the spot where the skirmishers were engaged, and was ordered to form his brigade in two lines on the right, or southern, side of the road. One might wonder about Hobart's frame of mind as he prepared to position his forces for combat. He had only recently retaken command of his brigade. The colonel had been captured at Chickamauga the previous year and had only made good his escape

---

[16] Robert W. Sanders, "The Battle of Bentonville, N.C.," *Confederate Veteran Magazine* 34/4 (1926): 299.

[17] McClurg, *Last Chance of the Confederacy*, 372–73.

from Libby Prison in Richmond on 9 February 1865.[18] Hobart assumed immediate command of the front line consisting of the 33rd Ohio, 94th Ohio, and 88th Indiana. Colonel Michael Fitch commanded the second line, composed of his own regiment, the 21st Wisconsin, the 104th Illinois, and the 42nd Indiana. Buell's Brigade was deployed on the left, or north, side of the road at the suggestion of General Slocum, in order to flank the Confederates, who were still imagined to be nothing more than cavalry. Buell's Brigade was likewise formed into two lines, with the 21st Michigan and 69th Ohio in the front and the 13th Michigan in the rear.[19]

Hobart and Buell advanced their first lines as soon as they were in position, and drove back the Confederate skirmishers for a few hundred yards until they reached the Cole house. Hoke's line then opened from their concealed works with artillery and musketry on the advancing Yankees, taking them completely by surprise.

The heavy skirmish fire combined with the sudden outburst of artillery and musketry from the Rebel line caused Slocum to cast doubt on Sherman's assumptions regarding the force in his front. He immediately sent forward Captain Foraker, Major Tracy, and Colonel Litchfield, of his staff, to investigate the true state of affairs.[20] Events had already moved past the point where Slocum could control them, however, and the battle was about to be joined. The only information his staff would be able to provide now would be an estimate of just how many Confederates were out there, ready to strike his division.

Hobart and Buell recoiled from the first Confederate volley and prepared to meet a more formidable force than they had first thought. Hobart, along with the first line, moved into a pine thicket on the left and front of the Cole field, and began to throw up entrenchments. The second line of his brigade, under Fitch, was placed on the right of the road, about 350 yards from the Cole house, in support of Battery

---

[18] Hughes, *Bentonville: The Final Battle*, 73.

[19] *The War of the Rebellion: A Compilation of the Official Records of the Union and Confederate Armies* (Washington, DC: Government Printing Office, 1895) ser. 1, vol. 47, pt. 1, Gen. Carlin's report, 448 and Buell's report, 468.

[20] Johnson and Buel, *Battles and Leaders*, 4:693.

C, 1st Illinois Artillery, which had just come up. Buell was recalled and his brigade was placed to the left and rear of Hobart. Hobart's Brigade was assigned this supporting role due to the fact that with an aggregate total of only 600 men, it was by far the smallest brigade in all of Slocum's left wing.[21] Carlin's 3rd Brigade, under Colonel David Miles, was now on the field and was ordered to form on the right of Fitch's line. As soon as the brigades were in position the order to charge was given.[22] It was now just about 9:00 A.M., and with the Federals advancing to the attack, the Confederates had yet to fully consolidate their forces. This had been delayed, owing to the fact that there was but one road leading from Bentonville to the battlefield, but Johnston had still managed to get most of his army in position before the Federals arrived. The main problem was that Hardee had not yet arrived from Elevation. As Carlin's division advanced toward the Confederate line, Hardee and the head of his column was just passing through Bentonville, 2 miles away.[23] In his original plan, Johnston had intended for Hardee's corps to form the middle of the line, between Stewart and Bragg, but his delayed arrival in the field necessitated a change of these plans. Johnston ordered General Hampton to place his artillery in the gap in the line where Hardee was supposed to be, after the cavalry had fallen back before the Union infantry through Bragg's lines.[24] With this line, incomplete as it was, Johnston kept one eye on the lines of blue infantry that were about to hit Bragg's blocking line and the other on the road from Bentonville looking for signs of Hardee's approach.

As Buell's Brigade advanced, he maintained his previous two-line structure and gave orders for the 13th Michigan to charge through the front line if they faltered for any reason. John Wesley Daniels, in the ranks of the 13th Michigan, was in charge "up the hill over a fence and into a wood under a severe front and flank fire from about twice

---

[21] Mark L. Bradley, *Last Stand in the Carolinas: The Battle of Bentonville* (Campbell CA: Savas Publishing Company, 1996) 172.

[22] *OR*, ser. 1, vol. 47, pt. 1, Gen. Carlin's report, 449.

[23] Thomas Lawrence Connelly, *Autumn of Glory: The Army of Tennessee, 1861–1865* (Baton Rouge: Louisiana State University Press, 1971) 526.

[24] Johnson and Buel, *Battles and Leaders*, 4:703.

our numbers."[25] The Confederates were pouring a murderous fire into the blue line, and as a member of the 21st Michigan remembered, "it was a tight place" and "it looked hard to see intimate friends blown to pieces before your eyes."[26]

The Union line had struck Hoke along the length of his works and extended on his right to include the division commanded by General H. D. Clayton. This division was part of D. H. Hill's corps, Army of Tennessee, and had been shifted to the left to cover the gap in the line caused when Hardee's corps was not yet up. Stewart's veterans from Nashville were therefore now holding the center of the Confederate line. Buell's Brigade on the Union left was marching straight into hornet's nest as they neared the Rebel works; still unknown to them, there was not only a force in front, there was also a concealed line already on their left flank. Charles Brown of the 21st Michigan observed that "as we charged they let us have the whole benefit of their whole line, besides a flank fire from the left of the 69th Ohio, with shell and grape. We came up so that men pelted each other with ramrods and buts [sic] of muskets & were finally compelled to fall back."[27]

As previously ordered, the 13th Michigan now prepared to charge through the stalled lines of the 69th Ohio and the 21st Michigan. John Wesley Daniels described the action: "The other regs. went within ten rods of the works and halted badly 'cut up' then our Reg. charged through them [their] line and within 5 rods of the enemy when our Major was killed and our color bearer wounded." Major Willard Eaton, commander of the 13th, has been cut down by a volley from the Rebel works. His men were quickly demoralized by the sight of their fallen commander. The regiment first halted, then "retreated to the cover of the ravine where we had formed and built hasty

---

[25] John Wesley Daniels Diary, 18, Bentley Historical Library, University of Michigan, Ann Arbor MI.

[26] Charles S. Brown to Etta, 26 April 1865, Charles S. Brown Papers, Perkins Library, Duke University, Durham NC.

[27] Ibid.

breastworks."[28] Buell's whole brigade joined in the retreat from the devastating fire. "We ran" one soldier stated, "but no mortal could have done better than our men did."[29]

Hobart and Miles were having a little better time of it on their part of the line, but not by much. Hobart's Brigade advanced on either side of the road for a distance of about 400 yards till they hit close to the center of Hoke's line. The two portions of the brigade were actually assaulting the works independently, as there was an "open uncovered space sufficient for a full Brigade front," along the road between the two wings.[30] The 19th Indiana Battery was unlimbered at the road and was covering the gap while it dueled with Hoke's guns. Hobart and his wing advanced with the 93rd Ohio, 87th, Indiana, and 33rd Ohio in line from left to right, with the 94th Ohio formed on the right of the 21st Michigan of Buell's Brigade. Hobart's orders were to discover what was in his front, and as his men advanced they ran into a line of Confederates "evidently with the same intention as Ourselves." The Federals fired a "well directed volley" that "drove them back to their works, from behind which we received a terrific fire."[31] With Buell's Brigade being thrown back on the left, the Confederates soon overlapped the 94th Ohio where the Michigan boys had been, and forced it to retire. Hobart, seeing his line giving way, ordered his other two regiments to fall back to their original works in the woods by the Cole House before they were all cut off and surrounded. Discovering the enemy to be in great force in his front, Hobart put his men to strengthening his works to prepare for the counterattack that he was sure would follow.

Colonel Fitch, with the other half of Hobart's Brigade, put his regiments in line with the 194th Illinois on the left near the road, the 21st Wisconsin in the center, and the 42nd Indiana on the right with

---

[28] John Wesley Daniels Diary, 18, Bentley Historical Library, University of Michigan, Ann Arbor MI.

[29] Charles S. Brown to Etta, 26 April 1865, Charles S. Brown Papers, Perkins Library, Duke University, Durham NC.

[30] James T. Reeve Diary, 15, James T. Reeve Papers, State Historical Society of Wisconsin, Madison WI.

[31] *OR*, vol. 47, pt. 1, Capt. W. N. Voris's report, 460.

its flank refused. Once his line was established, he set the men to work at fortifying the position as best they could under a constant fire from Hoke's entrenchments. Confederate movements led General Carlin to believe that an attack was imminent against Fitch's right, so he directed that the 104th Illinois be shifted to the extreme right and formed on the 42nd Indiana. While taking its position, the regiment very nearly marched directly into Hoke's fortified works. Carlin next ordered Fitch to advance a reinforced skirmish line to develop the enemy's position. The heaviest firing being along the right of his line, he "considered that the point of most danger and therefore gave the left less attention. Besides, two pieces of artillery were on my immediate left, and I suppose the other wing of the brigade on the immediate left of the artillery."[32] Fitch was mistaken about the position of Hobart's wing. The battery was standing alone in the center of the field now that the 104th Illinois had been driven back. The colonel did not have time to discover the gap, though, for his skirmish line was easily thrown back from the Confederate works and the continued heavy musketry on his right held his attention.

Colonel David Miles's 3rd Brigade had come onto the field while Fitch was positioning his line, and it extended the Union right, forming on the exposed flank of the Illinois boys. Miles was ordered to advance his brigade in support of Buell's movement on the left, and Fitch was to hold his regiments in readiness to exploit any breakthrough of the enemy lines the 3rd Brigade might make. Miles formed his regiments with the 21st Ohio on the left, the 38th Indiana in the center, and the 79th Pennsylvania on the right. At about 2:00 P.M., the command was ordered forward. The blue line "advanced through a swamp so densely covered with underbrush that it was impossible to advance in line." Even with the rough going, the Federals were able to push the Confederate skirmishers back upon their main line. When they were within 50 yards of the breastworks, the Confederates opened on them with a volley of musketry that stunned the brigade and forced it to halt. The Union soldiers were ordered to lie down and take advantage of whatever cover they could

[32] Ibid., Col. Fitch's report, 463.

find as they tried to fire back. Somehow a report was circulated in the ranks that the Federals were firing on their own men, and Captain James Low, commander of the 38th Indiana, issued orders up and down his line to stop shooting. As the fire from the Federal side slackened, that coming from the Confederate works intensified greatly, and Captain Low soon fell mortally wounded while still trying to prevent his men from replying to the murderous discharges in their front. "The men having no protection and being under orders not to fire, began to fall back to their former position."[33]

The Pennsylvania and Ohio regiments on the flanks were also having problems contending with the Confederates. Both flanks were in danger of being turned. It was soon apparent to Colonel Miles "that the enemy were moving on our left flank and were about to cut us off, when I changed front and in time to repulse their advance, and we held them well in check." Shortly after this repulse, Miles was ordered to charge again.[34] The 21st Ohio, being in an exposed position, was ordered to the right of the 79th Pennsylvania, and the Yankees pushed through the swamp amid a hail of bullets once more. This time they got to within 40 yards of the Rebel works before the attack stalled. Colonel Miles fell wounded leading the charge and command was passed to Lieutenant Colonel Arnold McMahon of the 79th Pennsylvania. The Union troops held their advance position for half an hour as they exchanged fire with the Confederate defenders, but the weight of numbers against them and their lack of cover compelled them to fall back. The brigade retreated to its original line to reform and replenish its dwindling stock of ammunition. The attack had been unsuccessful, but it had bought the Union army some badly needed time.

General James D. Morgan's 2nd Division was now on the field, extending the Union line to the right of the line held by Miles before the attack.[35] The charge of the Federals had forced the Confederates to defend their works momentarily, instead of allowing them to

---

[33] Ibid., Capt. D. H. Patton's report, 476.
[34] Ibid., Col. David Miles's report, 473.
[35] Ibid., Capt. D. H. Patton's report, 476.

mount an immediate offensive. Morgan's division was therefore permitted sufficient time to entrench his men behind strong log works. When the Confederate assault did come, they would find a formidable line along Morgan's front. These preparations would be in stark contrast to the hastily thrown up works that the men of Carlin's division had been forced to defend in order to buy Morgan's men the opportunity of entrenching properly.

General Slocum could no longer doubt that he faced more than just a division of stubborn cavalry. When the Confederate artillery had first opened on Carlin's troops, Slocum sent Major E. W. Guindon of his staff to assure Sherman that there was no need for alarm. The wing commander knew that Sherman would be able to hear the guns, and he wanted to set his mind at ease that there was nothing in his front that the left wing could not handle. When Carlin ran into Hoke's infantry all such delusions vanished, and reports were hurriedly sent back to Slocum with a true picture of the situation. Colonel Litchfield, the inspector-general of the XIV Corps, had been sent forward for information about the Confederates, and he reported back to Slocum with a revelation: "Well, General, I find a great deal more than Dribbrell's cavalry; there are infantry and artillery entrenched along our whole front, and enough of them to give us all the amusement we want for the rest of the day."[36]

Captain Tracy and Lieutenant Foraker had also returned with similar information, Captain Tracy having been wounded in the leg by a spent ball while gathering it. The Union army had come to view itself as being invincible since leaving Savannah, and some of the officers around Slocum were caught up in this feeling, refusing to concede that the Confederates were capable of mounting a force that could do them harm Major Mosely of Slocum's staff urged the general to make an all-out attack with Carlin's division at once. Mosely was sure that "it could not be possible that there was much force ahead of us," and he protested against waiting for the rest of the wing to come up because "if it should turn out that there was nothing to justify such caution it would look bad for the left wing." Slocum was convinced,

[36] McClurg, *Last Chance of the Confederacy*, 375.

however and he responded to Mosely's argument by stating: "I can afford to be charged with being dilatory or over-cautious, but I cannot afford the responsibility for another Ball's Bluff."[37]

The soldiers of Carlin's division needed no convincing. There was no denying that the Confederates had managed to concentrate a considerable force in their front that was too much for one division to handle. Instead of underestimating the strength of the enemy, the soldiers in the ranks credited the Confederates with having several times their actual number. Rumors from "people in the know" said that "The Rebs are estimated at 80,000 men.... and it is said the Gen. Lee commands them."[38]

Slocum knew that he was facing an entire Confederate army, but he did not know how large it was or who was in command. That was the information Carlin's division was to ascertain when it was ordered forward to develop the enemy works. The general had to be sure what he was up against before the engagement progressed much further. Three Confederate prisoners, captured during Carlin's assault, provided Slocum with all the intelligence he needed to make a decision that this would be too big a job for the left wing to handle alone. These three Confederates had actually gone out of their way to surrender to Carlin's men, and when that was accomplished, they insisted on being taken to see the commanding general. All three professed to be Union soldiers who had been captured by the Rebels. They said they had been given the option of joining the Confederate army or rotting in a prison camp, and that they had enlisted only with the intention of deserting as soon as they found themselves close enough to Union lines to make their escape possible. The Federal soldiers knew that there were a number of such "galvanized Yankees" serving with the Confederates, mostly in the position of pioneers, where they would not have to be counted on as combat troops, but the question was whether these men were indeed ex-Union soldiers, or had they been planted by the Confederates to spread misinformation. One spokesman for the trio informed Slocum that Joe Johnston had

---

[37] Johnson and Buel, *Battles and Leaders*, 4:693.

[38] John E. Risedorph Diary, 64, Minnesota Historical Society, St. Paul MN.

concentrated over 30,000 men in the Union front and that they were all strongly entrenched. Johnston had ridden among the troops that morning and the deserter had heard him address a portion of them, saying that "at last the long wished for opportunity had occurred," that they were "concentrated and in position, while Sherman's army was scattered over miles of country, separated by muddy and almost impassable roads," and they "could now easily crush him in detail," that a part of the 14th Corps was now in their power, and they "would now take in those two light divisions out of the wet." Slocum had doubted the information at first, not putting much stock in the credibility of a soldier he considered to be a double deserter, but a member of his staff recognized the spokesman as being from his home town of Syracuse, New York, and could vouch for the fact that at least part of his story concerning his Union military service was correct. Slocum therefore accepted all the information as being accurate. This intelligence, combined with the personal observations of his staff, prompted the general to assume a defensive posture on the battlefield.[39]

Orders were sent at once for the XX Corps to make their way to the front with all possible haste, as well as the two divisions that were guarding the wagon train of the left wing. Lieutenant Joseph Foraker, one of the staff officers who had reported on the strength of the Confederate line, was dispatched to General Sherman to report to him the true state of affairs and to request the assistance of the right wing. Foraker was an energetic young officer, only nineteen years of age, and his service on the field that day won him a commission as captain. Many years later, he would serve as governor of the state of Ohio.[40]

General Howard, continuing to hear the rumble of artillery as his column plodded on toward his appointed crossing of the Nuese, began to fear that something was amiss with the left wing; He dispatched a

---

[39] McClurg, *Last Chance of the Confederacy*, 374–75, and Johnson and Buel, *Battles and Leaders*, 4:692–93.

[40] New York Monuments Commission, *In Memoriam: Henry Warner Slocum 1826–1894* (Albany: J. B. Lyon Company Printers, 1904) 307 (Hereafter referred to as *Henry Warner Slocum.*) and Johnson and Buel, *Battles and Leaders*, 4:692–93.

messenger to inform Slocum that he could feel free to call upon General Hazen's division, the trailing division in the XV Corps line of march, should he feel the need of support. He followed that message up in the early afternoon by instructing his chief of artillery, Major Thomas Osburn, to ride back and personally inform Slocum that he could call upon the entire XV Corps for support if he was being hard pressed. Osburn met Sherman, after proceeding but a few miles toward Slocum's position, and the army commander informed him that he had recently heard from Slocum; that there was nothing but a division of cavalry in his front, and that the major need not continue on his long ride to deliver the message. Osburn, accepting Sherman's analysis, continued with his other duties, but neglected to inform Howard regarding his conversation with Sherman or his failure to deliver the message to Slocum. Therefore, the right wing commander continued marching forward under the belief that he had committed his support to the left wing, should they need it. Foraker had not yet arrived with his message from Slocum giving a true picture of the situation.[41]

For General Johnston, the surprise was now over. The Federals realized that they had walked into an ambush and were preparing to meet it. But the Confederates still held an advantage in numbers. If they could concentrate and launch an all-out attack before the other portions of the Union army arrived, victory could yet be achieved. Thus far, the only part of Johnston's plan that had not worked as scheduled was Hardee's unavoidable delay.

"Old Reliable" had arrived at Bentonville with the head of his column before Carlin's division engaged the Confederate line, but the road was clogged with A. P. Stewart's men, so he allowed his own tired troops to break formation and relax for a bit in the local churchyard until the road was cleared. General Hoke had already deployed his division, with his center being at the road, and his line extending at right angles on both sides of it. On his extreme right, he had placed his artillery, the only cannon that had been gotten onto the field at this point. Owing to the absence of Hardee, the Army of Tennessee

[41] Hughes, *Bentonville: The Final Battle*, 151.

had been shifted to the center of the Confederate line and was formed to the right of Hoke's artillery. Buell's Brigade and Hobart's regiments under his immediate command had struck the Confederates above the artillery where S. D. Lee's corps, under the command of D. H. Hill, had just recently arrived. Hill had observed Federal skirmishers coming toward him as his men were filing into position, and he dispatched Lieutenant S. A. Roberts, 39th Alabama, to take charge of the Rebel skirmish line and push the Yankees back, "which they did with spirit."[42]

Since the Confederates planned to take the offensive in this engagement, General Stewart had thought it inadvisable to entrench, but Hill determined to put to good use the time spent waiting for the other divisions by throwing up works. These were only about half completed when Buell and Hobart's men were seen advancing in line of battle. The Union skirmish line extended across the whole of Hill's front, but their line of battle was much smaller and overlapped General Stovall's Brigade, of Clayon's division, by only a slight margin to the right and left. The Federals had assumed that they were solidly on the right flank of the Rebels, but instead they were marching straight into the center of Clayton, Stevenson, and Coltart's divisions. When the Union troops got to within 40 yards of the works, the Confederates opened up: "The whole corps fired, many of the men without seeing any object at which to fire." With this concentration of firepower it is little wonder that Buell and Hobart were forced to retire. The Confederates were deprived of the services of one of their most dependable brigade commanders when General Daniel Reynolds was struck in the leg by a solid shot while bringing his men on the field. The limb was mutilated to the point of requiring amputation, and command of the brigade was passed to Colonel H. G. Bunn of the 2nd Arkansas Mounted Rifles.[43] Following the Union withdrawal General Hill once more sent forward his skirmish line.

---

[42] *OR*, ser. 1, vol. 47, pt. 1, Gen. D. H. Hill's report, 1089.

[43] B. L. Ridley, "Last Battles of the War," *Confederate Veteran Magazine* 3/1 (1895): 20.

Lieutenant Roberts led the men back to the position they had previously held, but fell mortally wounded in the process.[44]

Buell and Hobart's attack had done little to impede the plans of the Confederates. In fact, it had given the men of the Army of Tennessee a chance to gain a measure of confidence. After their disastrous defeats at Franklin and Nashville, the sight of Yankee infantry in retreat was a tonic to them. By comparison, the attacks of Miles and Fitch against Hoke's troops on the Confederate left proved to be more consequential to the outcome of the battle. Hoke had instructed his men to throw up works, as his assignment was to be the blocking force in the operation, and as such he was expected to receive the initial Federal assault. When the Union regiments south of the road attacked, the issue of their repulse was little in doubt to most Confederates on the field except the left wing commander, General Braxton Bragg. Fearing a movement against his flank, Bragg sent word to Johnston at once that he was being sorely pressed and would require reinforcements to hold. General McLaws's division of Hardee's corps was just arriving on the field when Johnston received the message from Bragg, and it was immediately ordered to the left in support of Hoke, instead of assuming its previously assigned position on the right. General Hampton disagreed with the change of plans and advised Johnston "that we should adhere to the one agreed on."[45] The commanding general felt it his duty to support Bragg, however, and the order stood.

This decision would prove to be the only mistake Johnston was to make on the field that day. The guides who were to lead McLaws's men into position got lost during the march, and the division did not reach Hoke's line until after the Federals had already been repulsed. The attacking wing on the right had been reduced by a full division for no real purpose, and McLaws was virtually left out of the fight for the rest of the day, as he received no further orders until late in the afternoon.

---

[44] *OR*, ser. 1, vol. 47, pt. 1, Gen. D. H. Hill's report, 1090.

[45] Johnson and Buel, *Battles and Leaders*, 4:703.

General Taliafero's division was now coming on the field, and they passed by a spot where Buell's Brigade had been thrown back. A. P. Ford observed,

> A number of the dead and wounded were still lying about, but the surgeons were busy with the latter, as the bloody, rough tables that we had just passed alongside of the road amply testified. Twelve or fifteen wounded Federals had gathered in from the immediate front, and they entreated our men for water, which some of us gladly supplied, even to the emptying of several canteens, at what we knew was an important time. One of our fellows—a thrifty fellow, who always manages to have things—produced a little flask of whiskey, and gave a good drink to a Federal who had his leg badly crushed. The blue-coat raised his eyes to Heaven with, "Thank God, Johnny, it may come around that I may be able to do you a kindness, and I'll never forget that drink of liquor." We were not allowed to remain long relieving the suffering, but soon were called to the "attention," and received orders to create it.[46]

With his men all up now, Johnston was ready to spring the trap, but it had been almost five hours since the opposing infantry had first engaged, and the Confederates would only have one chance to sweep the XIV Corps off the field before the lead elements of the XX Corps would arrive in support. Johnston set the time of the attack at 2:45 P.M., but General William Bate, then commanding on the far right of the Confederate line, reported that he had examined the Federal position and that their left flank did not extend beyond his line. Taliaferro's division was in reserve in his rear, and Bate suggested "that it make a detour, passing beyond my extreme right, and be thrown upon the left flank of the enemy." Bates's suggestion was

---

[46] A. P. Ford, "The Last Battles of Hardee's corps." *The Southern Bivouac* 8 (August 1885): 141.

accepted, and the attack was deferred for half an hour to give Taliaferro time to get into position.[47]

When the attack was launched at 3:15 P.M., Taliaferro was not yet fully deployed, but he was positively on the Federal flank. The Confederates came out of the woods and formed in perfect order so that the position of the officers could be distinguished, even at a distance. Several of them, including Hardee, were mounted, giving greater visibility to their men, but also making them much better targets for the Yankees. From his vantage point on Hoke's line, Colonel Charles W. Broadfoot, commander of the 70th North Carolina Junior Reserves, had the opportunity to take in the whole scene. "It looked like a picture at our distance, and was truly beautiful. It was gallantly done, but it was a painful sight to see how close their battle flags were together, regiments being scarcely larger than companies, and a division not much larger than a regiment should be."[48] One of Slocum's officers who viewed the military pageantry said that "the Rebel regiments in front were in full view, stretching through the fields to the left as far as one could see, advancing rapidly, and firing as they came. It was a gallant sight." He continued, "The onward sweep of the Rebel lines was like the waves of the ocean, resistless."[49] It was a scene of martial splendor, and it was also to be the last of its kind in the war. No one on either side could have known it, but when the Rebel line emerged from the woods it was to be for the last great Confederate charge of the war for the western armies. Four long years had come down to this one afternoon in the North Carolina swamps and pine forests. The long gray lines that had fought from Shiloh to Nashville had made such a charge on many occasions, too many occasions as testified to by the closeness of the tattered regimental flags. But the spirit of those earlier days was still evident in the men, and the now famous "Rebel Yell" came defiantly from the throats of thousands of hardened veterans who were not yet

---

[47] *OR*, ser. 1, vol. 147, pt. 1, Gen. William Bate's report, 1106.

[48] Mrs. John H. Anderson, "North Carolina Boy Soldiers at the Battle of Bentonville." *Confederate Veteran Magazine* 35/3 (1927): 175.

[49] McClurg, *Last Chance of the Confederacy*, 377.

ready to admit defeat. Seventeen-year-old Robert Sanders of Taliaferro's division noted that "Johnston's men, though cherishing but scant hope of final victory, seemed to fight as bravely and persistently as if they had been certain of a triumph in the end."[50]

Though the Confederates still held a slight numerical advantage, they were no longer attacking only the repulsed remnants of Carlin's division. Morgan was solidly entrenched now and elements of the XX Corps were on the field. Slocum had even dismounted the foragers and put them in line, along with his personal escort and most of his staff in an effort to bolster the line. General Alpheus Williams had responded to Slocum's call for help by pushing forward General William Jackson's lead division with all possible haste. Hawley's Brigade was the first XX Corps unit to reach Slocum, arriving at about 2:00 P.M., and it was closely followed by Brigadier General James Robinson's Brigade. Hawley was placed to the left of the XIV Corps at a right angle to the road, and Robinson was ordered to plug the gap between the troops of Buell and Hobart on the left and Fitch and Miles on the right. Before the movements could be completed, the Confederates attack hit Buell's Brigade full force and the Union left immediately began to crumble.[51]

The Confederates had been formed in two lines, and the men were instructed to yell to make the Yankees aware of that fact, "but, in moving forward for some one or two hundred yards, was in a thicket of small old field pines, and by the time we [the 40th Alabama] reached the south edge of the thick growth, our rear line was practically mixed in with the front line when we emerged into open ground."[52] Stovall's Brigade was in the lead in the assault on Buell and Hobart's works, and when his men started up a small hill on which they were located, the Federals broke and ran. B. F. Watson, of the 40th Alabama, was in Barker's Brigade behind Stovall, and he was surprised to discover that he "did not see a wounded man, nor one

---

[50] Robert W. Sanders, "The Battle of Bentonville, N.C.," *Confederate Veteran Magazine* 34/4 (1926): 299.

[51] *Henry Warner Slocum*, 308.

[52] R. A. Lambert, "In the Battle of Bentonville," *Confederate Veteran Magazine* 37/3 (1929): 221.

killed, of our men as we rushed up on the Federal works." Stovall's Brigade stopped at the works and Baker's passed to the front and pursued the Federals for about 300 yards through a growth of blackjack and pine. "When we were in about eighty yards," Watson continued, "they turned their backs and fled without firing on us at all except a few shots."[53]

It was the right of the Union line that first gave way under the pressure of the assault, that portion under the command of Colonel Hobart. Buell had observed a strong column moving around his left and toward the rear, and when he saw the Rebels in possession of the works on his right he knew that "my brigade, which still stood, was almost entirely cut off. In this condition, with both flanks turned and no reserve, I concluded that to remain there longer was to sacrifice my brigade. Hence I gave the order to all back." General Carlin had been with Buell's Brigade, encouraging the men by words and through exposing himself on the line. Buell waited for the general order to order the retreat, but Carlin's attention was so focused on the Confederates in his front that he was unaware that the right had already been folded. Buell, realizing that there was not a moment to lose, took the initiative without waiting for Carlin to be informed of the danger. "Half a minute's delay," he said, "and General Carlin, myself, and most of my brigade would have been captured."[54] General Hardee personally led the final charge over the breastworks on horseback "with his knightly gallantry," as Johnston describe it, the men following at the double quick.[55] With Taliaferro's division sweeping down on their left and rear, and the Army of Tennessee boys turning their right and pressing in front, Buell narrowly escaped the Confederate pincer move and fell back on elements of the XX Corps, where the command was reorganized and put in reserve.

All three of Buell's regiments had taken heavy casualties in their part of the engagement. The 13th Michigan lost 106 men, almost 20

---

[53] B. F. Watson, "In the Battle of Bentonville," *Confederate Veteran Magazine* 37/3 (1929): 95.

[54] *OR*, 1, vol. 47, pt. 1, Col. Buell's report, 468.

[55] Johnson and Buel, *Battles and Leader*, 4:704.

percent of the number they took into the fight. One young soldier from that regiment recorded an entry in his diary that could have been attributed to any man in the brigade: "Our Co. can stack only 17 guns tonight. We do not yet know how many are killed and wounded."[56]

General Carlin suddenly found himself without a division when Buell's men gave way. He had been so focused on the Confederate line advancing in his front that he did not even notice when Buell ordered the retreat. When Carlin finally did look around, he found that he was alone in the works, and Confederate infantry was preparing to swarm the position. Opting to take a bold course, he turned and walked deliberately for the rear, as if marching on parade. Miraculously, he reported that no shots were fired at him at this time. His luck would remain thus. Before eventually reaching his own lines, he would have many shots fired at him and would have a mounted Confederate officer level a pistol in his direction and demand his surrender, but Carlin did make it back to the blue line and safety.[57]

The onslaught overpowered the entire Union left and center, sweeping away all in its path. Robinson, in the center with only three of his regiments up, could not hold and was forced to fall back with Buell and Hobart for almost a mile where they then reformed among the other XX Corps units as they arrived. Colonel Alexander McClurg had been sent forward to give Slocum a report on the Confederate movements. McClurg stated that the "roar of musketry and artillery was now continuous. Very soon I met large disorganized masses of men slowly and doggedly falling back along the road. They were retreating, and evidently with good cause." McClurg made his way through this throng of beaten Yankees and had gone only a short distance further down the road when he came upon two pieces of the 19th Indiana Battery, also in the act of retreating. The colonel rode past the guns and was heading toward where the Union lines had been when the lieutenant in charge of the guns called after him: "For

---

[56] John Wesley Daniels Diary, 18, Bentley Historical Library, University of Michigan, Ann Arbor MI.

[57] McClurg, *Last Chance of the Confederacy*, 379.

Heaven's sake, don't go down there! I am the last man of the command. Everything is gone in front of you. The lieutenant commanding my battery and most of the men and horses are killed, and four guns captured. These two guns are all we have left."[58]

McClurg could see that Carlin's division was helpless to stem the tide, but General Morgan's division, on the right, though under attack was still on the field. If they could just hold on for a little while, General Williams might have time to get the rest of the XX Corps up and formed before the Confederates could drive the XIV Corps back into his troops while they were still in column of march. Two brigades of Jackson's division were already up, and General William Ward's division was on its way.

Sergeant C. H. Dickinson of the 22nd Wisconsin was eating lunch with his mess mates when a staff officer came riding up from the front, "his horse covered with foam, as though he had come through in a hurry," and began inquiring as to the whereabouts of General Ward.[59]

The general was asleep in an ambulance "within two rods of where our squad were making coffee, so we could not help hearing what was said."

> He says wake up General, for God's sake wake up: the General roused up, and in his gruff way he says, what's the matter now; the officer says, the enemy are in heavy force in our front, and we can't hold them, thay [sic] have already made one charge and have driven our men back, and thay [sic] are getting tired out; huh, Gen. Ward says, I'll bet I'm tireder than thay [sic] are now; and I don't believe thars [sic] many rebs nohow, I could put 'em all in my pocket
>
> Just then the Adjutant General came up, and the aid repeated what he had told Gen. Ward, and as he saw the General was in no condition to do business, he says, now

---

[58] Charles S. Dickinson Diary, 167, Charles H. Dickinson Papers, State Historical Society of Wisconsin, Madison WI.

[59] Ibid., 167–68.

> Adjutant, get the men under arms as quick as you can, and double quick them to the front.
>
> The Adjutant commence talking to the General and the Aid [sic] rode over to our fire.

Dickinson and his comrades asked how the fighting had started, and the officer recapped the events of the morning for them before riding back toward the front. He had scarcely departed before a second staff officer rode into camp and up to the ambulance where Ward was lying, saying, "for Gods sake, General, hurry up these men; we are hard pressed in front, and can't hold them." Upon looking around, the officer saw that the men were falling in line and were getting ready to march, so he "wheeled about, put spurs to his horse, and was soon out of sight."

The division moved forward with difficulty. The road was blocked by the train and the men "were obliged to go on both sides, and frequently in single file, as there was water in the ditches most of the way." The men were making good time, however, and with each step, the sounds of the battle became more audible. As the troops got nearer to Bentonville, "we could hear the rattle of musketry at times quite plainly, and it seemed as though when it sounded louder, and plainer than usual the men would lengthen step, as though afraid the turning point in the battle would be reached before we came on the field."[60]

Ward's men need not have had such anxiety over the battle being lost before they arrived. General Morgan's division was holding fast on the right, under extreme pressure, and was buying the time Slocum needed to concentrate his forces.

---

[60] Ibid., 167–68.

5

NONE BUT THE VALIANT

Hardee and Stewart's men were doing exactly as Johnston had planned when he devised the ambush. The Union left had been rolled up in short order, and half the XIV Corps men on the field were retreating with Robinson's XX Corps brigade. The Federals fell back through Cole's field and into a pine forest on its western side, where they tried to rally. "We pressed forward at a slow stride," said R. A. Lambert of the 42nd Alabama, "firing as we moved on among small brush and into big pine timber until, seemingly, there was no enemy directly in front of us."[1]

But the Confederate charge had lost some of its impetus already. The Federals had fled their works in such haste that they discarded all articles that would impede their flight. The line of their retreat was marked with baggage and knapsacks containing a variety of plunder gathered along the march from Savannah. As the Confederates marched past this discarded loot, many in the ranks stopped to examine the booty and pick up some needed articles. B. F. Watson of the 40th Alabama "grabbed up a frying pan and stuck the handle under my belt as a sort of shield."[2] Another Reb chose a more practical item: "on passing a badly wounded Federal soldier, I noticed that he had on a good looking canteen, and I took a notion to swap with him, but was in so much of a hurry I did not take time to parley with him

---

[1] R. A. Lambert, "In the Battle of Bentonville," *Confederate Veteran Magazine* 37/3 (1929): 221.

[2] B. F. Watson, "In the Battle of Bentonville," *Confederate Veteran Magazine* 37/3 (1929): 95.

on a trade—just simply jerked his off and threw mine down by his side and went on. I afterwards consoled myself with the thought of having done the poor fellow a real favor, as my canteen was full of water, while the one I got was empty."[3]

When the Confederates entered the woods it became difficult to maintain alignment and the attack started to lose its force. Combined with the men missing from the ranks, even momentarily, to look for plunder, the regiments began to become intermingled and disorganized, allowing the Federals to keep the retreat from turning into a rout.

When the left of the Union line broke, Colonel Miles attached his brigade to Morgan's division in the refuge of his well-fortified position. The addition of Miles's men in the works allowed Morgan to keep one of his own brigades, belonging to Colonel Benjamin Fearing, in reserve. General William Vandever and General John Mitchell's brigades would join Miles's men in the works. Morgan's division was all that stood in the Confederates' way now, and they braced themselves to receive the full impact of the attack.

Morgan had been given extra time to get ready for the Confederates. According to Johnston's original orders, Bragg was to have attacked with Hoke's division, launching successive assaults from left to right along his line as soon as Hardee and Stewart's men became hotly engaged. For some reason Bragg delayed his attack, and the assaults were not coordinated. It was more like two independent actions, in fact, as the momentum on the Confederate right was already fading by the time Bragg's men were sent forward. Indeed, Hardee had stopped in order to reform his lines by the time Bragg moved forward. Furthermore, two brigades, those of Smith and Pettus, were shifted from the left of Stewart's part of the line to his right to support General Bate, who was reporting a concentration of Yankees

---

[3] Lambert, "In the Battle of Bentonville," 221.

on his front and flank. This move weakened the left and opened an inviting hole for the Federals.[4]

General Davis unknowingly exploited this hole when he ordered Morgan's reserve brigade, under Fearing, to attack the Rebels in support of Carlin's retreating division and to plug the gap their withdrawal had created. Davis directed the move to the left, toward the road, and he rode up to Fearing just as the brigade was preparing to charge to give them personal encouragement. "Advance to their flank, Fearing," he shouted. "Deploy as you go. Strike them wherever you find them. Give them the best you've got and we'll whip them yet." The men took up the phrase "We'll whip them yet," and threw themselves furiously on a portion of Clayton's division on the north side of the road, driving them back until the Federals were taken in flank themselves by the brigades of Palmer, Baker, and Carter on their right.[5] James Burkhalter of the 52nd Ohio, Fearing's Brigade, said, "We were soon wholly engaged by a column to our right and striking squarely on the right flank of our column by which they succeeded in turning the flank and somehow demoralized the troops and rendered a rally very difficult, and on the right of the line almost an impossibility in the horrible situation." General Fearing was hit about this time, his wound resulting in the loss of the thumb and all four fingers on his right hand. His brigade was "driven back step by step for about 1/2 mile, where we again rallied in the edge of an open field and immediately advance to the timber near the edge of the open, where we immediately constructed a line of temporary breastworks," and awaited another Rebel thrust.[6] Fearing left the field, and command of the brigade went to Lieutenant Colonel James Langley of the 125th Illinois.[7]

---

[4] *The War of the Rebellion: A Compilation of the Official Records of the Union and Confederate Armies* (Washington, DC: Government Printing Office, 1895) ser. 1, vol. 47, pt.1, Gen. D. H. Hill's report, 1090.

[5] Alexander C. McClurg, *The Last Chance of the Confederacy* (Chicago: The Military Order of the Loyal Legion of the United States, Illinois; A. C. McClurg and Co., 1891) 381.

[6] James Burkhalter Diary, 93–94, Illinois State Historical Society, Spingfield IL.

[7] McClurg, *Last Chance of the Confederacy*, 381.

Palmer, Baker, and Carter's brigades swept past Fearing, to the south of the road, and advanced against the left and rear of Morgan's entrenched division. Bragg had finally ordered his men forward, and Hoke, seeing the flanking movement of his comrades on the Union left, wished to exploit the breach by throwing his men into it. He proceeded to move his men accordingly. The Federals saw that they were about to be completely surrounded and cut off, and for a moment, surrender was contemplated in the ranks. But Bragg countermanded Hoke's movements and ordered him to make a frontal charge against the works instead. Hoke's men charged into some of the most desperate fighting they had seen during the war. The roar of musketry was constant and two sides clashed together in violent hand-to-hand combat as the men clubbed each other in the dense thickets and swampy woods. Some veterans of the Army of Northern Viriginia called it the hottest infantry fight they had ever been in except for Cold Harbor.[8] "If there was a spot as hot as this at Gettysburg, I did not see it," stated one veteran sergeant. One Confederate veteran of the western theater stated that the fighting was hotter than anything he saw at Shiloh or Stones River. The firing was so furious that the men in the rear of the double Union line spent their time loading weapons for the men in the front. One Ohio soldier stated that the two muskets he and his partner were using got almost too hot to fire from the rapid and repeated use.[9]

The 60th Illinois had been serving as skirmishers when Hoke charged, and "they cut our skirmish line in twain leaving 2 companies of our regiment outside of the line surrounded." Companies C and K were the isolated units, and it was seen that "unless we did something quickly we were liable to be captured," so Lieutenant Allen, the only officer with the two companies, formed the men in line and charged back toward his own works. "We went forward with a yell then the fun commensed [sic]," said F. L. Fergerson of Company C, as "we had

---

[8] John G. Barrett, *The Civil War in North Carolina* (Chapel Hill: University of North Carolina Press, 1963) 334.

[9] F. M. McAdams, *Every-Day Soldier Life* (Columbus: Chas. M. Cott & Co., 1884) 145, and Mark L. Bradley, *Last Stand in the Carolinas: The Battle of Bentonville* (Campbell CA: Savas Publishing Company, 1996) 259.

the regimental flag with us and as soon as the rebels saw [it] they wanted it so they took after the color bearer with fixed bayonets but before they got the colors one of our boys put his bayonet thru [sic] the rebel and raised our flag." The two companies successfully cut their way through to their own lines with a minimum of loss. Fergerson said that "it looked for a while like we would all be killed or captured but there was but one of my company captured and none killed."[10]

Jeff Davis watched the action some distance in the rear and as he strained to see what was happening he remarked to an aide, "If Morgan's troops can stand this, all is right; if not, the day is lost. There is no reserve—not a regiment to move—They must fight it out."[11]

Morgan's men were doing just that. They had been called upon many times to attack Confederate works, and they were enjoying the novelty now of fighting from behind works themselves. Their fire was devastating Hoke's division. One regiment, the 36th North Carolina of Clingman's Brigade, suffered over 50 percent casualties in a matter of minutes, with 152 men falling of the 267 who had entered the fight. In the same attack, the 40th North Carolina lost their flag to the 14th Michigan in their front. The 40th North Carolina had served thus far in the Cape Fear River fortifications. This engagement was to be their first pitched infantry battle and they performed like veterans. In assaulting the Federal works, they sustained 57 percent casualties before being thrown back, losing their colors in the process. Union Corporal George W. Clute received the Medal of Honor for capturing the Tarheel colors. In the meantime, Private Henry Plant was busy earning his own Medal of Honor. The Confederates had shot down all of the color guard of the 14th Michigan and were about to capture their flag, when Private Plant grabbed it up and made his way, amid a desperate struggle, back to his own lines.[12]

---

[10] F. L. Fergerson's reminiscences in letter [undated], Frank L. Ferguson papers, Military History Institute, US Army, Carlisle Barracks PA.

[11] McClurg, *Last Chance of the Confederacy*, 295.

[12] Barrett, *Civil War in North Carolina*, 335, and Bradley, *Last Stand in the Carolinas*, 237–39, 242–43.

Hoke's men could not withstand the hail of fire coming from behind the log works, and the attack faltered and began to fall back. In all, the Confederates suffered 593 casualties in Hoke's command.[13] In the meantime, General Hill's three brigades had come into position in Morgan's rear and were advancing. The Federals were forced to jump their own works and fight from the opposite side in the face of this new threat. The Confederates were repulsed, and Federals jumped their works again to charge into their own rear, where they captured many prisoners. The 14th Michigan captured the flag of the 54th Virginia in the rear of its own works just minutes after it had captured the North Carolina flag in front of them.[14]

General Vandevere's Brigade came very close to making the same mistake that Captain Low had made earlier in the day. In the smoke and confusion of the battle, Vandevere was unsure if the men to his front were friend or foe. As one soldier of the division put it, "Many of the Rebs are dressed in our Blue clothes which decive [sic] us."[15] The confusion was cleared up and all doubts swept away when a demand for surrender was heard coming from the direction of the troops in question in an unmistakable southern drawl. The Federals opened on the blue-clad troops with assurance that they were not firing on their own men and drove them back. The Confederates had been just as confused by the actions of the Federal troops. One member of the 42nd Alabama described how the Yankees "began to wave hat and handkerchiefs over their works, so it was natural for us to suppose they were wanting to surrender, for we knew full well that we were in behind them; therefore, we rose up and told them to come over, and they in turn told us to come over, and thus we found there was a misunderstanding, so each line dropped back into a comparatively safe position for a short time, and the same thing took place for a second time."[16]

---

[13] *The War of the Rebellion: A Compilation of the Official Records of the Union and Confederate Armies* (Washington, DC: Government Printing Office, 1895) ser. 1, vol. 47, pt. 1, Gen. D. H. Hill's report, 1091.

[14] McClurg, *Last Chance of the Confederacy*, 384.

[15] John Batchelor Diary, 84, Illinois State Historical Society, Spingfield IL.

[16] Lambert, "In the Battle of Bentonville," 221.

At this most critical point of the battle, when the Confederates could have possibly taken sole possession of the field, Bragg's delay in attacking was indeed a costly error. But even more costly was the failure to issue orders of any kind to McLaws's division, who watched Hoke's charge without taking an active part in the attack. Johnston had detached the division from Hardee for service with Bragg when Hoke's troops were being pressed by Miles and Fitch, and he obviously intended them to temporarily fight as part of Bragg's command and to take part in the assault in that sector, but he issued no specific orders along those lines. Bragg, on the other hand, viewed McLaws's men as still being part of Hardee's wing and not under his immediate control, and therefore did not include them in his attack plans. The result of this miscommunication was that an entire division was left idle on the field instead of being thrown against Morgan's works. Given that along with Hoke and Taliaferro, McLaws commanded one of the larger divisions in the army, the mistake is further magnified.

Morgan's defense of the Federal left was aided by the timely arrival of Colonel William Cogswell's 3rd Brigade of Ward's XX Corps division. Cogswell's men had been quick marching all the way since the call for support had been received, but they were not to be given time to catch their breath when they reached the field. General Slocum directed that they be immediately sent to Morgan's Federal right. Emerging from the swamp, they stumbled on Hill's brigade in the process of assaulting Morgan's rear, and with a yell, they fell upon the Confederates. The combination of Morgan's men in front and Cogswell's in their flank and rear proved too much for the Confederates and the line first gave way, then started to retreat. Cogswell, in a spirited fight, pushed the Confederates back across the Goldsboro Road and reestablished a continuous Federal line on the south side of the road. Had it not been for the timely arrival of General Walthall's command, which plugged the gap and repelled the further advance of Cogswell, this breakthrough could have proved disastrous.[17] Although firing continued in this sector until after dark, there were no further attempts at an attack made by either side.

---

[17] *OR*, ser. 1, vol. 47, pt. 1, Gen. D. H. Hill's report, 1091.

Some 200 to 300 Confederates, primarily from Brigadier General A. M. Manigault's Brigade, had been cut off in a precarious situation behind the Federal lines. It was naturally assumed in the Confederate camp that they had all been made prisoners, but Captain Wood, Manigault's assistant adjutant general, showed up in camp the next morning with ten men and eight prisoners after an all-night march around the Federal army. These soldiers were not to be all of the men who escaped capture. It took Colonel Searcy of the 45th Tennessee a little longer to make his way around the Yankees and back to his own lines, but he did just that, nine days later with seventy of his men.[18]

Meanwhile, on the north side of the road, both sides were preparing to bring the issue of the day to a conclusion. Three regiments of Robinson's Brigade were formed on the north side of the road with their right resting on the road and the line running perpendicular to it. Colonel William Hawley's Brigade formed on a line with Robinson's position to the left, but there was a distance of 400 yards between Robinson's left flank and Hawley's right. The gap was intentional, and it was filled with all the artillery Slocum had on the field at the time, positioned just slightly to the rear of the infantry line on the side of a slight hill that gave it a better control of the field in front. The last brigade of Jackson's division, that belonging to Colonel Selfridge, was held in reserve behind the line. As the rest of General Ward's division came up they were sent to the left in prolongation of Hawley's line. Kilpatrick's Cavalry took its station on the far left to guard against any flank movements by the Confederates upon Ward's men as they came into line.[19]

As one of Ward's soldiers came in sight of the field he declared that "a wilder scene we never saw during the war; before us was an open plain, extending to right and left, more than half a mile, and in front the same distance, bordered on the whole front, by a dense swamp; the road we came on, ran over the hill, and down across the plain, to an opening in the swamp, hidden from view, was the rebel

---

[18] Ibid., 1090–91.

[19] Jay Luvaas, *The Battle of Bentonville March 19–20–21, 1865* (Smithfield NC: Bentonville United Daughters of the Confederacy, n.d.) 16–17.

army, and their line of works." The column marched down the hill past a "big field hospital tent; ambulances and wagons, were standing near, and a number of sick, and wounded men, and attendants, were busy, loading their wagons."[20]

This young soldier was taken with the signs of the fierce struggle that had already been fought.

> Riderless horses were galloping over the plain, Artillery was scattered over the hillside, some busily engaged, throwing shells into the swamp, others acted as tho [sic] trying to leave the field; their horses on the run towards the rear; thay [sic] might have been simply changing for a better position; who could tell, in such confusion.
>
> Down in the rear of the battle line, were scores of wounded soldiers; limping, and dragging themselves to a place of safety; it might have been an orderly confusion, but to a newcomer it looked like a stampede, a perfect rout.[21]

Hardee's men looked little better, even though they had thus far been victorious in the battle. The regiments were badly intermingled and the terrain had played havoc with their alignment. Colonel E. S. Gully of the 40th Alabama saw his regiment become so completely disconnected during the charge that he had only six men with him when he passed to the left and rear of the Federal line. Though effectively cut off from the rest of this men, he returned safely, several days after the battle, with three prisoners in tow.[22]

The advance on the Confederate right had lasted for about an hour before Hardee halted the line to reform. Time was now an enemy equal to the Yankees, for daylight was beginning to fade before "Old Reliable" had everything in readiness to move forward again. McLaws's division was finally given orders, and was directed to march

---

[20] Charles S. Dickinson Diary, 169, Charles H. Dickinson Papers, State Historical Society of Wisconsin, Madison WI.

[21] Ibid.

[22] Watson, "In the Battle of Bentonville," 95.

to the right wing to support the final push Hardee was about to make. For the third time that day, delay proved fatal to the Confederates. The orders to move were not received by McLaws until 6:00 P.M., as the sun was beginning to sink into the horizon. His division would not arrive within supporting distance of the rest of Hardee's troops until after dark, too late to participate in the final charge of the day.[23]

The Federals who would oppose Hardee's men were nearly exhausted. The XIV Corps boys were spent from a full day of fighting and would be held in reserve, but the XX Corps troops were not much fresher. They had marched upwards of 14 miles to reach the battlefield, most of the distance covered by a forced march at quick time. Instead of being allowed rest, they were about to face a Rebel army flushed with its previous success on that part of the field.[24]

Sergeant C. H. Dickinson describes the action as he saw it from the ranks of the 22nd Wisconsin:

> As our column came in view of the top of the hill, Gen. Slocum was sitting on his horse by the road side, and with a field glass, was calmly surveying the field.
>
> Just at that instant the rebels began pouring out of the opening in the swamp, in solid column, and deployed right and left, in front of our lines of battle for an assault.
>
> Where thay [sic] struck our line on the right of the road, the fighting was terrific; the volleys from our works were perfectly paralyzing in their effect on the assaulting column, a battery on the brow of the hill, high enough to fire over our line of battle, were throwing that opening, and doing terrible execution; after the battle, we found the dead piled there 6 men deep.
>
> As the head of our column came opposite Gen. Slocum's position, he pointed down where the fight was raging hot and heavy and say, Col. take your command down to the right of

---

[23] *OR*, ser. 1, vol. 47, pt. 1, Gen. William Bate's report, 1107.

[24] Ezra Button Diary, 69, John B. Tripp Papers, State Historical Society of Wisconsin, Madison WI.

> the road, and strengthen that line; right oblique, march; was the order, and just as we started, the tide of battle shifted to the left of the road.
>
> And there the fight seemed to rage with redoubled fierceness; one of our boys exclaimed, aint that a perfect hell; just then the Gen. gave the order, Col. move your men to the left of the road; the order was given left oblique, march; again the tide of battle changed, and from the crash, and horrid din, you'd thought all hell had broken loose on the left; again came the order from the Gen., Col. move your command to the extreme left, and open the battle immediately; the order was given, left oblique, double quick, march; and away we go on the run for the left, and only just in time, for thay [sic] were doubling our left flank, back towards the center.
>
> When our 2nd Brigade deployed in line on the left, we overlapped them, and turned their right flank; and we soon had them on the run for the swamp.[25]

The scene Sergeant Dickinson described was a bit more complex than his capsulated version suggests, but one can get a feeling for the ferocity and flow of the battle through his words. His description dramatically depicts the several critical junctures of the fighting when Slocum was not sure exactly where the reinforcements were needed most.

At 5:00 P.M., the Confederates emerged from the pine thickets in front of the XX Corps and dressed their ranks preparatory for the final action of the day. They had driven 1 1/2 miles from the original XIV Corps position that morning to the line now held by the Union army. The thin ranks had been further decimated by the fighting of the day, but the men were eager to settle the issue with this final attempt. All knew that this would be the final chance for victory, for Sherman and the right wing of the Union army would surely begin to arrive on the battlefield the next day. If the XX Corps could be driven

---

[25] Charles S. Dickinson Diary, 170–71, Charles H. Dickinson Papers, State Historical Society of Wisconsin, Madison WI.

from the field, the Confederacy might be granted a temporary stay of execution. Precious time would be bought for the cause, and perhaps some miracle yet be realized that would reward the sacrifices these Southern soldiers had made for their goal: independence.

Vice President Alexander Stephens had been involved in trying to work just such a miracle earlier in the year when he had headed up a commission that had attempted to treat with the Federal government for the purpose of reaching a negotiated peace. It had been the hope of the Confederate government that the people of the North had grown so tired of the bloodletting that they would finally be willing to allow the Southern states to go their own way. Lincoln had not been willing to negotiate for anything less than the full restoration of the country as it had been before the war had started, so the proceedings proved a failure. A Confederate victory at Bentonville would greatly strengthen the case Stephens had presented by giving a measure of credence to the assertion that a large number of Northern lives would yet have to be lost before the Confederacy would ever be forced to submit.

It is doubtful if any of the gray-clad soldiers facing the XX Corps line that balmy spring day paused to think of any such momentous matters of state. Their sole concern was the entrenched Yankee line in their front, especially the 400 yard gap between Hawley and Robinson's men where the artillery was located. The Confederate line surged forward just as the sun was beginning to set. Their gray and butternut uniforms could be seen moving in and out of the clouds of smoke that hung low to the field, from the powder discharges of thousands of muskets and batteries of artillery along with the smoldering stumps of trees which had caught fire during the battle.

The gathering twilight necessitated that Hardee send his men forward despite the fact that McClaws's division had not yet arrived from the Confederate left. Hardee could not know it, but McClaws had become confused by the sounds of battle as he marched his division forward. The sounds of musketry, still coming from the Confederate left, caused him to halt on several occasions and deploy the troops to fend off an expected attack from that sector. By the time he reached the Cole house, McClaws saw all the bodies and arms lying around the grounds and he thought that Hardee's attack had already take place, and that he had missed it. He had ordered his men to break ranks so that they might collect the arms and ammunition when he was found by another messenger from Hardee who corrected his misconception and put the division on the march once more.[26]

What Hardee knew for certain was that any further delay would make it probable that the attack would be postponed due to the darkness. If that happened, it was then reasonably certain that it would be canceled altogether, as the Federal right wing would undoubtedly be on the field in the morning, and it would then be futile to attempt offensive operations in the face of the overwhelming odds that would be stacked against them.

But the Federals were not about to allow the Confederates to regain the initiative. Skirmishers were thrown out from the XX Corps line as soon as it was formed, and they were pressing their Rebel counterparts with a vengeance. The Confederate skirmishers eventually managed to push the Yankees back, but were forced to give ground themselves when the Federal main line came up to support the skirmishers. Hardee ordered his troops forward, across the 300–400 yards that separated them from the Union works. At once, the massed batteries between Hawley's and Robinson's brigades began shelling the gray line with terrible effect. General Bate sent his corps straight for the gap, in an attempt to sever the Union lines at that point and divide their army in two. As Bate's men neared the Union position, they were greeted with a hail of grape and canister from the guns in front and a withering small arms fire from Hawley's and Robinson's brigades on their flanks. Forced to fall back, Bate reformed his line and threw it towards the artillery once more. The Union fire only intensified during the next charge, especially from the big guns. As one Confederate survivor put it, "The raging leaden hailstorm of

[26] Nathaniel Cheairs Hughes, Jr., *General William J. Hardee: Old Reliable* (Baton Rouge: Louisiana State University Press, 1965) 290.

grape and canister literally barked the trees, cutting off limbs as if cut by hand."[27]

Charles S. Brown of the 21st Michigan had made it through the fighting earlier that afternoon, and with his regiment now in reserve, he took the opportunity of observing the XX Corps guns in action. "There were 8 full batteries going for them as best they knew how & they would average 2 shots a minute to the gun as the Rebs charged on the batteries they began to fill up the guns with boxes of Cartridges."[28] Battery I, 2nd Regiment, Illinois Light Artillery, reported the firing of 217 rounds by their guns alone.[29] The carnage was ghastly, and the Confederates were driven back again. This scene was repeated a total of five times as Bates's men tried to force a wedge between the two Federal brigades, each time with the same disastrous results. Darkness finally bought an end to the charges, but sporadic firing continued for several more hours. General Bate estimated his losses to be a quarter of the men he had taken into the fight, and his dead and wounded littered the road in front of Robinson's position.[30] Bate also lost two of his commanders in the final charge of the day. Major W. H. Wilkinson, commander of Tyler's Brigade, was killed at the head of his brigade leading the last charge of the day, and Colonel Kenan of the 6th Florida, in the same charge, received a wound that required the amputation of his leg.[31]

Fortunes on the Confederate right went little better for the rest of Hardee's wing. As many as seven different charges were made by Rebel units against the XX Corps line, but each was successively weaker than the one before due to the ever-mounting casualties. Brigadier General John Kennedy, commanding Conner's Brigade of

---

[27] Samuel W. Ravenell, untitled article, *Confederate Veteran Magazine* 47/1 (1939): 124.

[28] Charles S. Brown to Mother and Etta, 18 April 1865, Charles S. Brown Papers, Perkins Library, Duke University, Durham NC.

[29] Thaddeus C. S. Brown, Samuel J. Murphy, and William G. Putney, *Behind the Guns: The History of Battery I 2nd Regiment, Illinois Light Artillery* (Carbondale: Southern Illinois University Press, 1965) 137.

[30] *OR*, ser. 1, vol. 47, pt. 1, 1108.

[31] Ibid., 1107.

McClaws's division, was brought on the field after the rest of the right was already engaged and was placed on the left of General Walthall's troops. The firing had died down some by the time Kennedy took his position, partly from an inability to see the enemy. "The smoke was so thick that it was impossible to see ten yards ahead," Kennedy reported, "hence I could form no idea of the force of the enemy in my front."[32]

Casualties continued to be heavy among the Confederate officer corps. General Pettus was shot down with a painful flesh wound and his nephew and aide-de-camp was killed. Lieutenant Colonel Boggess of the 26th Tennessee and Captain Hampton of the 63rd Virginia, both regimental commanders in Stevenson's division, also fell dead. Four officers on D. H. Hill's staff fell wounded during the engagement.[33] General Taliaferro's men, though not handled quite as roughly as those under Bate, still sustained heavy casualties, one regiment alone losing 190 men.[34]

The remainder of General McClaws's division made their way on the field as darkness was bringing an end to the heavy fighting and passed through General Bate's line to the front. Little could be done now though. General Bate was sure that "[h]ad these fresh troops been thrown in an hour earlier our victory could have been more complete and more fruitful of advantage."[35]

As the sounds of the battle faded in the night, General Hill was struck by the fact that the "natural darkness was much increased by the smoke of battle and from thousands of smoldering pine stumps and logs, it was greater than I ever witnessed before."[36] Confederate A. P. Harcourt seconded the general's description of the eerie scene the battlefield presented.

---

[32] Ibid., 1110.

[33] Ibid., 1091–92, 1096.

[34] Jay Luvaas, *The Battle of Bentonville March 19–20–21, 1865* (Smithfield NC: Bentonville United Daughters of the Confederacy, n.d.) 17.

[35] *OR*, ser. 1, vol. 47, pt. 1, 1107.

[36] Ibid., 1091.

> The battle...for the most part in a dense pine and turpentine forest. After the first day's firing this forest got on fire and at night, the scene beggars description, as lurid flames, fed by the rosin on the trees, would shoot up into the sky and suddenly drop back like so many tongues, while underneath the wounded moaned piteously for help or struggled to escape roasting alive. Sometimes huge logs of fire would drop from a great height, or a shell would knock off a blazing tree top upon a litter corps or other troops in motion or at rest. It was grim visaged war in his most weird, most grand and appalling aspect.[37]

The assault which had failed in the light of day could not be expected to bear positive results in such inky darkness. Commands were already badly intermingled and the situation would only be compounded by ordering a night assault. From 9:00 P.M., the regiments on the Confederate right received their instructions to withdraw to the rear to the positions they had previously held in the morning, but not before one last effort ended in disaster on Hoke's front.

Shortly after nightfall, General Mitchell had borrowed a rubber blanket and had just lain down to sleep when he was interrupted by an officer who told him that there was a staff officer with a message who needed to see him. The Union general sat up and listened as the young man reported that "Colonel Hardee presents his compliments to you, and asks that you will apprise your line that he is forming in your front to charge the Yankee lines on your left." These words drove the weariness from the general's body and he sprang to his feet and requested that the message be repeated. Mitchell then asked what Colonel Hardee had sent the message and was told that it was Colonel Hardee of the 23rd Georgia, commanding a brigade in Hoke's division. General Mitchell asked if the young man had had his supper, and when he learned that he had not, he was conducted to the rear with a staff

---

[37] A. P. Harcourt, "Terry's Texas Rangers," *The Southern Bivouac* 11 (November 1882): 96–97.

officer for that purpose. The Confederate was still not aware that he was in a Union camp or that he would be enjoying his supper as a prisoner, but to Mitchell "[t]he information was well worth a better supper than could then be improvised." The general drew in his picket line and informed his regimental commanders of the news he had received. Orders were given that the entire brigade line was to fire a volley when they heard a signal, which was to be the sound of a drum. Then the skirmish line was to resume its previous position without further orders. Mitchell had hardly relayed the messages before the Confederates reached the front of his brigade. They were so close that the Union soldiers could clearly hear their footsteps and the men talking among themselves. Mitchell had directed that the men fire low and, at the proper time, one loud tap was given on the bass drum and the brigade front erupted in a sheet of flame. "I never expect to hear again such a volume of mingled cries, groans, screams, and curses," wrote General Mitchell. "The next morning there was displayed in front of our works, among the dead, a line of new Enfield rifles and knapsacks, almost as straight as if laid out for a Sunday morning inspection." Mitchell later met Colonel Hardee in a Raleigh hospital and had the chance to talk with him. Hardee said that his men had spent most of the war in the fortifications in and around Wilmington, and that this had been their first battle. They had been kept in reserve during the fighting in the morning and afternoon but had been brought up in the evening for the sole purpose of making this charge. Hardee said that the men "were determined to go right over the Yankee lines; and, breathing fire, they had vowed to take no prisoners." The colonel described how the terrible shock of the Union volley had caused his brigade to crumble: "The fools thought they were discovered and surrounded. They ran, and I have no doubt they are still running, for we have never been able to get ten of them together since their flight."[38] No further effort was made by the Confederates during the night, as both sides concentrated on tending their dead and wounded and strengthening their respective defenses.

---

[38] McClurg, *Last Chance of the Confederacy*, 385–86.

One member of the 2nd South Carolina was walking the field that night when he came upon the freshly dug grave of a fourteen-year-old boy who had been killed in the fighting that day. "The sight of it awakened sad feelings," he later wrote. "I was myself only seventeen years of age, having volunteered at Charleston in 1864."[39] This lad of tender years was but one of the thousands who had fallen in the desperate struggle, and comrades searched the murky darkness well into the night seeking the whereabouts of missing friends. For most of the participants of the day's fighting, however, the first order of business was strengthening their defensive works, and this completed, the exhausted men on both sides collapsed to the ground for a few hours of badly needed rest.

Joe Johnston had succeeded in checking the advance of the Federal left wing and had brought them to battle on a site of his choosing, but the cost was more than the Army of the South could afford to pay. Confederate casualties on 19 March totaled 2,462 men, or just over 15 percent of the total engaged. Losses for the day were broken down to 239 killed, 1550 wounded and 673 missing and presumed captured. The largest number of these came from the Army of Tennessee, which lost 1,083 out of a total of a little over 5,000 men who were in the fight. Hoke's division suffered a loss of 740 men, followed by Hardee's losses of 526 and the cavalry losses of 113. General Slocum had been able to keep his army from being driven off the field, and in the morning he would be joined by two fresh Union corps. Johnston was to have no such addition of manpower. He would have to make the decision to stay and fight or to withdraw knowing that his force encompassed the sum total of Confederate fighting men in the area.[40]

Slocum had escaped destruction, but just barely. Though Union casualties were less than half those suffered by the Confederates, numbering slightly over 1,000, most of those had been sustained by the XIV Corps during the fighting of the morning and early afternoon

---

[39] Robert W. Sanders, "The Battle of Bentonville, N.C.," *Confederate Veteran Magazine* 34/4 (1926): 461.

[40] *OR*, ser. 1, vol. 47, pt. 1, 1058–59.

when the Rebels still held the momentum and the issue was very much in question. The rest of Sherman's army would jokingly refer to the engagement as the "Battle of Acorn Run" because the XIV Corps badge looked like an acorn, and they had been routed from the field. A certain amount of animosity had existed between the XX Corps men and the rest of Sherman's army due to the fact that they were Easterners who had been with the Army of the Potomac. They viewed the rest of the western army to be undisciplined and unsoldierly in their bearing, not at all what they had been used to in the east. The westerners viewed the XX Corps men as being "paper collar" soldiers; well drilled and pretty on parade, but lacking the fighting spirit that defined the troops from the west. It was with a great deal of chagrin that the XIV Corps men received the taunts of the XX Corps easterners who had come to their rescue, and many a fight was started, even years after the war, by the mere mention of "The Battle of Acorn Run."[41]

Federal losses numbered 152 killed, 821 wounded, and 171 missing for a total of 1,144.[42] The timely arrival of the XX Corps prevented the disaster that might have befallen Jeff Davis's corps and the entire wing. The majority of the Confederate losses occurred later in the day when their lines were thrown against the now fortified positions of the Federals.

Johnston had only partially gained his objective, and a partial victory at this point of the war was hardly better than a defeat. The day had witnessed the last grand, full-scaled attack to be made by the Confederates in the war, and it had restored the shaken confidence of the army, particularly among the members of the Army of Tennessee. Despite the tremendous casualties, the men were in high spirits following the fight and they submitted to their exhaustion that night with a feeling of accomplishment.

---

[41] Capt. Allan H. Dougall, *Bentonville* (Indianapolis: The Military Order of the Loyal Legion of the United States, Indiana, 1898) 218.

[42] Ashley Halsey, Jr., "The Last Duel in the Confederacy." *Civil War Times Illustrated* 1/7 (November 1962): 7–8, 31.

The day was not only the date of the final grand western charge of the war, it was also the day when the last Confederate duel was fought. The duel was fought between Privates Thomas R. Chew and Marx E. Cohen, Jr., both members of Halsey's Battery of horse artillery, formerly known as Hart's Battery. Both men hailed from Charleston, South Carolina, coming from well-respected families and had enlisted early in the war. Chew was a member of Hampton's Legion, having volunteered for service in June 1861. Since that time he had been with Battery A of the Legion's artillery battalion, and involved in some 143 battles and skirmishes. Cohen enlisted in the 5th South Carolina Cavalry Regiment in March 1862 and saw limited action until he effected a transfer from that unit to Hart's Battery in 1864. At twenty-three, he had studied medicine and had received his degree prior to entering the service. The night before the first day's fighting at Bentonville these two privates argued over an unknown issue. As Louis Sherfesee, guidon bearer of the battery later wrote, "On the evening of March 18, 1865, two of our comrades, Dr. Marx E. Cohen and Thomas Chew, had some words which ended in a challenge for a duel the next morning."[43]

The following morning found the camp busily preparing for the battle that was to come, but for Chew, Cohen, and a few other interested parties, preparations to meet the Yankees would have to wait. At sunrise the two principles, along with their respective seconds, Leonidus Raysor and William Verdier, walked, "[s]ome little distance" from the camp where the duel was to take place. Each man was presented a loaded revolver from his second, "took their positions, and at the word, emptied their revolvers at each other, but neither was hurt."[44]

Both men were visibly perplexed by their apparent inaccuracy at a distance of only 60 feet. On the walk back to camp, Cohen talked with Verdier, his second. "I can't understand it." Then his face became lit with the flash of sudden realization, and he demanded to know if the seconds had loaded the revolvers properly. It seems that

---

[43] Ibid.

[44] Ibid.

the two seconds had met the previous night and had agreed that there had already been enough bloodshed in the war without Confederates killing one another. Accordingly, they decided that they would load the revolvers with blanks. Verdier refused to admit the fact to Cohen when questioned; he merely smiled. "I understand now," Cohen raged. "I shall hold you to account for this!"[45]

But Cohen had no time to dwell on the deception. Before the dueling party made their way back to camp they could hear the sounds of "Boots and Saddles" being played in the camp, and they ran the rest of the way to saddle their horses and prepare to move out with the battery. Halsey's Battery was moved into the gap in the center of the line that had originally been reserved for Hardee's men with orders "to remain quiet until further instructions. Shortly afterward, the enemy opened on us." One of the early shell bursts killed Thomas Chew instantly, followed closely by another explosion which mortally wounded Marx Cohen. Leonidus Raysor, Chew's second, was then thrown to the ground when he was hit by a shell which completely severed one of his arms. The battery was finally allowed to respond to the Union barrage and it roared into action. Notwithstanding the tender attentions of his comrades, Cohen died from his wounds before the day was over, while Raysor eventually recovered from his. Verdier emerged the fighting unscathed, the only member of the last Confederate dueling party to do so.[46]

---

[45] Ibid.
[46] Ibid.

6

The Sounds of Thunder

General Sherman had indeed heard the sounds of fighting as he rode away from the left wing and toward General Howard's command. Though he was strongly convinced that his assessment of the Confederates in Slocum's front being nothing more than cavalry was correct, any doubts that the increased firing might have caused quickly disappeared once Slocum's first messenger arrived with reassurance from the general. By the time Lieutenant Foraker was dispatched to convey the true state of affairs, Sherman had put considerable distance between himself and the Union left. Foraker would have to ride the rest of the day to catch up with the general and deliver his message. An officer who was present in camp when the messenger finally reached Sherman left this account of the proceedings:

> At about half-past nine, one of General Slocum's aids came up at a dashing pace, and throwing himself from his horse, asked for General Sherman. We all gathered round, and listened attentively as he told the particulars of the battle. The Commander-in-chief would have made a good subject for Punch or Vanity Fair. He had been lying down in General Howard's tent, and hearing the inquiry for him, and being of course anxious to hear the news of the fight, he rushed out to the campfire without stopping to put on his clothes. He stood in a bed of ashes up to his ankles, chewing impatiently the stump of a cigar, with his hands clasped behind him, and with nothing but a red flannel undershirt and a pair of Drawers.

As Sherman listened, the messenger told how, "the enemy had made four distinct assaults on our line, and had been repulsed; but that just as he left they were coming again, and he feared we had lost the battle, as the enemy overlapped out troops on both flanks." The general, still in his night clothes, began issuing orders to the various staff officers in his presence which sent them scurrying off with marching orders for the commanders of the various portions of the right wing.[1]

Sherman probably regretted now a decision he had made that afternoon that overturned a directive from General Howard to General William Hazen.. The rumbling of artillery, along with the constant small arms fire should have alerted him that more than just stubborn cavalry was in Slocum's front, but he had convinced himself otherwise. It was too late for self-recrimination, however, and he ordered General Hazen, still commanding the rear division in the right wing of march, to retrace his steps and march back to Slocum.[2]

Hazen responded immediately, and his division marched with all possible haste. Sherman sent word to the left wing commander that help was on the way and should start arriving in the morning. Slocum was to assume a defensive posture for the time being, until the two wings could be concentrated. Sherman had erred once already today in his appraisal of the Confederate ability to bring his army to battle and he was not about to compound that mistake by taking any rash actions. Over the course of the previous summer, before Johnston was replaced by General John Bell Hood on 18 July, he had been given ample opportunity to observe the command decisions of his adversary, and he was well aware that Johnston was not one to commit his men recklessly to a battle. If Johnston had deemed it prudent to attack at this juncture then the Confederate commander had reasons to feel he could win. To be sure, he probably received the

---

[1] Alexander C. McClurg, *The Last Chance of the Confederacy* (Chicago: The Military Order of the Loyal Legion of the United States, Illinois; A. C. McClurg and Co., 1891) 389.

[2] Gen. O. O. Howard, *Autobiography of Oliver Otis Howard*, 2 vols. (New York: The Baker & Taylor Co., 1908) 2:446.

inflated estimates of the size of the Confederate army, placing it between 30,000 and 40,000 men, which had come to be accepted by most officers serving with the left wing. Knowing Johnston as he did, and without any positive information contrary to the estimates of the Rebel army, Sherman acted in the only acceptable manner open to him by ordering Slocum to assume the defensive.

The left wing commander did not have to wait for Sherman to order this posture. As soon as the firing had died down that evening, the sounds of spades being put to use were discernible all along the Union line. "Old soldiers know the value of protection even a little protection is much better than no protection," wrote James Congleton of the 105th Illinois. "We commence to dig as soon as we come in front of the enemy—often we use fence rails or timber—anything that will stop bullets. A little protection saves many lives and often wins a battle."[3]

Johnston, knowing he would be greatly outnumbered in the morning, had his men dig in as well. With his back to the Mill Creek River, he withdrew both of his flanks towards the stream, forming a bridgehead around the only serviceable span across the river. His lines now resembled a large V, and the configuration would give him the ability to use shorter interior lines in the event the Federals decided to attack him while he guarded the bridge that was his only means of retreat should he be driven from the field. The drawing back of his flanks was also in anticipation of the arrival of Union reinforcements. Johnston knew that the Federals would be coming down the Goldsboro Road towards Bentonville, and if he did not pull back his lines, the Yankee line of march would place them squarely on his flank and rear. Johnston has been criticized for remaining on the field after Sherman's army was concentrated, since it is felt that his small army would not be able to do the combined Union forces any real damage, while it placed him in a precarious position that could have resulted in the destruction of his entire army. This might be true if the general had planned to continue offensive operations, but Johnston had no

---

[3] James A. Congleton journal, 93, James A. Congleton Papers, Library of Congress, Washington, DC.

such delusions. In his autobiography, he states that he intended to allow the army time to secure their wounded before withdrawing, but it is also certain that Johnston would have welcomed the chance to defend his works against a Federal frontal assault. He was well aware how much strong works compensated for a disparity in numbers, and if Sherman could be tempted into it, the Confederates might yet be able to attain a victory comparable to Kennesaw Mountain.

While Sherman was turning his soldiers around and marching towards Bentonville, his wagons were given other orders. They were to proceed on towards Goldsboro and Kinston to effect a junction with General Schofield's forces, where they were to attain provisions before returning to the army. Clothes were not the only article the Federals were running short of—there was a definite shortage of food for both man and beast. As one Confederate soldier put it: "The Enemy at Bentonville were badly off for Provisions. His troops had positively nothing but parched corn. As to his animals that his Q.M. accounted were so fat, when we captured some Artillery the horses were actually too poor to pull the pieces off. We captured about three hundred mules and horses all in same condition."[4] One positive feature of the situation was that with the Confederate army at Bentonville, Schofield would be able to take possession of Goldsboro without a fight, and a source of supplies for Sherman's army would be ever closer with each step his men made in from the coast. In fact, elements of the 3rd Division, XVII Corps, had already made contact with portions of Schofield's advance.[5] General Jacob Cox, with his forces between Kinston and Goldsboro, was able to hear the sounds of the battle on the previous day: "on Sunday we had heard all day the very distant artillery firing, which we knew indicated a battle between Sherman and Johnston. It was a scarcely distinguishable sound, like a dull thumping, becoming somewhat more distinct when one applied his ear to the ground. We judged that this final battle in the Carolinas

---

[4] A. L. Brooks and Hugh T. Lefler, *The Papers of Walter Clark* (Chapel Hill: University of North Carolina Press, 1948) 136–37.

[5] Mary Ann Anderson, ed., *The Civil War Diary of Allen Morgan Geer: Twentieth Regiment/Illinois Volunteers* (New York: Cosmos Press, 1977) 205.

was near Smithfield, and we were not far out of the way, for Bentonville was only a little south, and either place about fifty miles from us."[6]

The first fresh Union troops to come to Slocum's aid were from the two divisions of the left wing that had been guarding the wagon train and from Hazen's division. General John Geary's XX Corps division left one brigade with the corps train and marched at midnight of 19 March for Bentonville, arriving there at 4:30 A.M. and being placed in reserve behind the line.[7]

Hazen's division also began to arrive in the middle of the night, followed by the rest of General John Logan's XV Corps. Blair's corps would have the greatest distance to march and would not begin arriving until the afternoon of 20 March. Blair had received his orders from Howard a little after 900 P.M. on the evening of 19 March when a breathless aide rode up to his headquarters wagon. Howard detailed the situation and directed him to get his corps "up here with at least two divisions disencumbered." Blair was to be on the road at 3:00 A.M. according to his orders, but had the commissary officers issue hardtack to the men preparatory to shoving off, and his columns were on the march by 1:00 A.M., two hours ahead of schedule.[8]

There was no sleep for most of the XVII Corps men that night. It would take them over twelve hours of hard marching to reach Bentonville. They retraced their route for the first 5 miles then, "turned to our right and marched in all twenty miles. Waded several bad swamps." At daybreak, the corps passed by Generals Sherman and Howard at Falling Creek Church, where they were allowed a brief time to rest while the rear of Logan's corps cleared the road in front of them. Blair began arriving on the field early in the afternoon of 20 March, and his corps extended the Union right near the Mill Creek

---

[6] Gen. Jacob Dolson Cox, *Military Reminiscences of the Civil War* (New York: Charles Scribner's Sons, 1900) 446.

[7] John Richard Boyle, *Soldiers True: The Story of the One Hundred and Eleventh Regiment Pennsylvania Veteran Volunteers* (New York Eaton & Sons, 1903) 290.

[8] Leslie Anders, *The Eighteenth Missouri* (Indianapolis: The Bobbs-Merrill Co., 1968) 314–15.

River, with Logan's corps formed on his left, connecting to the right of Slocum's force.[9]

One member of General John Smith's division of the XV Corps tells how part of his division had a bit of sport on 19 March before they got the word to march for Bentonville. "Pryor [sic] to our coming up the 2nd Brigade of our Div. Espied the whole wagon train of the Rebs. They threw off everything but their canteens and cartridge boxes and started on the double quick for the purpose of capturing it but they have not yet returned so with what success they have met with I cannot imagine."[10]

This same soldier tells how some captured Confederate dispatches might have helped to form Sherman's opinion that there were not enough Rebels in the vicinity to cause him any harm.

> A pretty good story for a true one is told of some Rebel communications that were intercepted between Gen. Lee & Johnston. The former sent word to the latter stating that Sherman could and must be stopped. Johnston sent back word saying that all he had to stop him, Sherman, with was three broken down Brigades and four Proclamations. The largest Rebel Army that I have seen on the march is the prisoners. Our Corps had about one thousand and I presume the rest of the Corps has about the same amount.[11]

As Howard's wing went into position, Johnston saw that his left flank was being badly overlapped by the Federal line. In order to extend his line, General McClaws was once more ordered to Hoke's portion of the line, forming on the left and extending back towards the river. Even with this addition the Confederates were still badly overlapped, and Johnston was forced to order a large portion of his cavalry, under General Wheeler, to form up on McClaws left and fight

---

[9] Ibid., 315.

[10] John E. Risedorph Diary, 19 March 1865, Minnesota Historical Society, St. Paul MN.

[11] Ibid.

dismounted so that he could present a front equal in length to that of the Federals. Though equal in length, the far left of the Confederate line was hardly equal in strength to the enemy. Wheeler did not have enough troopers to present a solid front and he was forced to space his men at intervals of three to four feet apart in order to cover the ground assigned to him. This was definitely the weak part of the entire Rebel line, and the only question was whether Sherman would probe with his men sufficiently to find it. Johnston had no reserves. A breakthrough by the Federals on that flank would put the Union forces in the flank and rear of the entire Confederate army.

At dawn on Monday, 20 March, "[a]ll of the troops were busy wiping out their guns, filling up cartridge boxes with fresh dry ammunition, and putting everything in order for the work of the day, for they knew, as well as did the general commanding, what was in store for them."[12] All of the troops on both sides anticipated that the action would pick up where it had left off the previous night. "The presence of Sherman, Howard, Logan, and Charles R. Woods [the commander 1st Division, XV Corps] on the field at that early hour, all mounted, and attended by their full complement of staff officers and escorts, giving orders and directing movements for the formations, indicated to a certainty that the first Division as the advance of the corps column would be in the storm center of the day's operations."[13]

The rain returned that day and Robert Bruce Hoadley, a soldier in the 26th Iowa, XV Corps, described the difficulties experienced while constructing works both from the weather and the Confederates. "Was engaged half a day, raining hard all the time. We had to build works under the Johneys [sic] fire, it was not very pleasant work, raining & Bullets flying one about as hard as the other, only the rain would not hurt, & the bullets would. My Company [G] lost 2 men badly wounded. That looks small, but when you come to see how few

---

[12] Henry Wright, *History of the Sixth Iowa Infantry* (Iowa City: State Historical Society of Iowa, 1923) 429.

[13] Ibid.

men we hav [sic], it is like taking a brother out of a family. We hav [sic] only 1 Sargt., 1 Corpl. and 9 men for duty."[14]

The Confederate fire Hoadley spoke of came from the skirmishers in front of the works. Major Walter Clark, one of the boy soldiers of the 1st Brigade Junior Reserves of Hoke's division, was in command of the skirmish line of the brigade that day. "It was a good wood for skirmishing with little or no undergrowth. We had a regular Indian fight of it from behind trees."[15]

The entrenching of the Union right wing was further slowed by a shortage of entrenching tools. When spades and axes were issued to the men of the XV Corps, the troops were instructed to work as speedily as possible. Only ten minutes were allotted to each company in a regiment to make use of the tools before they were to be passed on to the next company. Ten minutes was not a lot of time, but the men made the most of the tools, and passable works began to appear as the entrenching equipment was passed down the line.[16]

Though the Federal skirmishers attained success in pushing back the Confederate skirmish line on either side of Clark's position during the day, the sixteen- to seventeen-year-old boys who made up the reserves held fast to their position on the line and refused to concede an inch of ground. The courage exhibited by these boys, referred to as the "Seed Corn of the Confederacy" by Governor Vance, elicited high praise from General Hoke, their divisional commander. "At Bentonville they held a very important part of the battle field in opposition to Sherman's old and tried soldiers and repulsed every charge that was made upon them with very meager and rapidly thrown-up breastworks. Their conduct in camp, on the march, and on the battlefield was everything that could be expected from them, and,

---

[14] R. B. Hoadley Diary, 19 March 1865, Robert Bruce Hoadley Papers, Perkins Library, Duke University, Durham NC.

[15] Brooks and Lefler, *Papers of Walter Clark*, 136–37.

[16] Nathaniel Cheairs Hughes, Jr., *Bentonville: The Final Battle of Sherman & Johnston* (Chapel Hill: University of North Carolina Press, 1996) 184.

I am free to say, was equal to that of the old soldiers who had passed through four years of war."[17]

For the most part, 20 March saw no major fighting, but rather skirmish firing and artillery exchanges. Sherman, still cautious, lest the Confederates should have in their army the numbers of men that rumors claimed for them, decided to move slowly in developing the situation. One of Sherman's officers correctly summed up the strategy adopted by his commander when he stated, "I do not suppose there will be any heavy assault made by us in front, certainly not if the rebel position can be flanked, which is being now looked after."[18] Indeed, all of the action of 20 March was a result of Sherman's troops feeling out the position and strength of the Confederate works and were incidental to the commander's initiated offensive operations of any sort.

Sherman and his staff occupied a position in the rear of the reserves as he issued orders for the placement of the units coming on the field and received messages concerning the disposition of the Rebel forces. The skirmish firing could be heard distinctly from the general's vantage point, and he seemed to those around him to be lost in thought as he paced back and forth under the shade of some large trees, listening intently to the sounds.

> The cigar in his mouth was more often out than burning. Once he stopped an officer who was smoking and asked for a light. The officer obliged by handing him his own smoke. As the General lit his cigar, he seemed oblivious of those around him. His mind was on the noise of battle. Suddenly he turned, dropped the officer's cigar on the ground, and walked off puffing his own. The startled soldier looked at him a moment, then laughed, picked up the cigar, and continued his smoke.[19]

---

[17] Mrs. John H. Anderson, "North Carolina Boy Soldiers at the Battle of Bentonville." *Confederate Veteran Magazine* 35/3 (1927): 174.

[18] *Marching with Sherman*, 273.

[19] Melvin Grigsby, *The Smoked Yank* (Sioux Falls SD: Bell Publishing Co., 1888) 237.

While the XV and XVII Corps men were busy aligning themselves and constructing works on the right of the Union lines, many men on the left were occupied with trying to bring comfort to the fallen of the previous day's fight who still lay on the field between the two armies. W. C. Johnson of the 89th Ohio writes that he "was engaged most of the afternoon in assisting to remove the wounded of both sides, off the battlefield, who were wounded in yesterday's engagement; but the close proximity of the Rebel skirmishers had rendered it impossible to remove them at that time, at the close of the battle, night coming on soon after this, we did under heavy fire, shells almost continually bursting all around us."[20]

The wounded that were lucky enough to be reached by details such as the one Johnson was a part of were taken to the Federal field hospital where they waited their turn for attention from the already overworked surgeons. Over 500 men had already been operated on or had their wounds dressed over the night of 19 March and the morning of 20 March, Surgeon James T. Reeve spent that morning "[a]t work all day in Hosp. Principally at operating table. Amputated arms of Nugent and Kennedy and thumb of John Brady from the 21st [the 21st Wisconsin, his own regiment]."[21] Colonel William Hamilton, 9th Ohio Cavalry, made an interesting observation of the doctors at work and also gives some insight to how the hardships of the war had hardened its participants to scenes of horror: "A dozen surgeons and attendants in their shirt sleeves stood at rude benches cutting off arms and legs and throwing them out of the windows, where they lay scattered on the grass. The legs of the infantrymen could be distinguished from those of the cavalry by the size of their calves, as the march of 1,000 miles had increased the size of the one and diminished the size of the other."[22]

Many of the newly-arrived Federal troops were not impressed with the site of the battleground, among them was General Oliver O.

---

[20] W. C. Johnson Diary, 69–70, Library of Congress, Washington, DC.

[21] James T. Reeve Diary, 16, James T. Reeve Papers, State Historical Society of Wisconsin, Madison WI.

[22] John G. Barrett, *The Civil War in North Carolina* (Chapel Hill: University of North Carolina Press, 1963) 343.

Howard. The general noted that the area was "so much more woodland than open ground...and so much marshy or spongy soil that quick maneuvering was impossible."[23] He quickly deduced that cavalry and artillery would be difficult to move in this terrain and that any action would boil down to an infantryman's fight.

True to Howard's assumption, General Kilpatrick and his mounted men served mainly as spectators. They were assigned only to guard the extreme left flank of the army in the event that the Confederate cavalry should try to ride around the Union line, but they did mange to keep the Rebels to their front occupied with a harassing fire from the horse artillery. A Confederate battery responded and the shelling was kept up throughout the day, but with very little effect on either side.[24]

General Jeff Davis spent the night of 19 March upon the field with his men, arranging the lines and seeing that all was in readiness for the coming day.[25] The XIV Corps boys were still a little shaky from the day before, but it was expected that they should have ample time on 20 March to regroup. At about noon, however, the Confederates were observed withdrawing from in front of Morgan's division. The general ordered Vandever's 1st Brigade forward, but the 16th Illinois and the 14th Michigan became badly cut up in the process, "[t]he enemy having made arrangement to protect and cover that movement by construction a heavy line of works running nearly parallel to the Goldsboro road in which they had posted a six gun battery which opened with grape and canister on our advancing line." Despite a heavy fire from the Confederates, the 1st Brigade was successful in holding their advanced position and General John Pearce's 2nd Brigade then made a left wheel that put them again in full contact with the withdrawn Rebel lines in their front and should have put them in line with General Baird's 3rd Division, XIV Corps, on their right. Through some misunderstanding, Baird's line was not

---

[23] Anders, *The Eighteenth Missouri*, 315.

[24] John W. Rowell, *Yankee Cavalrymen: Through the Civil War with the Ninth Pennsylvania Cavalry* (Knoxville: University of Tennessee Press, 1971) 243.

[25] John Batchelor Diary, 85, Illinois State Historical Society, Spingfield IL.

where Morgan thought it should be however, and instead of linking up in a continuous line, Pearce's right was left exposed and dangling in the open. Morgan reacted quickly in filling this gap in the line by ordering the 2nd Brigade to cover the extended space temporarily while he brought up two regiments of Fearing's Brigade to plug the hole. There were many anxious moments spent waiting for Fearing's men to come up. One Union veteran understood the danger presented by the gap, commenting, "if the enemy had taken advantage of [it], must have proved disastrous to our army." He was also aware that the XIV Corps men had been just about used up the day before and it would not take much to start another stampede for the rear. Luckily, for the Federals, the Confederates were looking towards their own defensive arrangements and allowed the opportunity to pass unnoticed.[26]

The XV Corps had had to fight its way onto the field, as General Wheeler harassed their advance with a regiment of cavalry. Fighting dismounted, from behind hastily thrown up works, Wheeler was able to slow down the Federals progress by forcing the head of the column to repeatedly deploy for the battle. He did not have enough men to make the delay an appreciable one though, and was driven out of several lines of temporary works for a distance of 8 miles.

The 97th Indiana, of Colonel Robert Catterson's 2nd Brigade, 1st Division, was in the lead of the XV Corps and served as skirmishers, driving Wheeler's troopers out of their fieldworks. They were supported by the remainder of the brigade, consisting of the 100th Indiana and the 6th Iowa, and after pushing Wheeler back for a distance of 3 miles, they were relieved by the 6th Iowa. General Sherman personally directed Colonel Catterson to pressure the Confederates and advance as fast as the men could travel, and Captain Orlando J. Fast, the brigade adjutant general kept encouraging the men saying, "Keep a stiff upper lip boys, and give them the best you have." The 6th Iowa continued to force Wheeler's Cavalry to retire

[26] James Burkhalter Diary, 94–95, Illinois State Historical Society, Spingfield IL.

for another 5 miles, driving them out of six barricades.[27] A soldier in the 100th Indiana talks about the advance of the skirmishers.

> The Johnny's sent a lot of Cavelry [sic] around our flank, thinking they would capture our skirmish line which was well in advance. We were driving the Johnnys rapidly. They had a little 3-pound gun on the road and would stop and fire it sometimes. We were perhaps 80 rods away. Some of our boys had been firing at the men with the gun, but could not seem to have much effect. Then Capt. Pratt called me to try it with my Henry rifle. I got as close as I dared, for they were firing at us with their small arms too. By that time they had the gun limbered up and were starting away with it, but I was close enough now so I could see them good. The rider was on the rear mule. I pulled up my rifle, thinking I would shoot him which I could easily have done as his whole body showed plainly above the mule. Just as I was going to fire something seemed to say to me: "Don't kill the man; kill the mule" so I dropped my rifle a little and shot off the mule just behind the fore leg. He went down and that delayed them so much that we got the gun.[28]

One footsore Yankee plodded onward in the hope that this would be among his last campaigns. "If we are successful as I have not the least doubt but what we will be I think that we will all be home in less than one year."[29]

This march brought the head of the column to the junction of the Smithfield Road, and the men were halted to rest and replenish their almost exhausted supply of ammunition. After the cartridge boxes were refilled, the 46th Ohio took the lead. The regiment was armed with breech-loading Spencer rifles, and they at once opened

---

[27] Wright, *Sixth Iowa Infantry*, 430.

[28] Oscar Osburn Winther, *With Sherman to the Sea: The Civil War Letters Diaries & Reminiscences of Theodore Upson* (Baton Rouge: Louisiana State University Press, 1943) 158–59.

[29] John E. Risedorph Diary, 68, Minnesota Historical Society, St. Paul MN.

with a tremendous fire upon the Rebels. In fact, six of the seven regiments in Catterson's Brigade were armed with repeating rifles, giving his brigade firepower unrivaled in Sherman's army. Five regiments were equipped with Spencer's, while a portion of a sixth was armed with Colt revolving rifles.[30]

"At the sound of the bugles, the 46th Ohio charged with a yell, routed the enemy from a strong barricade and drove them back to their infantry lines, posted in heavy earthworks." General Wood immediately formed his division in line over the crossroads leading to Bentonville and Smithfield, connecting on his left with General Hazen's division, who in turn was connected to the XIV Corps extending on to his left. General John Corse's 4th Division extended the line to the right as it came up, with General John Smith's 3rd Division being held in reserve. Once his whole corps was on the field, General Logan ordered several charges by heavy skirmish lines along his front. The Confederates were forced to abandon their advanced rifle pits to the charging Federals, and Logan moved his line forward into them and fortified. This was as far as Logan was willing to carry the fight for the time being. The old antagonists of the Atlanta Campaign could see that Johnston's army was "posted behind strong parapets, fully as formidable and impregnable as their trenches in Georgia."[31] The movements were responsible for initiating a furious roar of musketry firing throughout the afternoon and through the night, but as both sides were well protected behind strong works, neither sustained many casualties.

All during the night, the skirmishers of both sides would indulge in scare demonstrations, pouring volleys into the opposing side, stirring the firing to a fevered pitch, but no charges were made. "Union shouts were answered with defiant Confederate yells, making the night horrid, a bedlam of noise and battle." Henry Wright of the 6th Iowa, now in the rear of the fortified works, got a good night's sleep along with his comrades, regardless of the noise of battle,

---

[30] Mark L. Bradley, *Last Stand in the Carolinas: The Battle of Bentonville* (Campbell CA: Savas Publishing Company, 1996) 323.

[31] Wright, *Sixth Iowa Infantry,* 431.

"knowing that brave and alert soldiers held the works between them and the enemy."[32] One young Federal lieutenant was concerned that the XV Corps had allowed the day to go by without taking the offensive. "We evidently took the enemy by surprise coming up in their flank," he confided to his diary, "and seems to me we lost a Golden Opportunity in not attacking them vigorously."[33]

In General Frank Blair's XVII Corps, some of his men did not make it up and on the field until close dark. His corps had the longest distance to march, being in the advance of the wing before it was turned around and marched backward, and with the XV Corps in front of them in the road, they were further delayed until General Logan's men cleared the way and got into position. General Joseph Mower, who Sherman once referred to as "the boldest young soldier we have,"[34] commanded the 1st Division which was bringing up the rear of the right wing. He was boiling for a fight, as was his nature, and just hoped that his division would not report too late to take part in the battle. As a rainy night began to settle across the land, Mower's division bivouacked south of the road. He had not missed any substantial action during the day and his troops would have the chance to get some rest after their 25 mile march. Soldiers would not be the only ones spending a rainy night in the open, as "many women & children [were] seen wandering about having been driven from their homes by the flying bullets."[35]

Federal leaders felt that Johnston would evacuate his position overnight, and, in fact, the Confederate commander was disposed to do just that. In the afternoon he had pushed preparations for a general retreat. The previous day he had been evenly matched with the Union forces under Slocum, pitting 16,895 of his men against 16,127 of the Federals. Of the force he took into battle, nearly 2,000 had been lost as casualties. Now that the right wing was up the odds against him

---

[32] Ibid., 432.

[33] C. C. Platter Diary University Archives, University of Georgia, Athens GA.

[34] *The War of the Rebellion: A Compilation of the Official Records of the Union and Confederate Armies* (Washington, DC: Government Printing Office, 1895) ser. 1, vol. 32, pt. 3, 325.

[35] Anderson, *Diary of Allen Morgan Geer*, 206.

were more than 2 to 1, and with Schofield's and Terry's armies advancing inland from the coast it seemed to the general that there was no longer an opportunity to do the Federals any harm. That evening he reconsidered the retreat and decided to remain one more day in his position "in the hope that [the enemy's] greatly superior numbers might encourage him at attack."[36]

Johnston might have been additionally bolstered by the fact that his losses from the battle of 19 March were being replaced through the timely arrival of another small portion of the Army of Tennessee. Approximately 2,000 of the western veterans made their way to the Confederate position on 20 and 21 March, filtering into the lines in several small detachments, with General Benjamin F. Cheatham in command.[37] Cheatham's arrival would be a welcome addition to an officer corps which had taken heavy losses the previous day. Another top-ranking Confederate had been force to relinquish his command on 20 March when General Loring was forced to go to the rear due to sickness, General Walthall succeeding him.[38]

Johnston might well have entertained thoughts of baiting Sherman into another disastrous frontal charge as he had done at Kennesaw Mountain the previous year, but the Union commander could remember the one-sided results of that bold move as well as Johnston could and he was not about to repeat it. Many on the Union side felt that Sherman did not want a battle here at all. The only major Confederate army of the western theater was in his grasp and he had the numbers on hand to ensure a victory should he decide to press it, but the Union commander was hesitant to commit his troops to any engagement, preferring instead to resume his march for Goldsboro. In this, the last of General Sherman's independent actions, he exhibited a reluctance to inflict any serious damage on the enemy.

---

[36] Nathaniel Cheairs Hughes, Jr., *General William J. Hardee: Old Reliable* (Baton Rouge: Louisiana State University Press, 1965) 290–91.

[37] Gen. Joseph E. Johnston, *Narrative of Military Operations Directed During the Late War Between the States by Joseph E. Johnston, General, C.S.A.* (New York: D. Appleton and Co., 1874) 393.

[38] B. L. Ridley, "Last Battles of the War," *Confederate Veteran Magazine* 3/1 (1895): 20.

While the general's skill in handling an army during the rigors of a campaign are beyond question, Sherman being recognized as a genius of supply and organization, there is some question concerning his battlefield handling of the army. He seemed to fight battles in a piecemeal manner, throwing his army into the fray by detachments rather than engaging all his forces, excepting, of course, Kennesaw Mountain, and that experience possibly only served to strengthen his resolve to stick to his own style of fighting. In General Oliver O. Howard's appraisal of Sherman's strengths he said, "Strategy was his strongest point. Take him in battle and he did not seem to me to be the equal of Thomas or Grant."[39] Sherman had been true to this assessment on 20 March, content to spend the day merely feeling for position, almost hoping that Johnston would evacuate and leave him free to continue the march.

---

[39] Barrett, *Civil War in North Carolina,* 342, and Hughes, *Bentonville: The Final Battle*, 43.

7

THE LAST HURRAHS

Both sides spent a miserable night on 20 March, with a pouring rain constantly punctuated with the thunderous booms of artillery. Though many old vets long since used to such inconveniences succumbed to their weariness and managed to get a few hours of sleep, others were not so fortunate, especially those Union troops who had lost much of their gear in the repulse of 19 March. One XIV Corps soldier said that the night was "very disagreeable for men without blankets or tents and some without hats."[1]

In the early morning hours of Tuesday, 21 March, engineers, pioneers, and heavy fatigue details from all the Union commands were busy strengthening their works and building parapets for the artillery. In the ranks, the men were sure that this day would bring with it a great deal more action than the previous one and they wanted to be ready for it. General Howard had risen very early in the morning to oversee the extension of his line to the right. He had General Mower's division under way at 8:00 A.M. for a position 5 miles north of the Goldsboro Road in heavy timber on the right of General Giles Smith's front. General Frank Blair met the column in march and personally led it to the appointed site to assure that there were no mistakes. The division threw up breastworks as soon as they reached their destination and prepared to hold the ground against any assault of the enemy. General Mower was not inclined to defensive measures however, and he asked General Blair if "[a]fter I get into position, will

---

[1] John Wesley Daniels Diary, 19, Bentley Historical Library, University of Michigan, Ann Arbor MI.

there be any objection to my making a little reconnaissance." "None at all," was Blair's answer, unaware that Mower's simple request would later bring on the heaviest fighting of the day.[2]

It was felt in the ranks that the placements of the Confederate line had been made with the idea in mind of attacking the Union right, and Major George Nichols could not understand why they were so intent upon staying on the field: "For some reason which does not yet appear, the Rebels contest every foot of ground with extraordinary pertinacity; more tenaciously than the occasion seems to require."[3]

To develop the Confederate intentions, Generals Wood, Corse, Hazen, and Smith all pushed forward their lines of battle until they were within 350 yards of the main Rebel works, capturing several lines of advanced rifle pits in the process.[4] At several points along the front the Union skirmishers "were not more than fifty yards from the enemy's lines and were held under heavy volley firing by the enemy from his main works."[5]

"Every few minutes the artillery in position in the rear of Corse and Wood opens fire, and the forest re-echoes the loud, sharp report, with terrible grandeur. Repeatedly the Rebels dash out of their works, making frantic attempts to retake the rifle pits out of which they have been driven; but are as often pushed back, leaving their dead and wounded to mark the scene of their discomfiture."[6]

Joe Johnston could see all the increased activity of the Federals against his left, but he did not know what it meant. So far, his right had not been pressured at all. It was possible that the Federals were massing for an attack on the Confederate left. That would explain the lack of activity on the other flank, but Johnston needed to be sure before he made any changes in his current lines: "To ascertain why our right was unmolested, Stewart's and Taliaferro's skirmishers were thrown forward. They found the Federal troops in their front drawn

---

[2] Anders, *The Eighteenth Missouri*, 316–17.

[3] Maj. George Ward Nichols, *The Story of the Great March, From the Diary of a Staff Officer* (New York: Harper & Bros. Publishers, 1865) 266.

[4] Ibid., 264.

[5] Wright, *The Sixth Iowa*, 432.

[6] Nichols, *The Story of the Great March*, 265.

back and formed obliquely to the general line; the left retired, and intrenched [sic]."[7]

The Federals had not been inactive in this sector. They had merely been busy adjusting and strengthening their positions. Fearing's Brigade had been marched into the works during the night of 20 March and positioned themselves in line. They were supposed to be occupying the section that the 3rd Division of the XIV Corps had just vacated but the light of day showed that there had been a mistake committed. A large gap existed that was only covered by the skirmishers of the 1st Division, XIV Corps, along with some XX Corps men

> who had but partially recovered of the stampede they had on the 19th, and without any very heavy demonstration would have quickly repeated their disgraceful conduct of a few days before. Report of our situation was immediately reported to Generals Morgan, Carlin, Davis and other high officials, who after examining the place temporarily provided for the defect by sending the 1st Division of the 20th Army Corps in, but only to stay about an hour when they were withdrawn and a heavy line of works constructed in the rear of the advanced lines and all the troops ordered into them, cautioned to be vigilant.[8]
>
> From information received from deserters and prisoners, we learned that Hardee's corps was massed on our front ready to make a charge and was only delayed by the heavy demonstration made on our right by General Howard.[9]

This anticipated charge was nothing more that the reconnaissance Johnston had ordered to find out what the Yankees were up to. The Confederate commander did not intend to take the offensive; rather, he was still waiting and hoping that Sherman would oblige him

---

[7] Johnston, *Johnston's Narrative*, 390.

[8] James Burkhalter Diary, 95–96, Illinois State Historical Society, Spingfield IL.

[9] Ibid., 96.

by storming his works. The Confederate deserters and prisoners had seen the Rebel skirmish line preparing to move forward and explore the Union lines and had mistaken its meaning. Some of this mistaken information was intentional, however. The Confederates were aware that Federal high command was still not sure about the exact size of Johnston's army, and they used that fact to advantage. A few planted deserters fueled the fire of apprehension among the Union troops that an attack was forthcoming, in an effort to pin the left wing of the Union Army in place. When these intentional fabrications were added to the mistaken reports of legitimate prisoners and deserters, it produced the desired effect of keeping the Yankees off balance and allowing Johnston to concentrate on his own threatened left wing.[10]

Scattered small arms fire erupted as the Confederate skirmishers felt for the enemy line, accented by the booming of artillery from both sides. Though losses were light, they continued to add to the total carnage of the battle. One private in Morgan's division describes how acute the lack of officers was in his company: "Lieutenant Summers put in command of my company, belongs to Co. K. Was killed by a solid shot. All my Co. officers are killed wounded or captured."[11]

Throughout the morning and afternoon a brisk fire was maintained along the front line, especially on the Confederate left and center. At noon, the rain started to fall again in torrents, but it did not diminish the exchange of fire from the opposing works. Private Levi Green

> found our boys cautiously advancing, and taking possession of old rebel pits. I worked my way up to one and commenced to use my Spencer, for I had good opportunities. The rebels would fire heavy volleys from their main line, but we would lay low until slackened, then raise, fire, and yell.[12]

---

[10] Bradley, *Last Stand in the Carolinas*, 357.

[11] John Batchelor Diary, 85–86, Illinois State Historical Society, Spingfield IL.

[12] Levi Nelson Green Diary, 21 March 1865, Minnesota Historical Society, St. Paul MN.

> Our men brought us out shovels and we began to dig as well as shoot. The rebels kept up a tremendous fire on us, and seemed determined to retake their line. They drove our men on both left and right of us, but we held our guard for quite a distance, and poured such a galling fire into the rebel flank that they fell back, and our boys rallied and held the ground.

Green described himself as "a sweet looking bird" from his time in the trenches "covered with mud from top to toe."[13]

But the threat to the Confederate right never materialized. Sherman declined to accommodate Johnston's desire for a chance to fight from behind his works. Skirmishing and sniper fire, punctuated by the occasional roar of artillery, served to keep both sides at a respectful distance. The Federal snipers were particularly annoying to the Confederate center, where they had occupied the Cole house, along with the other outbuildings, making it hazardous for the Confederates to show their heads above the works. In the afternoon, the skirmishers of Generals Hill, Walthall, and Bate were advanced, "and with small loss drove the Yankees from their position about the Cole's house. All the buildings there were burnt to prevent their further use by the Yankee sharpshooters."[14]

The day probably would have witnessed nothing more than a continuation of the skirmish fighting had it not been for the approval of General Blair for Mower to explore the Confederate lines. Blair was obviously consenting to what he thought was a request to merely scout out the enemy position. He was not aware that Mower intended to use the permission to make a full-scale advance against the Rebel works. Recognizing the precarious position the Confederates were in with their backs against the river and surrounded on three sides, Mower sought to push his men in behind the strong works and possibly bag the whole lot. Though General Blair had given permission for him to probe the works to his front, no superior officer on the field, including Blair, was aware of what Mower was about to do.

---

[13] Ibid.

[14] *OR*, ser. 1, vol. 47, pt. 1, 1092.

By 2:00 P.M., Mower had gotten Brigadier General John W. Fuller's 1st Brigade and Colonel John Tillson's 3rd Brigade into position and was ready to go. Tillson's Brigade would form the left of the line and Fuller's the right, with Tillson having orders to keep his left in contact with the right flank of General Giles Smith's 4th Division position. The rain, which had been falling heavily, slackened, serving as a sign to begin the advance. A large swampy area fronted Fuller's lines, but at the command, "in we went. In our front the marsh was so deep and such a tangle of vines that all the mounted officers were speedily on foot and the intrenching [sic] tools thrown away."[15]

As the troops were wading through the swamp, Captain Jacob DeGress of Mower's staff appeared in front of Fuller's line to announce that all barefoot men were ordered to the rear. This order applied to a considerable number of Fuller's men, as many were without shoes. In the 39th Ohio alone, there were 130 men who were barefoot. But the Federal line was not much depleted by way of this directive. Only a small number of men actually heard the order, and, of those, precious few fell out of the line and went to the rear.[16]

Fuller was so detained in passing through the entanglement that his brigade fell considerably behind Tillson, and Mower was forced to hold up the advance until the men were through the swamp and the division line could be reformed. The delay gave the Confederates time to react to the movement, and skirmishing erupted at the far edge of the swamp followed by continuous shelling from high ground in the Rebel works.[17] The shelling "however did us no harm as they were high and wide of their mark."[18]

By three o'clock, Mower had his men through the swamp, reformed, and was pressing rapidly against the Rebel works. The rain had now returned, and was falling in torrents on the advancing Yankees. As Sergeant Adelbert M. Bly of the 32nd Wisconsin,

---

[15] Anders, *The Eighteenth Missouri*, 317.

[16] Bradley, *Last Stand in the Carolinas*, 376.

[17] Ibid., 318.

[18] Adelbert M. Bly Diary, 21 March 1865, Adelbert M. Bly Papers, State Historical Society of Wisconsin, Madison WI.

Tillson's Brigade, stated, "We advanced upon them so fast that the greatest consternation overtook them and took from them two caissons."[19] Federal skirmishers had shot down two of the gunner's horses, preventing the caissons from being removed from the field. The men in both brigades were cheering wildly as they pushed through a little ravine and up the sides of a small hill where the dismounted Confederate cavalry was stationed. The gray-clad troopers, spread thin to cover their extensive front, could not hold against the massed Federal infantry. They fell back toward the Mill Creek Bridge, exposing the flank and rear of the entire Confederate army as they retired.

Mower halted his men on the top of the hill to reform them for a second charge, and from his vantage point he could see the opportunity for the Union army his movements had created. A messenger was dispatched at once to General Blair with news of what the two brigades had accomplished thus far, and a request that the corps commander convince Sherman to attack all along his line so that Johnston might be sealed off. Colonel Charles Sheldon of the 18th Missouri felt that "there could have been but one result, providing Mower could hold his position. Johnston's army must either surrender, or lose all its artillery and stores, besides many prisoners, in a disorderly scramble to cross the almost impassable creek at other points than the bridge."[20]

General Blair supported Mower's advance with a heavy skirmish fire that quickly spread along the front until all of the Union and Confederate lines were involved in the exchange. Mower then resumed his charge into the Rebel rear. He captured General Johnston's headquarters, the general and his staff narrowly avoiding being taken prisoner in the process. By 4:00 P.M. the Federal advance was within 50 yards of the Mill Creek Bridge and it looked as if everything was going according to Mower's plans and the Confederates were in a desperate position. The 27th and 39th Ohio

---

[19] Ibid.

[20] Anders, *The Eighteenth Missouri*, 318.

Regiments made the furthest penetration.[21] It was these two regiments that came close to capturing General Johnston when they over ran the old log house he was using for a headquarters. Captain W. H. H. Mintern of the 39th Ohio rushed forward and was successful in capturing Johnston's sash, sword, and belt, along with his bridled and saddled horse and his personal correspondence.

However, the Union attack had already started to unravel. Colonel Tillson sent word to Mower that he was not in contact with Giles Smith's right flank. Mower's two brigades were therefore advancing alone with both of the wings exposed and open to a counterattack. The general realized that he "had obliqued to the right in moving through the swamp," and he made arrangements to correct the mistake by ordering an oblique to the left, in a southwesterly direction, so that he could link up with Smith once again. But the momentum now swung to the favor of the Confederates as hastily gathered reserves were thrown against Mower's force from all sides. The general was accompanying Tillson's Brigade when the counterattack was launched, and the roar of musketry in his immediate vicinity drowned out all else, leaving Mower unaware for some minutes that Fuller's Brigade was also engaged. It was not until he requested that the 39th Ohio, Fuller's closest regiment to Tillson, be sent to aid the left wing that he learned the true situation. Fuller, being sorely pressed himself, declined to give up the regiment.[22]

Mower's line was pushed past the Rebel works and forced back down the hill and into the ravine they had previously crossed, with some units of Fuller's command being pushed even further to the fringes of the swamp itself. In the center of his line, where the two brigades met, the 32nd Wisconsin and 39th Ohio held firm and prevented the retreat from being turned into a rout. The two regiments stood shoulder to shoulder, and even back to back, as the lines were pressed rearward, and kept up a deadly fire on the advancing enemy. Sergeant Adelbert Bly stated that

---

[21] Ibid.

[22] Ibid., 318–19 and Charles Smith, *The History of Fuller's Ohio Brigade* (Cleveland: A. J. Watt, 1909) 273.

> [a]fter the first moment of panic among them [the Confederates] they succeeded in rallying and poured their troops from their front line down upon our left flank and from their rear line upon .our right flank, they charged first with cavalry and this followed by two lines of infantry this completely turning and forcing back both our flanks and getting in our rear. Some of our Reg. was wounded by ball from the rear. Our Regt. Was on the left of the center and stood fast never giving an inch and poured as destructive a fire into the rebels ranks as ever was done by any regiment.

As with Morgan's stand two days before, these two regiments held off the Rebel counterstroke just long enough to give the Federals time reform their lines before they could be shattered.[23]

As soon as Mower's predicament became apparent to General Howard, he ordered General Blair "to support him with his whole corps if necessary, and Logan to advance and seize the skirmish rifle pits along his front." Mower was still attempting to hook up with the rest of the Union army on his left, and he ordered for Fuller's Brigade to pass behind Tillson's to fill the gap, but his right was still too heavily engaged to make the move. One of his officers tried to convince the general to attack again himself to try and drive off the Confederate infantry and cavalry that was stinging his force in front, flank and rear, but Mower's only response "was profanely expressive of his utter contempt for the 'aforesaid cavalry.'" His plans were all coming apart, but his combative spirit remained unchanged. Casting a disdainful gaze in the direction of some "[r]oystering, cheering, and defiant" Confederate troopers, Mower shook his fist in the air, raised himself up in his stirrups, and yelled to one of his aides, "God, man, wouldn't you like to wade in there with a saber!"[24]

---

[23] Anders, *The Eighteenth Missouri*, 319 and Adelbert M. Bly Diary, 21 March 1865, Adelbert M. Bly Papers, State Historical Society of Wisconsin, Madison WI.

[24] Anders, *The Eighteenth Missouri*, 319–20.

By 5:00 P.M. the Rebel counterattack had subsided to the point that the Union line was ordered forward to the top of the hill once more, where it was halted to reform and await the fresh supply of ammunition Mower had sent his division staff officers to procure. With all this accomplished by 5:30 P.M., Mower was ready to push his double line of infantry forward when he received a message direct from General Sherman ordering him to retire his force and come into line with the rest of the XVII Corps. Sherman had also sent word to General Blair that he was to desist in his demonstrations against the Confederate works immediately. Through some oversight, General Howard was not informed of the Union commander's decision, and when he saw the XVII Corps retiring he approached Blair and proceeded to scold him. "The withdrawal is by Sherman's order!" the general snapped, bringing the matter and the battle to a close.[25]

It had been a close call for Johnston's army. The Confederate chieftain was well aware how lightly his left was defended with General Wheeler's dismounted cavalry, but he had no more men to put into the line. His only hope was that Sherman would choose to test the works at some other points where his more solidly entrenched infantry would be able to hold. At 4:00 P.M., with Wheeler's troopers finding it hard to hold their ground, Johnston gathered together what little infantry reserves he could find and ordered General Taliaferro's division to change position from the Confederate right to the left. He had scarcely sent the message before General Hampton appeared at headquarters to announce that the Federals had broken through, inaccurately estimating that the entire XVII Corps was involved in the attack due to the increased activity along Blair's line in support of Mower's charge.[26] Hampton continues the narrative:

> The general directed me to return to the point indicated to ascertain the exact condition of affairs, and as I was riding back I met a courier, who informed me that the enemy in force had crossed the branch, had driven back the cavalry

[25] Ibid., 320–21.
[26] Johnston, *Johnston's Narrative*, 390–91.

> pickets, and were very near to the main road leading to the bridge. This attack rendered our position extremely dangerous, for if the attacking force had been able to attain possession of the road we could not have withdrawn without very heavy loss, if we could have done so at all.[27]

Hampton had just ridden past the remnant of Cummings Brigade of Georgians before meeting the courier. The brigade was under the command of Colonel R.J. Henderson, and at just around 300 men in strength, was no larger than most regiments, over half the brigade having been captured at Nashville. "Realizing the importance of prompt action," Hampton "ordered this command to move at once to the point threatened, and also ordered up a battery which I had passed."[28]

General Evander Law was temporarily in command of Butler's cavalry, the latter being too ill to assume his post. His men were on the extreme left of the Confederate line, dismounted, and in skirmish line. General Wheeler's troopers were to his right in temporary breastworks. Law had been worried over the thinness of his skirmish line before the Federals attacked and he had sent word to Wheeler requesting that he extend his men to the left. Wheeler refused on the grounds that he was already much too thin himself to resist an infantry assault. At that moment, one gun of Captain William E. Earle's South Carolina Battery, which Law had placed on his skirmish line, opened on Mower's troops coming out of the swamp. General Law rode over to the gun, and from its slightly elevated vantage point he could see the heavy lines of blue infantry heading straight for his position. "Capt. Earl, get your gun out of here," he yelled. The gun was moved to safety but one of the caissons, in turning, got a tree stuck between the wheel and the limber and had to be abandoned. This was the caisson, and the only caisson that Mower's men captured when they over ran Law's lines. The cavalry skirmishers could not

---

[27] Robert Underwood Johnson and Clarence Clough Buel, *Battles and Leaders of the Civil War,* 4 volumes (New York: The Century Company, 1884–1888) 4:704.

[28] Ibid., 704–705.

hold in the face of such overwhelming odds and they began to retire, shooting as they went.[29]

Meanwhile, General Johnston had given Hardee the responsibility of making a counterattack with the small number of reserves that were already at hand. Time was of the essence, and he could not afford to wait for Taliaferro's division to arrive from the right. If the Union threat was not thrown back now all would be lost. The 8th Texas Cavalry, Terry's Texas Rangers, had just been issued two quarts of corn for horse and rider when the rattle of musketry broke out. The regiment numbered only about eighty men, but they had picked up one new recruit earlier that day in the person of Willie Hardee, the sixteen-year-old son of the general. Willie had left school to seek his father's permission to join the army. He had served on his father's staff, but had turned down a spot on General Johnston's staff on the grounds that he would not hold rank until he won it. With his father's grudging approval, he was entered on the rolls as a private in the 8th Texas Cavalry. When the Federal attack came he was busy detailing the latest news around headquarters.[30]

The 8th Texas and the 4th Tennessee Cavalry proved to be the only units readily available to "Old Reliable," but he ordered them to prepare to charge at once. A. P. Harcourt, one of the Rangers, noticed that "In the old general's face was read an anxiety and suspense never observed there before. In a short time an open space was reached where four hundred yards beyond the Federals were seen, busy as bees, throwing up breastworks across the highway leading to the bridge. 'There they are, boys, charge them!' said Hardee as he reined up and sent his aide back for more troops. Word passed among the rangers, 'Close order and reserve fire,' and on they went, a living wedge into a wall of blazing fire. Disincumbering [sic] themselves of their guns after they were emptied [by throwing them to the ground] and seizing their six-shooters, they spurred right on for the Federal

---

[29] James G. Holmes, "The Artillery at Bentonville," *Confederate Veteran Magazine* 3/2 (1895): 103.

[30] A. P. Harcourt, "Terry's Texas Rangers," *The Southern Bivouac* 11 (November 1882): 96–97.

center, already shattered and wavering as if with wonder at such a cavalcade of yelling, desperate madmen."[31]

Colonel Henderson and Cumming's Georgians had already made contact with the enemy. Their ranks augmented through the addition of some of the dismounted cavalry that had been driven back, they struck Mower's men on top of the hill, driving them off: "They fell back to their second line, leaving a line of ditching tools and knapsacks as far as we could see in the open piney woods. We had passed this line some thirty or forty yards when they began to pepper us at a lively rate. We halted some eighty yards away, and all that could got behind trees. We were giving them the best that we had in the shop, when we heard a yell to our right, and the 8th Texas Cavalry...dashed by us at breakneck speed right into the line of infantry."[32]

In fact, Hardee's counterstroke was coming from several different directions. Henderson's infantry was attacking Mower directly in front, though he did not have enough men to cover the length of the Federal line. The 8th Texas and the 4th Tennessee struck the Yankees on their front and left flank while, almost simultaneously, General Hampton assailed their right flank with Brigadier General Pierce Young's Brigade, and General Wheeler attacked their rear with Brigadier General William Allen's Brigade. The various charges were timed perfectly, and though the attackers were outnumbered by the Federals, the viciousness of their charges, combined with the fact that they were falling at different points on the Union line, created the desired effect and drove the Yankees back to the edge of the swamp. General Hardee not only directed this assault, he personally led it.[33] Captain G. K. Miller of the 8th Confederate Cavalry, Anderson's Brigade, occupied the temporary works to the right of Law's skirmish line. From his vantage point he was able to watch both the Federal breakthrough and the Confederate

---

[31] Ibid.

[32] M. J. Davis, "Eighth Texas Cavalry at Bentonville," *Confederate Veteran Magazine* 23/3 (1915): 184.

[33] Hughes, *General William J. Hardee*, 91.

counterattack. A veteran of many hard-fought battles, Miller thought this to be "as brilliant a charge as the war furnished." There was a sizable representation of German immigrants among the Union regiments in Mower's command, and Captain Miller "had an interesting conversation with several of the prisoners, but being short on Dutch, while they were utter strangers to English, history will lose the result of the interview."[34]

Most of the 113 casualties suffered by the Confederate cavalry at Bentonville occurred during this charge, including Lieutenant Newton G. Park of Company G, 2nd Arkansas Mounted Rifles. An older brother, Corporal James Park, had been in the regiment when Newton enlisted and had tried to convince him to sign up for a short period so the two could go home together, "but Newton replied that he preferred to sign up 'for three years or longer, until this cruel war can be brought to a close.'" Lieutenant Park signed his enlistment papers for three years on 22 March 1862. His time had expired the day he fell mortally wounded while fighting against Mower's brigades and he died in the arms of another brother, Corporal Burrell Park, Company K, 19th Arkansas Infantry.[35]

General Hardee had been delighted by the success of the attack, and he turned to a staff officer and remarked that he had seen "many a charge of cavalry, infantry and artillery on the plains of Mexico and elsewhere, and had seen the old United States dragoons charge and the Commanches charge, but had never witnessed the equal of the charge just made." While reveling in the success of his mission, the general began riding back with General Hampton, and "Old Reliable" said, "General, that was 'nip an tuck,' and for a while I thought 'tuck' had it." As the generals rode on, they passed two litter bearers bringing Willie back from the front with a mortal wound. The youth had kissed his father before riding off with the Rangers and had been shot down as he gallantly raced to the head of the charge. The general dismounted and went over to comfort his boy, then returned to

---

[34] G. K. Miller, untitled article, *Confederate Veteran Magazine* 3/2 (1895): 71.

[35] Lt. Col. Wesley Thurman Leeper, *Rebels Valiant: Second Arkansas Mounted Rifles (Dismounted)* (Little Rock: Pioneer Press, 1964) 278.

Hampton and rode off to finish the deployment of the troops. Parks was shot down on the last day of his enlistment and young Hardee on the first. Willie was taken to Raleigh with the other wounded. He died at Hillsborough and buried in the St. Paul's Episcopal Church Cemetery.[36]

After the battle, General Stephen D. Lee sent a message through the lines for right wing commander General Howard. In it he informed the general of young Willie's wounding. Lee knew that Howard would want to know of it, for he had been Willie's Sunday school teacher at West Point while Hardee was serving as commandant of cadets. Howard had developed a strong bond with the boy during those years and was greatly attached to him.[37]

Not all of the Confederates who were ordered to resist Mower's assault did so in such a glorious fashion. Captain D. Augustus Dickert related,

> Late in the day the enemy made a spirited attack upon us, so much so that General McClaws sent two companies of boys, formerly of Fizer's Brigade of Georgia Militia. The boys were all between sixteen and eighteen, and a finer body of young men I never saw.
>
> He also sent a regiment of North Carolina Militia, consisting of old men from fifty to sixty, and as these old men were coming up on line the enemy were giving us a rattling fire from their sharpshooters. The old men could not be induced to come up....
>
> The colonel, a venerable old graybeard, riding a white horse, as soon as the bullets began to pelt the pines in his front, leaped from his horse and took refuge behind a large tree. I went to him and tried every inducement to get him to

---

[36] Harcourt, "Terry's Texas Rangers," 96–97, and Walter Branham Capers, *The Soldier-Bishop: Ellison Capers* (New York: Neale Publishing Company, 1912) 116–17.

[37] John M. Gibson, *Those 163 Days: A Southern Account of Sherman's March From Atlanta to Raleigh* (New York: Bramhall House, 1961) 231.

> move up his men on a line with us, but all he would do was to grasp me by the hand and try to jerk me down beside him.
>
> "Lie down, young man," said he, "or by God you'll be shot to pieces. Lie down!"
>
> The old militiaman, I saw, was too old for war, and was "not built that way."
>
> But when I returned to the skirmish line, on which were my own brigade skirmishers, reinforced by the two boy companies, the young men were fighting with a glee and abandon I never saw equaled. I am sorry to record that several of these promising young men, who had left their homes far behind, were killed and many wounded.[38]

General Johnston met the troops as they returned to the Rebel lines. "It was the first time we had seen 'Old Joe' since he was relieved of his command at Atlanta," wrote one member of Cummings' Brigade. "We gave him three cheers. He raised his hat and spoke some words that I failed to catch, but some that were nearer him said he told Colonel Henderson to compliment that brigade for him; that they had saved the army. That set us on fire again and we would have charged Old Nick himself if Joe Johnston had ordered us to."[39]

With reinforcements now on line and the captured works retaken, Johnston called off the pursuit of the Federals and fortified his works for another attack, which never materialized. Much controversy has arisen out of the charge of Mower's men, and the battle was debated by the veterans on both sides as long as they lived. General Hampton's mistaken assessment that the entire XVII Corps was attacking when he reported the breakthrough seems to be at the root of some of the confusion. Many Confederate accounts of the fighting insist that an entire Union corps was pushed back by an attacking force of slightly over 300 men. These reports are principally from members of Cumming's Brigade or Terry's Texas

---

[38] D. Augustus Dickert, *History of Kershaw's Brigade* (Dayton OH: Morningside Bookshop, 1976) 287.

[39] Davis, "Eighth Texas Cavalry at Bentonville," 184.

Rangers, and exhibit a lack of knowledge of what was transpiring on other parts of the battlefield. The facts are that Mower had only two brigades of his division under his command during the charge, and while the attacking Confederates were not as numerous as the Union force, they were considerably stronger than 300 men.

On the Union side, much has been made about Sherman's orders for Mower to retire. The standing argument is that the Confederate attack had nothing whatsoever to do with the withdrawal, and that the lines retired only under orders. The facts seem to render this argument mute, however, as Mower's men had already been pushed back to the edge of the swamp before receiving orders from Sherman to return to his place in the line. While it is true that Mower was reforming for another go at the Confederates at the time, he had most certainly been pushed back to his present position by a much smaller force.

Despite many attempts to set the record straight, the dispute over the number of men engaged and the reasons for the retreat of the Federal infantry was argued in veteran's magazines and other publications for years. As with all soldiers in all wars, unfounded rumors circulated through the ranks would invariably become accepted truth and incorporated along with the soldier's own memories, perpetuating the debate. On the night of 21 March, one XX Corps soldier who had not even seen the fight recorded in his diary, "It is said that the 17th Corps captured 5000 prisoners."[40]

Mower's return to the Federal line ended the battle for the day, though skirmish fire was kept up till around 3 a.m. Artillery joined in the fray and one Union soldier remembered that the firing was "kept up at short intervals during the afternoon and far into the night, making the day hideous and night lurid, by the fire of fifty guns on each side." The rain continued to fall heavily, making the prospect of sleep difficult for the men on both sides. The accumulation in the

[40] Charles S. Dickinson Diary, 171, Charles H. Dickinson Papers, State Historical Society of Wisconsin, Madison WI.

trenches was such that "we had to cut brush, and throw on the water to sleep on."[41]

Johnston's gamble had failed. Sherman had shown that he was not going to allow himself to be drawn into making any large-scale offensive thrusts, so no advantage was to be gained from remaining on the field. Besides, reports were coming in that the armies of Generals Terry and Schofield were close at hand, and that Schofield had already taken possession of Goldsboro. He could come down behind Johnston's position and cut off the Confederate retreat, or at the very least, the addition of these two armies would swell Sherman's numbers to over 100,000 men in the Confederate front. Either way, the Confederates would find themselves in danger of destruction or capture.

The Confederate commander had no choice but to arrange for the withdrawal of his army. For some of his men there was no need to wait to be told that the battle was over—or the war, for that matter. Some went straight home after the battle and were never heard from again, while others joined up with marauding bands of deserters, bringing more hardships to an already ravaged countryside. Though those who left were a very small minority, their departure further weakened Johnston's already undermanned army.[42]

In later years Johnston would be criticized for fighting a battle at Bentonville at all, and especially for remaining on the field on 20 and 21 March, after failing to crush the left wing the first day. The battle had cost the Army of the South many casualties it could not replace, and in the face of the host of Yankees in his department, these losses have been viewed as purposeless. In the general's defense, it might be said that he had no good choices to make, considering the odds against him. The decision to fight at Bentonville was merely the lesser of the evils and the only viable option for an officer of Johnston's stature to honorably choose. The general realized that he was taking a long chance in attacking even one wing of Sherman's army, but he also

---

[41] Levi Nelson Green Diary, 21 March 1865, Minnesota Historical Society, St. Paul MN and Wright, *Sixth Iowa Infantry*, 433.

[42] Barrett, *Civil War in North Carolina,* 341.

knew that he would have no chance once the three Union armies were joined. The real marvel here is that he came so close to winning on the first day. There can be many explanations for this near-victory: the overconfidence of the Union army, the bad roads that delayed the arrival of support, or the complete surprise with which the Federals attacked. General D. H. Hill offers yet another reason: "The Yankees fought worse than I have ever known them to do on any previous field of battle. It may be that even a Yankee's conscience had been disturbed by the scenes of burning, rapine, pillage, and murder so recently passed through."[43]

Sherman would claim victory on the basis that the Confederate army was compelled to retreat, leaving him in possession of the field. Johnston would claim that the Federals had been checked in their advance and would claim a Southern victory. Both men were right. Sherman, to be sure, gained the military victory at Bentonville in every sense of the word. He was in possession of the field and the enemy had been forced to retreat from a position of their own choosing. But Johnston was also correct insofar as the battle had reestablished, to some degree, a level of Union respect for the Confederate military. He had succeeded in giving Sherman a check, and in doing so, had also molded his various units into an army in reality instead of one in name alone. One Union soldier was not quite sure who had won: "I don't know as it was any victory to the rebels but the 2 Corps were brought to a halt and that is so unusual that we termed it a whip"[44]

The fighting had produced a total of 4,252 casualties to both sides. By late-war standards it was hardly larger than a large skirmish, but the regiments were instructed to add it to their battle flags. The Confederates had suffered the greatest loss, with a total of 2,606 casualties, or approximately 15 percent of the total engaged. The Union losses were 1,646, less that 3 percent of Sherman's available force. For most of Sherman's army it had been only a skirmish. The real fighting had taken place before the XV and XVII Corps had

---

[43]*OR*, ser. 1, vol. 47, pt. 1, 1092.

[44] Charles Berry, Sr., Diary, 15, Iowa State Historical Society, Iowa City IA.

arrived on the field, two divisions each from the XIV and XX Corps shouldering the brunt of the battle. During the last two days at Bentonville, Union losses were 502, while the Confederates suffered only 162 casualties. With these numbers it is easy to see why many Union soldiers considered Bentonville nothing more than a large, noisy skirmish, but to the Confederate soldiers and the members of the four Federal divisions that broke the tranquillity of that beautiful Sunday morning with all the savagery that war contains, it was indeed a battle.[45]

[45] Victor Hicken, *Illinois in the Civil War* (Urbana: University of Illinois Press, 1966) 297.

8

THE END IN SIGHT

By 2:00 A.M. on the morning of 22 March, all of the Confederate wounded who could bear it had been removed from the battlefield and Johnston was ready to withdraw the army. The darkness of the night and the heavy woods combined to make their progress painfully slow, and by sunrise the rear of the column was still in Bentonville. At 8:00 A.M. the column was halted for a rest. The rear was still only 2 miles north of the Mill Creek Bridge. General Wheeler had been assigned to cover the retreat and he posted his rear guard along the bank on the north side of the creek to contest any Yankee crossing.[1]

The Union soldiers were surprised to find the enemy gone. "This morning at early daylight we advanced skirmish lines and found the enemy had withdrawn during the night in the direction of Smithfield. After full and satisfactory evidence that the enemy had left, the troops were ordered out of their works and into the open field, where they can dry their blankets, which have become thoroughly drenched in these last few days in the swamps and trenches."[2]

Sherman directed that units be sent forward to determine the exact location of the Rebel army, but he made no efforts to organize a pursuit of Johnston with his whole force. Johnston had directed that the bridge over Mill Creek be destroyed, but it had become so waterlogged by the recent rains that Wheeler's men could not get it to

---

[1] Gen. Joseph E. Johnston, *Narrative of Military Operations Directed During the Late War Between the States by Joseph E. Johnston, General, C.S.A.* (New York: D. Appleton and Co., 1874) 392.

[2] James Burkhalter Diary, 96, Illinois State Historical Society, Spingfield IL.

burn. The flooring was taken up, but that could be speedily replaced by the Federals. Wheeler's rearguard fought with tenacity and by 9:00 A.M. had only yielded a mile of ground. At 10:00 A.M. the Confederate cavalry was at the crossing of Black Creek on the Smithfield Road and were once again in position to resist the Union advance. A column of infantry tried to force their way across the bridge but Wheeler prevented it: "Three color bearers of the leading brigade fell dead within fifty feet of my position. They then retreated out of range and made no further pursuit whatever."[3]

Sherman showed no concern for trailing the fleeing foe. Instead, he issued orders for the XIV and XX Corps to resume their march for Goldsboro and link up with Schofield. In later years the general would show regrets for his failure to deliver the final blow to Johnston's army, especially on 21 March. "On the 21st of March, it began to rain again and we remained quiet until about noon, when General Mower, ever rash, with two brigades of the First Division, broke through the rebel lines on his extreme left flank and was pushing straight for Bentonville, and the bridge across Mill Creek; I ordered him back to connect with his own corps and lest the enemy should concentrate on him, ordered the whole rebel line to be engaged with a strong skirmish fire. I think I made a mistake there and should have rapidly followed Mower, with the whole of the right wing, which would have brought on a general battle and it could not have resulted otherwise than successfully to us, by reason of our vastly superior numbers. But at the moment, for the reasons given, I preferred to make a junction with Terry and Schofield before engaging Johnston's Army, the strength of which was utterly unknown."[4]

One XIV Corps soldier took special notice of the field where Mower's fight had taken place as his regiment "marched over a portion of the Battlefield of Yesterday between our forces, [XV and XVII] Corps and the retreating Rebels, which gave evidence of its

---

[3] *The War of the Rebellion: A Compilation of the Official Records of the Union and Confederate Armies* (Washington, DC: Government Printing Office, 1895) ser. 1, vol. 47, pt. 1, 1031–32, 1113.

[4] Charles Smith, *The History of Fuller's Ohio Brigade* (Cleveland: A. J. Watt, 1909) 275.

having been a fearful, almost a hand to hand struggle being in the woods, many of the trees had numbers of 'Ramrods' sticking out of them, showing that our men, upon reloading, did not take time to remove their guns; the bark of the trees peeled off and the trees almost completely filled with bullets of the contending forces, and covering both friend and foe, tells the story of the fearful contest of yesterday."[5]

Slocum's wing did not go into camp until late that night after making a hard march of 10–12 miles through the deep, sandy ground. Meanwhile, Howard's men spent the day burying the dead and collecting the wounded. During the day, some of the veterans of the right wing had the opportunity to witness a scene that was impressive even to these battle-hardened soldiers: the river was on fire. It seems that a large quantity of resin had been stored at a factory on the bank of Mill Creek that had somehow been set on fire. The burning resin flowed down the bank into the water, where it cooled and hardened. The lava-like resin filled the river with its molten, burning fluid for a distance of several hundred yards below the factory. Rain finally extinguished the burning above the water line, leaving a natural bridge from shore to shore. One soldier claims that it was used by the troops to cross Mill Creek.[6]

General Johnston, in his retreat, was forced to leave behind 108 of his most seriously wounded men. These were taken in by the Federal search parties and were administered such care as the Union surgeons could provide. The Harper House, home of Mr. and Mrs. John Harper, was located 4 miles west of the battlefield and had been used as a hospital by the XIV Corps since the fighting of 19 March. After the battle, some fifty-four of the badly wounded Confederates Johnston left behind were carried there and for three months the sixty-two-year-old Harper and his forty-four-year-old wife ministered to their needs, though they were almost destitute themselves from the

---

[5] W. C. Johnson Diary, 72–73, Library of Congress, Washington, DC.

[6] Henry Wright, *History of the Sixth Iowa Infantry* (Iowa City: State Historical Society of Iowa, 1923) 433–34, and Oscar Osburn Winther, *With Sherman to the Sea: The Civil War Letters Diaries & Reminiscences of Theodore Upson* (Baton Rouge: Louisiana State University Press, 1943) 160.

passing of the armies. Twenty-three of their charges died while under their care. Of these, three were taken home by their families for burial. The remaining twenty were buried by Mr. and Mrs. Harper on the ground near their home. The couple built a simple rail fence around the cemetery, but the graves were unmarked as they had not the means to purchase headstones for such a large group. But John Harper kept a list of who was buried where, and for the next twenty-nine years he and his wife tenderly cared for them.[7]

Federal troops also cast their eyes upon some of the true horrors of war. As many as five bodies of Union soldiers were found that had been mutilated, one of them still hanging from a noose. It was obvious that they had been prisoners who were murdered, and the Federal troops reacted to the sight by vowing to take no more Rebel prisoners, and became so agitated as to induce the officers to increase the provost-marshal detail to prevent the killing of Confederate prisoners. All white males in the area were rounded up, and John Harper, a local minister and whose father's house was being used as the XIV Corps hospital, and John Hood, a local mechanic, were among the group. Harper asked to be taken before those Union troops who had been wounded in the battle and left behind by the Confederate army. He had carefully ministered to the needs of these suffering Yankees, as well as his countrymen, and the wounded Yankees proclaimed him to be a friend who could not possibly have been involved in the killings. Harper was freed, along with the rest of the male civilians, there being a lack of any evidence with which to hold them, and it was never determined exactly who had committed the atrocities or why.[8]

Though Johnston had surrendered the field and was still badly outnumbered and almost hemmed in by the Federal forces in the area, many in the South viewed the battle as an important Confederate victory and a sign of positive things to come. Two days after the battle General McClaws wrote to his wife that Johnston would soon be

---

[7] "Died in the Last Ditch," *Confederate Veteran Magazine* 2/3 (1894): 200.

[8] Mark L. Bradley, *Last Stand in the Carolinas: The Battle of Bentonville* (Campbell CA: Savas Publishing Company, 1996) 402–403.

in a position to force Sherman and his army out of the state altogether.[9] In the Confederate capital, the news of the battle was greeted with unbounded enthusiasm. Rebel War Clerk John B. Jones recorded in his diary

> It is reported that Grant is reinforcing Sherman, and that the latter has fallen back upon Goldsborough. This is not yet confirmed by any official statement. A single retrograde movement by Sherman, or even a delay in advancing, would snatch some of his laurels away, and enable Lee to obtain supplies. Yet it may be so. He may have been careering the last month on unexpended momentum of his recent successes, and really operating on a scale something more than commensurate with the forces of his command. Should this be the case, the moral effect on our people and the army will be prodigious, and a series of triumphs on our side may be the consequence.[10]

President Davis likewise celebrated the victory and tried to bolster public spirit through it, and even Robert E. Lee was relieved when he heard the news, thinking that Johnston would be able to hold his own against Sherman and keep a second army from menacing his rear.

Johnston did not share in the euphoria occasioned by the news of the battle. He realized that there was little he could do now to stop the combined Union forces from going anywhere in the Confederacy at will. As one Union soldier put it, "I should think those fool Johnnys would quit. They might as well try to stop a tornado as Uncle Billy and his boys."[11] Johnston continued to urge Lee to unite their two armies against either Grant or Sherman. In one of his messages to the Confederate commander he stated that "it is no longer a question

---

[9] John G. Barrett, *The Civil War in North Carolina* (Chapel Hill: University of North Carolina Press, 1963) 341.

[10] John B. Jones, *A Rebel War Clerk's Diary*, vol. 2 (Philadelphia: J. B. Lippincott & Co., 1866) 458.

[11] Winther, *With Sherman to the Sea*, 160.

of whether you will leave present position; you have only to decide where to meet Sherman. I will be near him."[12]

The mood in Richmond could not be could not be altered by Johnston's admonitions for action. To a government and public hungry for good tidings, the news of the battle at Bentonville was welcome indeed. It was perceived to be another example of what Southern soldiers could do in the face of adversity. Being outnumbered had become a natural state of affairs for Confederate soldiers during the war, and the spectacular victories they had won in the face of long odds created a feeling among the public that their army was capable of performing almost any miracle. Now, with all the evidence of the North's military might pointing to a foregone conclusion, they clutched at the perceived Confederate victory at Bentonville as proof that the recent setbacks were now over and the hated Yankees would once more be driven from Southern soil.

In a letter to General Lee dated 22 March, President Davis said, "I have been very much gratified by the success of General Johnston at Bentonville, and hope this is only the first of the good tidings we may receive from that quarter. It is a plain case for the application of the maxim with regard to the employment of a small army against a larger one. Sherman's forces, worn by long marches, and necessarily comparatively ignorant of the country in which he is operating, must offer opportunities for surprises and attacks in detail."[13] Davis was oblivious to the fact that the Confederates had marched just as far as the Yankees, and as the confusion with the maps at Bentonville seems to point out, were equally ignorant of the country they were operating in. But Davis planned to augment the numbers in the Army of the South through the transfer of soldiers from the Trans-Mississippi Department. He had prodded General Kirby Smith to cross the Mississippi with as large an army as he could muster in January, but had received no reply from the department commander. Flush

---

[12] Craig L. Symonds, *Joseph E. Johnston: A Civil War Biography* (New York: W. W. Norton & Co., 1992) 352.

[13] Don C. Seitz, *Braxon Bragg: General of the Confederacy* (Columbia: The State Company, 1924) 519.

with the news from Bentonville, he reiterated this desire to General Lee. "My belief is that efficient if not the only mode of getting over any considerable portion of troops from the trans-Mississippi would be to send a commander, who knows the necessities on this side of the river, and whose views were sufficiently comprehensive to embrace the whole question of defense in the Confederate States, with discretionary power to send such force as he believed ought to be transferred. My judgement [sic] is that General Bragg fulfills the conditions here enumerated."[14]

To the Confederate president, plans for the concentration of all available Southern forces in the east seemed logical. Davis felt that Bentonville had purchased the Confederacy a breathing spell that would afford him the time needed for these transfers, but time was a commodity in short supply for the South. Johnston knew that reserves from Texas cold never reach him before the issue was forced to a conclusion. Any measures adopted would have to be done with the realization that his and Lee's armies were all that could be counted on to stop the Federals. In his messages to General Lee, Johnston demonstrated his firm grasp on the desperate finality of the situation and the need for immediate and positive action.

True to this analysis, Johnston withdrew his army to the north, allowing Sherman a free hand to proceed to Goldsboro. Instead, the Confederate commander opted to protect the rail line, which still connected his army with Lee's. It was, in fact, the practical option open to him. If he chose to oppose Sherman's march he would be caught between the Neuse and Roanoke rivers, forced to fight a battle with his back to the sea and his right flank severely threatened. If he fell back behind the Roanoke in an effort to dispute its passage, he would expose his rear to Grant's army. By retiring north toward Smithfield, Johnston was abandoning any thoughts of restraining or retarding Sherman's movements, but it was the only course that did not assure the certain and immediate destruction of this army.

The XIV and XX Corps reached Goldsboro on 23 March, where the 26th Illinois, at the head of the column, dispersed a rearguard of

---

[14] Ibid., 520.

Confederate cavalry with a "first class yell" before entering the town.[15] General Sherman had met with General Terry at Cox's Bridge on the Neuse on 22 March, and the two officers rode together to Goldsboro where they found General Schofield. At last, all three commands were combined. General Schofield had occupied the town on 21 March at 4:00 P.M. after its evacuation by the Confederates under the command of Colonel D. Pool and its subsequent surrender by Mayor James H. Privett.[16]

General Jacob Cox chronicles the meeting of the armies: "On Thursday, the 23rd, Sherman joined us in person, and we paraded the Twenty-third Corps to honor the march-past of Slocum's Army of Georgia, the Fourteenth and Twentieth Corps, as they came in from Bentonville. Sherman took his place with us by the roadside, and the formal reunion with comrades who had fought with us in the Atlanta campaign was an event to stir deep emotions in our hearts."[17]

Sherman's troops "who had traversed the Carolinas were ragged and dirty, their faces were begrimed by the soot of their camp fires of pine knots in the forests, but their arms were in order, and they stepped out with the sturdy swing that marked all our Western troops." Schofield's men, by comparison, had just been issued fresh uniforms and received jibes and ribbing, "as if we were new recruits or pampered garrison troops." One of Sherman's warriors sarcastically cried out, "do they issue butter to you regularly now?" Schofield's ranks replied, "Oh yes! To be sure! But we trade it off for soap!" This exchange brought a round of laughter from all within earshot. Once the ragged veterans of Bentonville learned that the well-clothed soldiers who were greeting them were the same troops who had been with them in Georgia and had fought the battles of Franklin and Nashville, a cheer ran through the ranks to welcome their long-lost comrades.[18]

---

[15] Victor Hicken, *Illinois in the Civil War* (Urbana: University of Illinois Press, 1966) 297.

[16] Barrett, *Civil War in North Carolina,* 343–44.

[17] Gen. Jacob Dolson Cox, *Military Reminiscences of the Civil War* (New York: Charles Scribner's Sons, 1900) 447.

[18] Ibid., 447–48.

Sherman found a message from Grant waiting for him in Goldsboro that had arrived the previous day. "I congratulate you and your army in what may be regarded as the successful termination of the third campaign since leaving the Tennessee River less than one year ago," wrote the Union commander. He also informed Sherman of his own intentions for the upcoming campaign against Robert E. Lee, so that their actions could be coordinated accordingly.[19]

Sherman took the opportunity on 23 March to issue a congratulatory message of his own to the soldiers of his army.

> The General commanding announces to this army that yesterday it beat on his chosen ground the concentrated armies of our enemy, who had fled in disorder leaving his dead, wounded and prisoners in our hands and burning the bridges on his retreat.
>
> On the same day Maj. Gen. Schofield from New Berne entered the occupied Goldsboro and Maj. Gen. Terry from Wilmington stormed Co's [sic] Bridge Crossing and laid a Pontoon Bridge across the Neuce River, so that Campaign has resulted in a glorious success after a march of a most extraordinary character, near five hundred miles over swamp and rivers deemed impossible, to others, at the most inclement season of the year and drawing our chief supplies from a poor and wasted country.
>
> I thank the Army and assure it that our Government and people honor them for this new display of the physical and moral qualities which reflect honor upon the whole nation.
>
> You shall have rest and all the supplies that can be brought from the rich granaries and store houses of our magnificent country, before embarking on new and untried dangers.[20]

Sherman's promise of rest met with the wildest approval of the troops, and he kept his word by allowing the army to remain in camp

---

[19] Ibid., 448.

[20] S. S. Farewell Diary, 25 March 1865, Iowa State Historical Society, Iowa City.

at Goldsboro for seventeen days. The promised supplies were also forthcoming, but they were not immediately available to the soldiers, causing Sherman to show a bit of temper, one of the few times he did so during the campaign. In an angry letter to his quartermaster general, L. C. Easton, the general demanded action:

> I have made junction of my armies at Goldsborough a few days later than I appointed, but I find neither railroad completed, nor have I a word or sign from you or General Beckwith of the vast store of supplies I hoped to meet here or hear of. We have sent wagons to Kinston in hopes to get something there, but at all events I should know what has been done and what is being done. I have constantly held out to the officers and men to bear patiently the want of clothing and other necessaries, for at Goldsborough awaited us everything. If you can expedite the movement of stores from the sea to the army, do so, and don't stand on expenses.[21]

In light of the fact that Sherman had officially given the need to supply his army at Goldsboro as the main reason for his refusing to pursue Johnston's Confederates, the absence of those same supplies caused his decision to look like a bad one.

Even without the government stores at hand, Sherman decided it was time to do away with the method of supply that had seen him safely through the all-but concluded campaign. He ordered all foragers dismounted and returned to their respective regiments at once. The decision quieted the fears of the citizens of Goldsboro, but it did not end the depredations against the Southern countryside entirely. Many of the foragers, long since accustomed to the freedom of independent action, refused to rejoin their commands and struck off in small groups to continue their raiding. Though these men continued to make life difficult for civilians in the area, they were more easily controlled by Confederate cavalry since they no longer enjoyed the benefit of operating with the army

---

[21] Barrett, *Civil War in North Carolina,* 346.

On the morning of 23 March, General Howard's right wing took up the march from Bentonville toward Goldsboro, the XVII Corps in the advance. After only a few miles, contact was made with the XXIV and XXV Corps of General Terry's command. The Confederate cavalry remained active during the march, Hampton's troopers remaining vigilant for an opportunity to inflict damage on the moving column. Once, after the column had crossed the Neuse, "the rebel cav. made a dash from the left of the road and drove in our flankers but they saw nothing in the road to encourage them to come on, went into camp in good season, and our and the rebel picket line were not more than 80 rods apart they seem to be picketing all the country to the North of the road on which we are traveling."[22] On another occasion, Private Conrad Cramer recorded how a scouting party of the 111th Ohio was set upon by a portion of the 3rd Alabama Cavalry, resulting in one Federal soldier being killed and another mortally wounded.[23]

The right wing entered Goldsboro on 24 March, making the concentration complete. Sherman now had slightly over 100,000 troops under his command and it would be impossible for Johnston to do anything to stop him. The arrival of the right wing was marked with another review for the benefit of Generals Schofield, Terry, and Cox. The appearance of the troops was again of interest to their comrades. Their uniforms certainly drew comment: "long since worn out, now ragged, faded, weather beaten and much 'soiled' from the constant long wear and tear, especially tear, and rough usage, and not having come in contact with a proper application of 'soap and water' in many a long day, many of the boys wearing citizens clothes, almost barefoot, truly a sight that almost beggars description and in strong contrast to the appearance of the troops under Gen. Schofield."[24] A great many of the men, "wearing *Rebel* clothes and the ones that

---

[22] Ezra Button Diary, 72, John B. Tripp Papers, State Historical Society of Wisconsin, Madison WI.

[23] Conrad Cramer Diary, 30 March 1865, Conrad Cramer Papers, Greensboro Historical Museum, Greensboro NC.

[24] W. C. Johnson Diary, 74, Library of Congress, Washington, DC.

have *them* are in luck".[25] As the troops filed by, General Blair took note of the poor condition of their pants. "See those poor fellows with bare legs!" he remarked to General Sherman. "Splendid legs! Splendid legs!" Sherman replied. "I would give both of mine for any one of them."[26]

The ill-clad veterans were heartily welcomed by their old comrades. "No 'New Minister' was ever more hospitably received by his congregation or had bigger 'donation' party than we received," wrote one of Sherman's men. Though the rations the general expected to find at Goldsboro had not yet arrived, "when it became known that our 'Haversacks' were empty over they came bringing their 'Commissary Supplies' (we having drawn no rations for some days) and most cheerfully offering to divide their last crackers, etc., with us."[27]

For many in the ranks the end was in sight. "I think that the rebellion is played out, as the term is in the army," one soldier wrote. "I guess Davis, Lee and crew begin to see that it is a failure and I am satisfied that the southern people and the privates in their army desire peace. As they fail we gain strength. There never was a more confident army than Sherman's. I believe that when he leaves here he will have an army sufficient to cope with the whole Confederate army, Lee, Johnston combined."[28] Others were not quite so sure. The war was not yet over and some were convinced that more blood would have to be shed before its conclusion. Confederate pickets kept touch with the Union army, though at a more respectable distance of a mile away, and men who strayed from the camps were often killed or captured. For those who left and did not return it was assumed that the Rebels had gotten them, as evidenced by the following excerpt: "[At] five a.m. a detail was sent out from the Brigade in search of the body of Capt. Crawford of the 85 Ind. who was reported killed yesterday.

---

[25] John E. Risedorph Diary, 71, Minnesota Historical Society, St. Paul MN
[26] Barrett, *Civil War in North Carolina,* 345.
[27] W. C. Johnson Diary, 75, Library of Congress, Washington, DC.
[28] Charles Berry, Sr., Diary, 15, Iowa State Historical Society, Iowa City IA.

They came in about dark having found the body alive and well and running a grist mill some twelve miles away."[29]

While the troops were resting and refitting, General Sherman decided to reorganize the army for the final campaign. Slocum's wing was redesignated as the Army of Georgia. Howard's wing retained its name as the Army of the Tennessee; Schofield's remained the Army of the Ohio. The XVII Corps also adopted a new emblem for its corps badge while at Goldsboro, an arrow "symbolic of swiftness, of surety in striking and of destructive power."[30]

General Johnston was also looking to the reorganization of his army at Smithfield. On 25 March he issued orders for the consolidation of many of his regiments that had fallen drastically below adequate strength, a move which was necessary if unpopular with the soldiers who had come to cherish the history their own unit. Some 153 regiments were merged together to form 32 units that were still short of being full strength.[31]

The condition of the Tennessee regiments serves as an illustration of the army as a whole. In the 1st Tennessee there were just 125 men left out of a total enlistment of 1,200. In the 19th Tennessee there were just 64 remaining out of a total of 1,000, and the 5th Tennessee which once boasted 1,300 hearty souls could now muster but 30 men. The 9th Tennessee had only 40 men present and there were three regiments that together only totaled 50 men, and a colonel was the only surviving field officer for all three. In the 154th Tennessee one of the companies had only one soldier left, and he was disabled.[32] Even with the combining of units most of Johnston's regiments were still far under half strength. Still the consolidations had put some numbers in the new units, which did away with the

---

[29] Ezra Button Diary, 73, John B. Tripp Papers, State Historical Society of Wisconsin, Madison WI.

[30] Smith, *Fuller's Ohio Brigade*, 277.

[31] Robert Underwood Johnson and Clarence Clough Buel, *Battles and Leaders of the Civil War*, 4 vols. (New York: The Century Company, 1884–1888) 4:699.

[32] Christopher Losson, *Tennessee's Forgotten Warriors: Frank Cheatham and His Confederate Division* (Knoxville: University of Tennessee Press, 1989) 246.

pitiable spectacle which had presented itself at Bentonville when the regimental flags had been almost side by side.

There was also a shortage of muskets in the ranks that needed to be addressed. Just under 1,400 men, or slightly less than 10 percent of Johnston's effective force was without arms. The shortages were to be found predominantly in the Army of Tennessee, and persisted into the first week of April when a shipment of 1,500 Enfield rifles arrived.[33]

General Johnston also had a review of the troops while they camped at Smithfield, but there the similarities between himself and General Sherman ended. The Union commander was enjoying the full confidence and support the government and the people back home, while Johnston was becoming embroiled in a political controversy stemming from this adversarial relations with General John Bell Hood and President Davis. Hood had just recently submitted his official report of his tenure as commander of the Army of Tennessee, in which he devoted the first third of the text to denouncing Johnston's abilities and substantiating his claims that his own failures were due to the fact that Johnston had already destroyed the morale and fighting ability of the army before Hood took command. In his hotel room at the Spotswood in Richmond, Hood had read a copy of his report to Isham Harris, Confederate governor of Tennessee. When Harris suggested that Hood's criticism of Johnston had no place in a report which was to chronicle only his own actions the general "broke down" and agreed with the governor's assessment. He said he knew it was wrong, but it was too late now to change things as the report had already been submitted to and accepted by the administration. Harris suggested that "Hood was a puppet in the hands of other who were sacrificing him to gain their own ends—and striking though him a blow at Genl. Johnston."[34]

Johnston was furious when he found out that President Davis had sent Hood's report to Congress with a recommendation that it be printed, especially since he had repressed efforts to distribute

---

[33] *OR*, ser. 1, vol. 47, pt. 3, 754–55.

[34] Symonds, *Joseph E. Johnston*, 352.

Johnston's own report of his actions during the Atlanta campaign. He telegraphed Hood that he would prefer charges for the accusations that had been made and that the whole matter would be settled by court-martial. Hood replied that he would "be ready to meet any charges you may prefer."[35]

This situation was not the only intrigue Johnston faced as he prepared his army for what must be the final showdown with the Yankees. Sniping was also evident within his own army from the disgruntled and sulking Braxton Bragg. Along with Hood, Bragg enjoyed the friendship and unconditional support of President Davis, regardless of his success or lack thereof in command. His being placed in a subordinate position to Johnston had caused ruffled feathers with Bragg and he was determined that honor and position be restored. In numerous messages, sent directly to Davis, Bragg complained of his present status and made pleas for the president to rectify the situation. Of course, these messages also served to poke criticism, most of it tainted, at Johnston. The following excerpt is exemplary of the tone and content of the correspondence:

> Mr. President: Since my note from near Smithfield a change has been made in my position. Finding myself with nothing but a small division in the field, and virtually ignored in regard to that and all other command, orders being constantly sent to my subordinates without notification to me, I asked and was allowed to turn over Hoke's division to him. I have retired to this point where I have nothing to do but mourn over the sad spectacle hourly presented of disorganization, demoralization, and destruction. The condition, Mr. President, cannot be exaggerated, and no language can paint it. All three corps of the Army of Tennessee are up, and our infantry now foots about as follows, effective: Hoke's command (Department of North Carolina) of Tennessee, 3,500, including reserves; Hardee, 5,000; Armyof Tennessee, 3,500. About 5,000 stragglers from the

[35] Ibid., 353.

> latter are reported coming with S. D. Lee somewhere in the rear. The balance of the men are scattered over the States of North and South Carolina, Georgia, Alabama, and Mississippi, living at free quarters on the people. It is a most sad and humiliating picture. Officers seem paralyzed, men indifferent to everything but plunder, and the people, as they well may, appear disgusted and dismayed. This state of things cannot last, and no one is so blind as not to see the inevitable result.... You should not permit yourself to hope even for any result here, and in your movements, official and personal, you should be governed accordingly. This is intended for you eye only, but the facts may be obtained from any eye witness.[36]

Bragg had good reason to caution the president that the message was for his eyes alone. He had grossly misrepresented the situation in Johnston's army and had given an inaccurate account of the withdrawal from Bentonville. Overall, the morale in Johnston's army was high after the battle. The men had struck the first positive blow against Sherman's army that had been landed in months. They had delivered a serious check to a force roughly equal in size to their own and had only withdrawn in the face of overwhelming odds. Bragg misrepresented the withdrawal as a rout and claimed that the army had barely escaped, contrary to every other account of the retreat, both Union and Confederate. As for his claims that depredations were being committed on the civilian populations, there were, to be certain, bands of deserters who were marauding through the countryside, just as there were bands of renegade Yankees, but none of them were soldiers of either army. To insinuate that Johnston was allowing this to happen, or had the power to prevent it, is an unfair account of the situation. Lastly, Bragg accuses the members of the Army of Tennessee of being laggards and of not doing their duty for the cause. This observation is perhaps his greatest slander in the entire letter. Possibly Bragg was not fully aware of just how completely the army had been destroyed at Nashville, and possibly he was not aware that

[36] Seitz, *Braxton's Bragg*, 521–22.

portions of it had been sent to Mobile to bolster the garrison there, but it is hard to contemplate how he could have been so uninformed. The fact is that the surviving members of that army were returning to the ranks at a commendable rate. Men who had been wounded in the actions at Franklin and Nashville were reporting for duty with their injuries but partially healed. A few of the western veterans even froze to death riding on top of railroad cars while attempting to rejoin General S. D. Lee at Augusta. The official response given by President Davis toward the battle at Bentonville shows that he was either discounting much of what General Bragg had to say, or he was trying to bolster public morale. It is difficult to determine which course he was following, as he continued to give Bragg his complete support until the very end of the conflict. Bragg's comments on the battle in his letter are made all the more suspect because of the fact that this was the sum total of his comments on the subject. Of the numerous high ranking officers with the Army of the South, only two failed to submit reports on the battle of Bentonville: Generals Hoke and Bragg.[37]

While being assailed by some of his fellow officers, Johnston continued to command the utmost confidence of his ranks. As Sergeant Augustus Smyth wrote, "We are organizing meanwhile drilling and getting ready to move when the Yankees or Johnston is ready. Deserters are returning rapidly now that Johnston is in command. Every train brings them in by the fifties and hundreds. This rest here will do wonders for our army which is very much demoralized by that long weary retreating march. Everyone is delighted at Johnston's being put in command. We feel that he can be a match for Sherman."[38]

General Johnston did receive some good news while his army rested in and around Smithfield. General S. D. Lee finally arrived from Augusta on 29 March with 5,000 more men from the Army of

---

[37] Nathaniel Cheairs Hughes, Jr., *Bentonville: The Final Battle of Sherman & Johnston* (Chapel Hill: University of North Carolina Press, 1996) 126.

[38] Augustine Thomas Smythe to Miss Lou, 30 March, 1865, Augustine Thomas Smythe Papers, Southern Historical Collection, University of North Carolina, Chapel Hill NC.

Tennessee. Though this addition greatly increased the size of his army, many of the men with Lee could hardly be listed as effectives. They had been badly used up in Hood's Tennessee Campaign and the hard marching from Georgia had further worn them down. Many of them were unfit for combat when they arrived, but they were finally concentrated with the main body and if Sherman would only lay about Goldsboro, as seemed to be his intention at present, they would rest and regain their strength for the next struggle.

While the Union army was camped around Goldsboro, General Sherman traveled to City Point, Virginia for a meeting with General Grant and President Lincoln. In conjunction with the president, the two chief northern commanders mapped out a strategy that would, it was hoped, bring the fighting to a close. The two-day meeting lasted through 27 and 28 March. Lincoln had been in ill health, dragged down by the enormous burdens of his office, and the trip to see his commanders was made partly from a desire to get free of Washington and his official cares, as well as a desire to be at hand when the final plans for the war were made.[39]

Sherman arrived on the afternoon of 27 March, having taken passage aboard the steamer *Russia* for the final leg of his journey from Fortress Monroe. Grant and his staff were there to meet him when the ship arrived and one of the officers present described the meeting of the generals after a lengthy separation.

> Their encounter was more like that of two schoolboys coming together after a vacation than the meeting of the chief actors in a great war tragedy." After an introduction in camp, which included being presented to Mrs. Grant, Sherman took a seat with Grant and the other officers around the campfire where he delighted his audience with the story of his celebrated campaign. The story of the campaign was cut short after an hour when General Grant said, "I'm sorry to break up this entertaining conversation, but the President is aboard the

[39] J. G. Holland, *The Life of Abraham Lincoln* (Springfield: Gurdon Bill, 1866) 507.

"River Queen," and I know he will be anxious to see you. Suppose we go and pay him a visit before dinner?" The two generals were soon seated in the cabin of the ship with Lincoln, where they spent an hour talking with the President before returning to camp…. Grant had already explained to Sherman how Sheridan was to destroy the railroads south of Petersburg, and Sherman urged that Sheridan should continue south after the completion of his mission to join with his own army. When Sheridan heard of this talk he became irritated and earnestly protested against the move. Grant put an end to the discussion by announcing that Sheridan would not join Sherman, but would remain in his present position with the Army of the Potomac.[40]

The next morning Grant and Sherman went once one to see the president aboard the "River Queen". Admiral David Porter accompanied the military commanders on this trip, and was the only other officer present…. Lincoln expressed his hopes that the war could be brought top a close without the need of fighting another costly battle, to which Grant replied that the necessity of further fighting would rest on the shoulders of the confederates. He went on to inform the president of his plans to prevent Lee from slipping out of the siege lines at Richmond and Petersburg to join Johnston. Sherman assured Lincoln that even in the event of such an occurrence, he would be ready and able to meet their combined force and hold them in place till Grant could arrive to decide the issue. Lincoln also spoke of the course he wished to pursue after the war was over in regard to the Southern states. He expressed a desire to be lenient toward the South and even intimated that it would be better if all the Confederate political leaders would escape to another country….[41]

---

[40] Gen. Horace Porter, *Campaigning With Grant* (New York: The Century Company, 1897) 417–22.

[41] Ibid., 423–24.

This would be the last time that Sherman would see President Lincoln. He had been impressed with the commander-in-chief's attitude about the treatment of the Southern states once the Confederacy was beaten, and the tone of Lincoln's conciliatory stance stuck with him as he traveled back to North Carolina. Though his name had become hated throughout the South for the ravages during his March to the Sea and through the Caronlias, Sherman had spent several years living in the South before the war and developed an affinity for the people. He viewed the total warfare he waged as being more humane in the long run since it was sure to bring the war to a speedier conclusion that the more conventional style of fighting.

Sherman's return to the army at Goldsboro did not immediately signal the commencement of the last leg of the campaign. The general continued to allow his men to rest and recuperate from their taxing march and he took the opportunity to stage more reviews. On 29 March uniforms were issued to many of his troops, the first they had gotten since Savannah. When the march resumed, the men of Sherman's army would no longer look like the tattered ragamuffins who had marched into Goldsboro. They would look like the victorious army they were.

9

THE FINAL MANEUVERS

General Johnston's hope that he and General Lee would be able to combine their armies against either Sherman or Grant were unknowingly dashed by the conference at City Point. The Union high brass was anticipating such a move, even if Lee was not, and all of their dispositions were designed to eliminate its possibility. After proper refitting, Sherman was to march his army across the Virginia state line to a position south and west of Petersburg where he would make contact with the Army of the Potomac. From here, he would be able to prevent the two Confederate armies from joining and would be able to strike in any direction which military necessity dictated.

Johnston and his army found the situation deteriorating rapidly. The men were scantily clothed and were now receiving less than half rations per day. The general had petitioned Richmond for 5,000 pair of badly-needed shoes, but there were none to spare. Amidst the shortage, some of his men took to emulating the conduct of the Yankee foragers, confiscating foodstuffs and clothing from the surrounding countryside to augment their meager supplies. A great many deserted under the hardships, so many that General Johnston—the same officer who had granted amnesty to all returning deserters from the army a year before in Georgia—ordered General Bragg to oversee the arrest and round-up of all soldiers in the area absent without leave. Bragg, in turn, assigned Brigadier General Leventhorpe, of the North Carolina Home Guard to perform the task with the endorsement: "A prompt and vigorous enforcement of the general's views would materially strengthen his force, and at the same time relieve the community from many of the outrages it now suffers."[1]

With a vastly superior enemy in his front and his own force diminishing in size with each passing day, Johnston was now asked to divide his army. General Lee was concerned that with no Confederate army to oppose him, Major General Thomas would march up from Nashville and move against his flank. Lee suggested that Beauregard lead a detachment from Johnston's army into east Tennessee to block any movements from the Federals in that area. Lee was still either overestimating the number of men in Johnston's command or underestimating the number of Federals he faced. It is impossible to believed that he would have suggested such a move if he had been in possession of the facts. Johnston was already outnumbered almost five to one. Beauregard vetoed Lee's suggestion, stating that he did not have enough men at present, nor did he think he could raise enough, to give the project any chance of success.[2]

Johnston was having enough difficulty dealing with the immediate dangers to his command without planning to meet an enemy that was not coming. Major General Stoneman's Federal cavalry was raiding through the state with several thousand troopers and Salisbury was being threatened by one of these Union columns. General Bragg was given the responsibility of dealing with Stoneman, while Major General Bradley T. Johnson, at Salisbury, was telegraphed with a promise of support: "Colonel Hoke reports 3,000 of a column of the enemy moving east in Caldwell County. You must assemble all forces in your vicinity to meet it. Governor Vance will send all his disposable force, and I shall collect and forward all detachments, including a battery of artillery. You will assume command of the whole and make all dispositions to defeat the enemy's purpose. Should any troops be passing, you will call on them for temporary assistance. Keep me fully advised."[3]

---

[1] Don C. Seitz, *Braxon Bragg: General of the Confederacy* (Columbia: The State Company, 1924) 522.

[2] Ibid., 523.

[3] Ibid.

The Confederates were rightly concerned about any activity on the part of the Federals in the vicinity of Salisbury or Greensboro. Both of these cities lay along the main supply and transportation route still left open to the Confederacy. If the line were cut, Johnston's army would be truly hemmed in and would lose not only a crucial source of provisions, but also a viable escape route back into the Deep South. If compelled to retreat out of North Carolina, Johnston's army could use this route to march back down to Georgia, which would prolong the war for weeks or months, while the Federals forces followed and tried to corner them.

With pressure from all sides there was little Johnston could do but sit back and await further developments. He was running out of room to maneuver, unless he went south along the Greensboro-Salisbury line, and his force would not permit him to engage the Federals in anything more than light skirmishing and picket fire. He had detailed a battery of artillery to Colonel Lipscomb with instructions that it be positioned to prevent the navigation of the Cape Fear River by the Federals, but it was a token act of resistance. Nothing would be able to stop Sherman when he decided to move again, and the best the Confederates could hope for was to harass the Federals and cause them as much inconvenience as the muddy roads of the North Carolina countryside.

On 31 March Johnston once more pressed Bragg for an active response in dealing with the desertion problem. Bragg responded, "All the Senior Reserves at my disposal, about 130, have been turned over to General Holmes, to be employed in the duty you desire. The means, however, are totally inadequate. The country is perfectly infested, and the most atrocious outrages are being committed. Nothing but an active cavalry force can accomplish the object."[4]

He could not know it then, but there would soon be no army to bring the deserters back to. Sherman was making the arrangements to set in motion the final march of the western army and the Confederacy and Johnston's army had only three more weeks to live. On 5 April, Sherman issued Special Field Orders, No. 48, to his "Army

---

[4] Ibid.

Commanders, Corps Commanders and Chiefs of Staff Departments" detailing the next march which was to begin on 12 April.

> The left wing (Major-General Slocum commanding) will aim straight for the railroad-bridge near Smithfield; thence along up the Neuse River, northeast of Raleigh (Powell's); thence to Warrenton, the general point of concentration.
>
> The center (Major-General Schofield commanding) will move to Whitley's Mill, ready to support the left until it is past Smithfield, when it will follow up (substantially) Little River to about Rolesville, ready at all times to move to the support of the left; after passing Tar River, to move to Warrenton.
>
> The right wing (Major-General Howard commanding), preceded by the cavalry, will move rapidly on Pikeville and Nahunta, then swing across to Bulah [sic] to Folk's Bridge, ready to make junction with the other armies in case the enemy offers battle this side of Neuse River, about Smithfield: thence, in case of no serious opposition on the left will work up toward Earpsboro.[5]

On 6 April, the day after he issued Special Field Orders, No. 48, Sherman received word of the fall of Richmond and Petersburg.

> I at once altered the foregoing orders, and prepared on the day appointed, viz, April 10th, to move straight on Raleigh, against the army of General Johnston, known to be at Smithfield, and supposed to have about thirty-five thousand men… Promptly on Monday morning, April 10th, the army moved straight on Smithfield; the right wing making a circuit by the right, and the left wing, supported by the center, moving on the two direct roads toward Raleigh, distant fifty miles. General Terry's and General Kilpatrick's troops moved

---

[5] Gen. William T. Sherman, *Memoirs of W. T. Sherman by Himself*, 2 vols. (New York: Charles L. Webster & Co., 1891) 2:341–42.

> from their positions on the south or west bank of the Neuse River in the same direction, by Cox's Bridge. On the 11th we reached Smithfield, and found it abandoned by Johnston's army, which had retreated hastily on Raleigh, burning the bridges.[6]

With Lee finally pried out of his trenches around the Confederate capitol, it now became imperative that Sherman apply pressure to Johnston's army. With the Confederacy virtually disintegrating before his eyes, the general not only wished to prevent any junction of the two armies; he also wanted to make sure that Johnston's army was not permitted to get away. Sherman's main fear was that the Army of the South might be divided into small groups to carry on guerrilla warfare that could prolong the conflict for months or even years.

If the Union generals knew how close the end really was, the average soldier in the ranks did not. They realized that the Confederacy could not last much longer, but it was generally accepted in the ranks that one or more battles would have to be fought before the struggle was over. As one soldier put it, "Our Generals must evidently expect a visit from Lee or Johnston or they would not be in such a hurry. My opinion is that the decisive battle of the war is to be fought near this place for the whole Rebel army seems to be concentrating and we have at least one hundred and thirty thousand men."[7] Though this soldier overestimated the size of the Union army by almost thirty thousand men, he clearly reasoned that the massive force had been put together for some purpose. Another soldier felt that there was still some hard campaigning to do. "We were ordered to send all our sick back, take none with us except those that could march 15 or 20 miles per day & carry their load so I think we hav

---

[6] Ibid., 343–44.

[7] John E. Risedorph Diary, 76, Minnesota Historical Society, St. Paul MN.

[sic] got some pretty hard marching to do, well all right, it is putting down the Rebellion fast."[8]

Sergeant J. G. Berstler anticipated more than just marching. In a letter home he wrote, "You are aware in this that we have got through with our great expedition and are now fitting out for a new one some place else. I do not know where but I think in the direction of Richmond and then comes the tug of war then comes war in reality war that will make this nation tremble let us have it any shape that will satisfy Mr Jonnie [sic] Reb that they must be good citizens as soon as this is done the War is over and piace [sic] and plenty will again abound."[9]

When the Union army reached Smithfield on 11 April, "the fighting became quite spirited."[10] Lieutenant Colonel Thomas Doan's Brigade of Baird's division, XIV Corps, was at the head of the column, lead by the 75th Indiana. The Hoosier "skirmishers pushed rapidly through the streets of the village, firing as they progressed; unfortunately they could not reach the bridge spanning the Neuse River in time to prevent its destruction by the enemy." But Sergeant David Floyd proudly proclaimed, "The town was captured by our regiment at 1 o'clock, p.m."[11]

Daniel Herron, of Company B, 75th Indiana, holds a special distinction in the war arising during this action. He was severely wounded during the fighting, one of the last men in Sherman's army to be hit by a Confederate bullet. "It was the second time he had been shot in the war, the first wound occurring at Chickamauga when a bullet had struck him in the breast. Luckily for Herron, he was carrying a deck of cards in his breast pocket and it dissipated the force of the shot. Though the deck was entirely penetrated and he was knocked down by the force of the blow, he soon arose and fought

---

[8] R. B. Hoadley Diary, 11 April 1865, Robert Bruce Hoadley Papers, Perkins Library, Duke University, Durham NC.

[9] J. G. Berstler to Cousin, 26 March 1865, Griffith Family Papers, Iowa State Historical Museum and Archives, Des Moines IA.

[10] David Floyd, *History of the Seventy-Fifth Regiment Indiana Infantry Volunteers* (Philadelphia, 1893) 373–84.

[11] Ibid.

through the rest of the battle. At Smithfield, he was not so lucky, receiving a serious wound in the hip."[12]

Rumors of the surrender of Lee's army at Appomattox Court House were running rampant through 10 and 11 April, but it was not until the army reached Smithfield that any official confirmation was received, that coming from Grant on the night of 11 April. In his message, the general-in-chief informed his lieutenant of the terms Lee had been given and Sherman wired back: "The terms you have given Lee are magnanimous and liberal. Should Johnston follow Lee's example, I shall of course grant the same."[13] On 12 April, Sherman announced the wonderful news to his army:

> The general commanding announces to the army that he has official notice from General Grant that General Lee surrendered to him his entire army, on the 9th inst., at Appomattox Court-House, Virginia.
>
> Glory to God and our country, and all honor to our comrades in arms, toward whom we are marching!
>
> A little more labor, a little more toil on our part, the great race is won, and our Government stands regenerated, after four long years of war.[14]

News of the surrender was spread through the army all during 12 April, and the sounds of cheering rent the air from all directions. Captain Edwin Marvin of the 5th Connecticut said that he "never saw such wild demonstration and such enthusiastic rejoicings in my life."[15] Lieutenant Augustus Ricks was serving on General Cox's staff when the general received the word from Sherman.

---

[12] Ibid.

[13] John M. Gibson, *Those 163 Days: A Southern Account of Sherman's March From Atlanta to Raleigh* (New York: Bramhall House, 1961) 242.

[14] Sherman, *Memoirs of W. T. Sherman*, 2:343–44.

[15] Edwin E. Marvin, *The Fifth Regiment Connecticut Volunteers* (Hartford CT: Wiley Waterman & Eaton, 1889) 381.

> As I was riding by the general's side, speculating with him as to Johnston's probable movements, an orderly rode slowly toward us, bearing a message. General Cox opened it in the usual businesslike manner, and read it over, as he would have done an ordinary official communication. There was nothing in the manner of the messenger to indicate that he was the bearer of any unusual or important news, and he sat listlessly on his horse while a receipt was being written for the message. Happening then to cast my eyes toward the general, I noticed his face suddenly brighten, and in great animation he turned and directed the escort and staff to be drawn up in line, that he might read to them a message from General Sherman. It was done in a hurry, and with head uncovered he read a brief dispatch stating that General Lee, with his entire army, had surrendered to Grant at Appomattox. It was the message long looked for, long fought for, and though it came to us on the roadside so unexpectedly, its full significance was at once appreciated. It meant home, and wife, and children, and happy meetings throughout the land.[16]

So it was throughout the army. Marcellus Darling of the 154th New York later recalled,

> early in the morning, off at a distance, shouting was heard. The men were just at breakfast. The shouting came nearer, and then we saw General Geary riding down the line slowly, and as the men fell in line he said something, and shouting was renewed. We thought little because such things were not uncommon. But when he came to our part of the line he halted and said: "Dispatch from General Grant announces that Lee with all his army surrendered on April 9,

---

[16] Augustus J. Ricks, *Carrying The News Of Lee's Surrender To The Army Of The Ohio* (Cincinnati: The Military Order of the Loyal Legion of the United States, Ohio; Robert Clarke & Co., 1888) 235.

> at Appomattox". And then we shouted and threw our hats in the air.[17]

The Confederates were just finding out about the surrender too, but there was no cheering in the Rebel ranks. Rumors of big events had been circulating in Johnston's army as well as Sherman's, but the first confirmation many of the Confederate soldiers had was when they began to see members of Lee's army on their way home from Appomattox. Confederate Commissary Officer R. P Howell was still affected by the memory of meeting one of Lee's paroled soldiers many years later when he wrote his memoirs of the war: "Never shall I forget my feelings at that moment. I wept like a child and said I was sorry I had not been killed in the war. After a lapse of thirty-four years it wrings my heart to write about it. I told my drivers to take their teams and go home the best way they could. I bade them goodbye and, with a heavy heart, rode my black mare, Nellie Grey, home."[18]

General Johnston had anticipated some news from Lee, but not the surrender of his army. Word had reached the general of the evacuation of Richmond and Petersburg, but he had still clung to a hope that the two forces might yet be merged when he withdrew from Smithfield toward Raleigh. In fact, Johnston had known of Sherman's intentions to march on Smithfield in advance. On the morning of 10 April, the day the offensive was to begin, Dibrell's scouts brought several Yankee officers that had just been captured into camp. The officers had just received their marching orders and had gone to a house outside Greensboro to bid some ladies goodbye when they were taken prisoner. With this information in hand, Johnston planned the evacuation of Smithfield and made arrangements for the rear guard to destroy the bridge over the Neuse. His newly consolidated army moved out in three corps, commanded by A. P. Stewart, William

---

[17] Mark H. Dunkelman and Michael J. Winey, *The Hardtack Regiment: An Illustrated History of the 154th Regiment, New York State Infantry Volunteers* (Rutherford NJ: Fairleigh Dickinson University Press, 1981).

[18] R. P. Howell reminiscences, 14, R. P. Howell Papers, Southern Historical Collection, University of North Carolina, Chapel Hill NC.

Hardee, and Stephen D. Lee. At 7:00 A.M. on the morning of 11 April, the army started for Raleigh and were 3 miles west of the city on the Hillsboro Road by night. As the soldiers marched past the female Seminary in Raleigh they were heartened by the sight of all the girls in front of the building: "the beautiful schoolgirls greeted us warmly. Each one had a pitcher of water and a goblet. We drank, took their addresses, and had a big time."[19] For awhile the war was far away. For a while there were no hardships, no retreat, and defeat was not looming on the horizon. There was only gaiety and the remembrances of happier times gone by, but only for a while.

Though the people of Raleigh tried to show a brave front to their soldiers marching by, the fear in their faces was plain to see. They were proud of the ragged, dirty scarecrows who had marched down the main street and they serenaded them with "Dixie" and other stirring songs, but they could see the exhaustion and hunger in their countenances. The once mighty army was now fleeing for its life and could not make a stand to save the capital of the Old North State. They were heading west, and Sherman's dreaded Yankees were not far behind.[20]

On 12 April, Johnston received a telegram from Jefferson Davis, then at Greensboro, which gave him his first official confirmation he had received that Lee's army had indeed surrendered. The president directed him to turn over command of his army to General Hardee so that he might join Davis in Greensboro immediately for a conference. General Beauregard was to accompany Johnston on the trip. When the two generals reached Greensboro and met the president, they were hardly prepared for his line of questioning. Johnston had obviously believed that Davis had sent for him with the idea in mind of bringing an end to the war, but that was not the case. After a few words of greeting the president said, "I have requested you and General Beauregard...to join me this evening, that we might have the benefit of your views on the situation in this country." Johnston was stunned

---

[19] B. L. Ridley, "Last Battles of the War," *Confederate Veteran Magazine* 3/2 (1895): 70.

[20] Gibson, *Those 163 Days*, 242.

by the question and he answered caustically, "My views are, sir, that our people are tired of war, feel themselves whipped, and will not fight... My men are daily deserting in large numbers...since Lee's surrender, they regard the war as at an end."[21]

As far as Johnston was concerned, there was no longer a country. The only thing to do now was to open communications with General Sherman and try to find out what sort of terms he might grant for a surrender. The army had done all that courage and pride could demand of men and any further prolongation of hostilities would be a crime against men who had already sacrificed more than duty required. For Davis, the Confederacy still existed, but it was to be found in the Trans-Mississippi Department, not in North Carolina.

Johnston returned to the army on 13 April, 2 miles east of Hillsboro. On that same day, Sherman's army marched into Raleigh and took possession of the city. It was here that "Uncle Billy" exhibited one of his rare indulgences of humor. The Union soldiers "planted the stars and stripes on the State House and as they were putting the flag on the cupola, Gen. Sherman rode up and said with a smile "this is a good time to rauleigh [sic] around the flag."[22] Sherman's humor was more than offset by the actions of General Kilpatrick and his men upon entering the town. The cavalry was the first to enter the city.

> The mayor and distinguished citizens met Kilpatrick on the outskirts of Raleigh, and surrendered the town, and assured General Kilpatrick that the city had been entirely evacuated by the Rebel soldiery. No advance guard was needed, and with banners and guidons unfurled and music playing, General Kilpatrick rode into the city, at the head of his Division. In passing up Fayetteville street, from the Governor's house to

---

[21] Cass Canfield, *The Iron Will of Jefferson Davis* (New York: Fairfax Press, 1978) 117.

[22] F. L. Fergerson journal, 3, Frank L. Ferguson papers, Military History Institute, US Army, Carlisle Barracks PA.

the Capital, with no thought of an enemy near, General Kilpatrick was suddenly fired upon by one of Wheeler's men.

As at Fayetteville, the Confederate was soon captured. He was a Texan by the name of Walsh, and Kilpatrick ordered him to be hung immediately, refusing his request to be able to write to his wife before he died.[23]

The Federals were not the only ones guilty of atrocities during the march, however. On at least one occasion, the Confederates committed an outrage of their own, as an Ohio private remembered: "At another place they had, through some of their women, induced our officers to leave a safeguard of two men, whom the guerrillas took, as soon as the army was fairly out of sight, tied them with arms behind them to a tree, cut their tongues from their mouth, and nailed them to a tree besides their owners."[24]

Friday 14 April, proved to be a black day for both sides. General Johnston, with his army at Hillsboro, sent a message to Sherman requesting a temporary cessation of hostilities so the two men could open peace talks. On that same day, President Lincoln would be assassinated at Ford's Theater by John Wilkes Booth. Word of the president's murder spread rapidly through the army and a spirit of retribution took hold of the men.

> We have just heard of the death of Lincoln. May the Lord have mercy upon the country we pass through, & the Rebs we catch if we go any further upon this campaign, I never saw a more exasperated set of men than the Army. Honestly the Army had rather experienced another Bull Run afair [sic] than to have had this happen few men will I stop from committing any outrage or crime they may choose to.

---

[23] *Ninety Second Illinois Volunteers*, Journal Steam Publishing and Bookbindery, Freeport, 1875, 238, and Spencer, Cornelia, *The Last Ninety Days of the War in North Carolina*, Wateham Publishing Co., New York, 1866, 238.

[24] Pinney, Nelson A., *History of the One Hundred and Fourth Ohio Volunteer Infantry During the War of the Rebellion from 1862–1866,* Werner and Loman, Arkron, 1866, 81.

> Sherman & Johnson [sic] are treating now I hope they wont come to terms by jove I would like to see Wm S. turn his army loose over what is left of the S[outhern] C[onfederacy] by jove I would not give much an acre for it after a corps or two had gone over it. this is the worst news we have ever heard yet. I hope Andrew Johnson will put down the screws tight by thunder the army will sustain him if he hangs every man & burns every house in the whole South.[25]

In the Confederate camp General Benjamin F. Cheatham was being cornered by his men to tell them what they should do. Cheatham consented to talk to the troops, telling them that what he was about to say would be grounds for his dismissal from the service under normal circumstances, but he had faith in their loyalty and would therefore be frank with them. "Boys," he said, "I have gained a reputation as a fighter, but the credit belongs to you, not to me... We have been in many tight places, but none where you ever failed me or failed your country. How many brave men have fallen, your decimated ranks attest." The general continued in a vein of praise for the men and their sacrifices before confiding that Johnston and Sherman were beginning the process to negotiate the surrender of the army. He advised the soldiers to become loyal citizens when they returned home. Towards the end of his speech, the general's eyes began to mist, and "tears ran down the faces of his veterans." "The effect was appalling," one soldier remembered, "the soldiers walked quietly away without a word, except to reassure their commander that he might continue to depend upon them under all circumstances."[26]

In the time intervening between Lincoln's assassination and the news reaching Sherman's army, General Johnston had decided that the surrender of his army was the only logical option open to him. The terms granted to Lee's Army of Northern Virginia had indeed been

---

[25] Charles S. Brown to Mother and Etta, 18 April 1865, Charles S. Brown Papers, Perkins Library, Duke University, Durham NC.

[26] Christopher Losson, *Tennessee's Forgotten Warriors: Frank Cheatham and His Confederate Division* (Knoxville: University of Tennessee Press, 1989) 247.

lenient, and if Johnston could obtain similar provisions and guarantees from Sherman for his own capitulation, then at least his men would be afforded the protection and consideration due a paroled enemy. Accordingly, Johnston sent a message to Sherman on the morning of 14 April requesting a cessation of hostilities until the two commanders could meet to discuss the terms of surrender. Sherman replied at once that he was in agreement with the request and set 17 April as the date for the meeting. General Hampton and Colonel McCoy, of Sherman's staff, were assigned to work out the details of the meeting.[27] Sherman had anticipated Johnston's request, and with a view toward an early reconciliation, had already ordered that there was to be no further destruction of railroads or private property.[28]

General Cox had gone even further in an effort to stop the vandalism and destruction in his corps. He issued a circular during the march to Raleigh which promised a death penalty for anyone found guilty of committing the crime:

> Since we left Goldsborough there has been a constant succession of house burning in the rear of this command. This has never before been the case since the corps was organized, and the prospect of speedy peace makes this more than ever reprehensible. Division commanders will take the most vigorous measures to put a stop to these outrages, whether committed by men of this command or by stragglers from other corps. Any one found firing a dwelling-house or any building in close proximity to one, should be summarily shot. A sentinel may be left by the advance division at each inhabited house along the road, to be relieved on succession from the other divisions as they come up, those left by the

---

[27] Robert Underwood Johnson and Clarence Clough Buel, *Battles and Leaders of the Civil War* (New York: The Century Company, 1884–1888) 4:755.

[28] *The War of the Rebellion: A Compilation of the Official Records of the Union and Confederate Armies* (Washington, DC: Government Printing Office, 1895) ser. 1, vol. 47, pt. 3, 188–89.

rear division reporting to the train guard and rejoining after the next halt.[29]

On the day of his death, one of Lincoln's war predictions was at last coming true. General Grant related that in almost every discussion he had with the president where maps were involved, Lincoln's finger would wander down to the region between the Raonoke and Cape Fear Rivers in North Carolina, saying, "Somehow I think the matter will be ended about here."[30] On the previous night, Lincoln had also had his recurring dream of the "dark and indefinite shore," which he confided he had had before several of the significant battles of the war. His interpretation of the dream was that the surrender of Johnston's army was about to take place, as that was the only significant matter yet to be attended to in the war.

Several hundred miles south of Raleigh, at Charleston, South Carolina, a ceremony was taking place on the same day that appropriately signaled the end of the war at the precise spot where it had begun. With full military pageantry, the flag of the United States was once more being raised over the rubble that was now Fort Sumter. Among the distinguished officers and guests present for the ceremony was General Robert Anderson, the original defender of the fort and the North's first war hero. General P. G. T. Beauregard had been in command of the Confederate forces in Charleston four long years ago when the fort was surrendered, and in the process had become the South's first war hero. Now it was to be his turn to furl his flags and surrender.

---

[29] Albion W. Tourgee, *The Story of a Thousand; Being a History of the Service of the 105th Ohio Volunteer Infantry in the War for the Union from August 21, 1862 to June 6, 1865* (Buffalo: S. McGerald & Son, 1896) 370–71.

[30] Ibid.

10

Enemies No More

The roar of artillery had erupted from the Confederate column as it marched out of Raleigh on the Hillsborough Road on the morning of 13 April, but it was not the signal for impending battle. As Hart's South Carolina Battery marched past the railroad depot, General Hampton rode up and ordered Lieutenant Bamburg, commander of the rear section, to unlimber one of his guns and set fire to the military stores contained in the building. The fourth gun of the section was set up in the road, and after firing about six shots into the depot, smoke was seen coming from it. Though the shots were not directed against any enemy, it was the last time that the artillery of the Army of the South fired their guns.[1]

M. M. Buford of the 8th South Carolina Cavalry had the duty of escorting the Federal messengers bearing Sherman's response to the request for a truce. The dispatch was borne by a "lieutenant and some petty officers with a flag of truce," and Buford set out with them in search of General Johnston, who he knew to be somewhere between Durham and Hillsboro. As they were riding along, Buford noticed "that one of the Yanks was riding a very fine bay horse that he had captured from Charles Bennett, of our company, only a few days before. I wanted very much to take the horse from him, but of course could not."[2]

---

[1] A. Wood, "The Last Shots by Gen. Johnston's Army," *Confederate Veteran Magazine* 16/6 (1908): 585.

[2] M. M. Buford, "Surrender of Johnston's Army," *Confederate Veteran Magazine* 28/3 (1920): 170–71.

On the morning of 17 April, Sherman was entering a car to leave for his appointed meeting with Johnston when he was stopped by a telegraph operator at the station. There was a message coming in over the line which impressed the operator as being important, and he thought the general might want to read it before he left. The dispatch was from Secretary Stanton and contained the news of the assassination of Lincoln and the attempt on Secretary Seward's life. Sherman realized the potential danger this tragedy posed for his peace negotiations. Wary of his army's reaction, he asked the operator if anyone else had been apprised of the situation, and being told that the operator and the general were the only two people to thus far learn of the news, Sherman ordered him to keep it a secret until he returned that evening.[3]

Sherman boarded the train with his staff and proceeded toward the meeting place, the Bennett house, four miles west of Durham. It hardly seemed the location for the two great commanders to discuss the virtual ending of the greatest war in American history. One observer described it as "a plain little farmhouse...having only two or three rooms."[4] But a momentous act was taking place at the modest home of James Bennett, and forever after it would be known simply as Bennett Place.

Johnston and his staff, along with General Hampton, greeted Sherman and his staff at the farmhouse, but the Confederates were not prepared for the news they were to receive. Sherman's announcement of the murder of the president cast a somber mood over the proceeding and seemed to affect the Rebel officers as genuinely as it did Sherman's own staff. The Confederates voiced a shared opinion that Lincoln's death was as much of a tragedy to the South as it was to the North, and that the road to reunification would be much rockier without his guidance. Their sincere expressions of loss and their forceful denunciations solidified Sherman's own convictions that

---

[3] Robert Underwood Johnson and Clarence Clough Buel, *Battles and Leaders of the Civil War*, 4 vols. (New York: The Century Company, 1884–1888) 4:755.

[4] Wood, "The Last Shots by Gen. Johnston's Army," 585.

the conspirators had acted on their own and not as part of any Confederate design.

So much time was spent discussing Lincoln's death and its possible ramifications on the peace process that the specifics of the surrender terms could not be fully covered. It was decided that the two commanders would meet again the next day at the same place to conclude the negotiations. When General Sherman returned to Raleigh that evening, he issued orders for the announcement of the president's death to the troops the next morning.[5] Joyous as they were over the impending end of the war, the news cast gloom and despair in the ranks. Lincoln had been more than a president, more than the commander-in-chief. While the army respected and even admired many of its officers, it truly loved "Honest Abe." He had been a constant during the war. Commanding generals had come and gone, but he had always been there. Lincoln had, in some ways, come to symbolize the nation's determination and dedication to see the war through. Now, when the final result was at hand, he was gone.

On Monday morning, 18 April, General Sherman again traveled to Bennett Place to continue the surrender negotiations. He was accompanied by his staff and General Kilpatrick on this day. General Johnston brought Wade Hampton to the meeting again, and also in attendance was General John C. Breckinridge, the recently appointed Confederate secretary of war, and General J. H. Reagan, the Confederate postmaster general. Secretary Breckinridge had brought along a bottle of spirits and the officers joined in a few toasts while they were exchanging pleasantries. Sherman brought an end to the drinking by lightheartedly suggesting that if it continued and Breckinridge became any more persuasive in his arguments, it might become hard to figure out who was surrendering to whom.[6]

Johnston sought to receive terms better than those afforded General Lee and his army by arguing that his army was not in the same situation as Lee's. Instead of being cut off and surrounded by

---

[5] Harry Vollie Barnard, *Tattered Volunteers: The Twenty-Seventh Alabama Infantry Regiment, C.S.A.* (Northport: Hemitage Press, 1965) 47.

[6] Johnson and Buel, *Battles and Leaders*, 4:756.

Federal troops, as Lee's had been, Johnston's army still had room to maneuver and could march south to continue the war. The hard marching of his troops had placed a distance of approximately 80 miles between his position at Greensboro and Sherman's at Raleigh. Therefore, he had attained a head start of at least four-days march on the Federal army that was pursuing him, and with that lead could easily escape Sherman and his army. Johnston was not surrendering out of a conviction that his own army had reached a hopeless position; rather he had come to the conclusion that the Confederacy itself had been defected and he wished to prevent, if possible, the further loss of lives for a cause he viewed as lost. Breckinridge, in his capacity as secretary of war, offered to negotiate for the surrender of all Confederate armies still in the field, and Sherman quickly agreed. The terms were then discussed and accepted by both parties, pending approval by the president and the Federal Congress, who were not then in session. Sherman, remembering his last meeting with Lincoln and the conciliatory tone of the president's words, became all the more magnanimous in his dealings with the Confederates since this accord was to encompass all of their military forces and end the fighting everywhere. The result was more than military in nature. They broached civil matters, over which Sherman had no authority. In addition, the terms were extremely lenient toward the South at a time when the country was still mourning the death of the president. The following is the text of the treaty agreed to on 18 April:

> Memorandum, or Basis of Agreement, made this 18th day of April, AD 1865, near Durham's Station, in the State of North Carolina, by and between General Joseph E. Johnston, commanding the Confederate Army, and Major-General William T. Sherman, commanding the Army of the United States in North Carolina, both present:
>
> The contending armies now in the field to maintain the status quo until notice is given by the commanding general of any one to its opponent, and reasonable time—say forty-eight hours—allowed.

The Confederate armies now in existence to be disbanded and conducted to their several State capitals, there to deposit their arms and public property in the State arsenal; and each officer and man to execute and file an agreement to cease from acts of war, and to abide the action of the State and Federal authority. The number of arms and munitions of war to be reported to the Chief of Ordinance at Washington City, subject to the future action of the Congress of the United States, and, in the meantime, to be used solely to maintain peace and order within the borders of the States respectively.

The recognition by the Executive of the United States of the several State governments on their officers and legislatures taking the oaths prescribed by the Constitution of the United States, and where conflicting State governments have resulted from the war the legitimacy of all shall be submitted to the Supreme Court of the United States.

The reestablishment of all the Federal Courts in the several States, with powers as defined by the Constitution of the United States and of the States respectively.

The people and inhabitants of all the States to be guaranteed, so far as the Executive can, their political rights and franchises, as well as their rights of person and property, as defined by the Constitution of the United States and of the States respectively.

The Executive authority of the Government of the United States not to disturb any of the people by reason of the late war, so long as they live in peace and quiet, abstain from acts of armed hostility, and obey the laws in existence at the place of their residence.

In general terms—the war to cease; a general amnesty, so far as the Executive of the United States can command, on condition of the disbandment of the Confederate armies, the distribution of the arms, and the resumption of peaceful pursuits by the officers and men hitherto composing said armies. Not being fully empowered by our respective principals to fulfill these terms, we individually and officially

> pledge ourselves to promptly obtain the necessary authority, and to carry out the above programme.

By delving into the political questions of franchisement for the Confederates and by guaranteeing the authority of the governments of the respective Southern states, Sherman had gone far beyond the scope that Grant's terms to Lee had covered. Had Sherman been informed fully of the proceedings surrounding Grant's terms, however, he would never have undertaken to write such an agreement. When General Lee had contacted Grant to request a meeting between them to discuss a surrender, the message was forwarded to Secretary Stanton in Washington. He received the following telegraph in reply:

> Office United States Military Telegraph, Headquarters Armies of the United States. Lieutenant-General GRANT: The President directs me to say to you that he wished you to have no conference with General Lee, unless it be for the capitulation of Lee's army or on solely minor and purely military matters. He instructs me to say that you are not to decide, discuss, or confer upon any political question; such questions the President holds in his own hands, and will submit them to no military conferences or conventions. Meantime you are to press to the utmost your military advantages.[7]

Sherman's ignorance of the above communication between Lincoln and Grant induced him to pen a treaty which could not possibly be acceptable in Washington, even if Lincoln had not been killed. As it was, the easy posture toward the South that the president had shown was being replaced by a hard-line approach, led by Secretary Stanton.

Lincoln's policies towards the South had never been very popular with Stanton, and now that the president was dead, he saw an opportunity to use the grief of the nation in supplanting his own

---

[7] Charles Willis Thompson, "The Golden Anniversary of Peace within the Union," *New York Times*, 4 April 1915, 1.

views about the handling of the Confederacy. When the draft of Sherman's agreement arrived in Washington, the secretary took it at once to James Speed, the attorney general, and secured his support in opposing its content. Stanton called a cabinet meeting in which he and Speed revealed for the first time the nature of Sherman's message. The secretary denounced the terms as outrageous, and the attorney general alluded to Sherman's actions as being treasonous. Speed accused Sherman of trying to make himself a dictator "at the head of his victorious legions," and cautioned that this was the first step in accomplishing that plan. The cabinet was taken aback by the accusations and voted unanimously to disapprove of the treaty. Stanton issued a stern rebuke to Sherman personally, then he proceeded to report the whole affair to the press, according to his own bias.[8]

General Grant was ordered to proceed at once to North Carolina to Sherman's headquarters and to personally direct operations against the enemy. President Johnson and Secretary Stanton had expressed their outrage over Sherman's actions to Grant and asserted that they were close to treason. "At this General Grant grew indignant, and gave free expression to his opposition to an attempt to stigmatize an officer whose acts throughout all his career gave ample contradiction to the charge that he was actuated by unworthy motives."[9]

Grant left Washington on the morning of 22 April for Sherman's headquarters, arriving there on 24 April.

> When I arrived I went to Sherman's headquarters, and we were at once closeted together. I showed him the instructions and orders under which I visited him. I told him that I wanted him to notify General Johnston that the terms which they had conditionally agreed upon had not been approved in Washington, and that he was authorized to offer the same

---

[8] Gen. Horace Porter, *Campaigning With Grant* (New York: The Century Company, 1897) 504.

[9] U. S. Grant, *Personal Memoirs*, 2 vols. (New York: Charles L. Webster & Co., 1885) 645.

> terms I had given General Lee. I sent Sherman to do this himself. I did not wish the knowledge of my presence to be known to the army generally; so I left it to Sherman to negotiate the terms of the surrender solely by himself, and without the enemy knowing that I was anywhere near the field. As soon as possible I started to get away, to leave Sherman quite free and untrammeled.[10]

Grant had not followed his orders to the letter. Through his actions he had given his subordinate and friend not only a vote of confidence, but also an opportunity to erase the slanders being perpetrated against him by being solely responsible for securing the surrender of Johnston's army. Had Grant strictly obeyed his directions, William T. Sherman quite possibly might have been unjustly denied the full fame and credit his accomplishments deserved. The general-in-chief showed in this time of political and social upheaval that he could be a statesman and diplomat, as well as a warrior.

Sherman drafted two messages to Johnston as soon as he had been briefed by Grant, and both were in the Confederate chieftain's hands by noon. The first message consisted of only a single sentence, and provided Johnston with a severe jolt: "You will take notice that the truce or suspension of hostilities agreed to between us will cease in forty-eight hours after this is received at your lines, under the first of the articles of the agreement." In the second message, Sherman gave Johnston some insight into what was the cause for the first: "I have replies from Washington to my communication of April 18. I am instructed to limit my operations to your immediate command, and not to attempt civil negotiations. I therefore demand the surrender of your army on the same general terms as were given to General Lee at Appomattox, April 9, instant, purely and simply."[11]

---

[10] John M. Gibson, *Those 163 Days: A Southern Account of Sherman's March From Atlanta to Raleigh* (New York: Bramhall House, 1961) 279–80.

[11] Ibid., 278.

Sherman's message took Johnston completely by surprise. He had been having difficulty in persuading President Davis to agree to the terms, generous as they were, and had only that day received word from Davis approving the treaty. The president would not be convinced that the war was over, but he was finally ready to concede that Johnston's army was finished: in fact, it was melting away. In the five days after Sherman and Johnston's second meeting, approximately 8,000 men had deserted from the Army of the South. Anxious about the treatment they would receive once they were surrendered, many simply went home instead of facing the possible prospect of detainment in a Northern prison. Davis planned to leave Greensboro and head further south until he could reestablish the seat of government at some safe location, possibly in the Trans-Mississippi Department. Johnston's army, it was now plain to Davis, could be of no further service in his plans, and thus would be permitted to capitulate.[12]

The president had directed Johnston to acquire from Treasury Agent J. N. Hendren over $30,000 in silver coin to be used for military expenses, but after it was decided that the army was to be surrendered, Davis altered the directive by ordering that the money be sent to him instead. General Johnston declined to send the money to Davis. To his mind, the army was the last remaining vestige of the Confederacy. The soldiers had not been paid for months and they would need to have some money to help them get back home once they were paroled. He therefore decided to distribute the funds equally between the remaining members of his army, officers and enlisted men alike. Johnston placed the welfare of his troops foremost in his decisions, accounting in large measure for his enormous popularity in the ranks. Though the funds were to be distributed equally, there is evidence that this did not occur, as different soldiers recorded receiving between $1.25 and $2.50 apiece. It was a token sum, hardly enough to allay the expenses they would incur on their homeward

---

[12] Ibid., pg, 277–78 and R. A. Lambert, "In the Battle of Bentonville," *Confederate Veteran Magazine* 37/3 (1929): 222.

treks, but to men who had not been paid in months it must have seemed a windfall.[13]

General Johnston telegraphed the contents of Sherman's latest message to President Davis, now in Charlotte. The president once more balked at the peace proceedings. He ordered that the army be disbanded instead of surrendering, and that it be given instructions to reassemble again at a later place and time. Once more, Johnston disobeyed the orders of his superior. Convinced that it would be criminal to prolong the war any longer, he penned a letter for Sherman:

> I have the honor to have received your dispatch of yesterday summoning this army to surrender on the terms accepted by Gen. Lee at Appomattox Court house.
>
> I propose, instead of such surrender, terms based on those drawn up by you on the 18th for disbanding this army—and a further armistice & conference to arrange these terms.
>
> The disbanding of Gen. Lee's army has afflicted this country with numerous bands having no means of subsistence but robbery, a knowledge of which would, I am sure, induce you to agree to other conditions.[14]

Colonel Rawlins Lowndes of General Hampton's staff was selected that night to carry the message to Sherman. Accompanied by a single man, M. M. Buford of the 5th South Carolina Cavalry, Lowndes struck out for the Federal camp under a flag of truce. Trooper Buford related the story of the trip:

> On our way to Sherman's headquarters we came to the Yankee picket line at one o'clock at night. The vidette on the post could not speak English and seemed at a loss what to do. The vidette on the next post called out to him: "Damn it, make them dismount!" We dismounted and awaited the

[13] Gibson, *Those 163 Days*, 280.

[14] Buford, "Surrender of Johnston's Army," 170–71.

> appearance of the officer who had been called to escort us, when we remounted and accompanied him to headquarters. (As indicating the discipline in the Federal army, I afterwards learned the vidette was arrested and punished for permitting us to get so close before he halted us.)
>
> When we reached General Sherman's headquarters we were treated very nicely. Soldiers were sent out to hold our horses. Colonel Lowndes went in, but I stayed out and held my own horse. When Colonel Lowndes had delivered his message and we had started back to our headquarters, he said to me: "Buford, why didn't you let that soldier hold your horse?" My reply was: "I don't let no Yankee hold my Horse."[15]

Johnston's message had arrived none too soon. Sherman had already issued orders for his army to resume the march against the Confederate army at noon of that very day. Grant not only approved of the conference, he urged Sherman to accept, and the general sent back a response that he would meet Johnston at the Bennett House again at noon, the hour his legions were supposed to have marched out to crush the remaining Confederates. His message did not arrive at Confederate headquarters until after sunrise, and Johnston only had time to scratch off a quick note to Davis about the developments before he hurried off to the meeting place.[16]

Though both officers still held the same views regarding the ending of the bloodshed, this third meeting proved to be more difficult than the others. Sherman was bound by the terms Grant had given Lee and could offer no deviation. Johnston, on the other hand, acknowledged the generosity of Grant's terms but insisted that they did to go far enough in certain areas. In particular, he was concerned over the actions of some of Lee's men as they made their way back home. Without money, food, or transportation, some had committed numerous criminal acts upon the civilians in the country through which they passed. Johnston wanted to accept the terms, but he

---

[15] Gibson, *Those 163 Days*, 286.

[16] Johnson and Buel, *Battles and Leaders*, 4:757.

wished to have them amended in some way so that his men and the Southern citizens would be protected. Sherman showed compassion for Johnston's concerns, but he felt he was unable to address them given his current status with the government. At last, the impasse was ended when Sherman summoned General Schofield into the conference. Schofield was a very persuasive man who had shown his talent as a diplomat on various occasions. The general came through with a solution that was acceptable to both commanders. After the surrender of Johnston's army, Sherman would be expected to march the bulk of his troops to Washington for disbandment, leaving Schofield and a small force in North Carolina to maintain order. As the ranking officer on the scene, Schofield would then have the authority to oversee the particulars of the Confederate demobilization, and he promised to do everything in his power to prevent the conditions Johnston feared. Schofield then sat down at a table and wrote out the formal document:

> Terms of a Military Convention, entered into this 26th day of April, 1865, at Bennett's House, near Durham's Station, North Carolina, between General Joseph E. Johnston, commanding the Confederate army, and Major-General W. T. Sherman, commanding the United States Army in North Carolina:
>
> 1. All acts of war on the part of the troops under General Johnston's command to cease from this date.
>
> 2. All arms and public property to be deposited at Greensboro, and delivered to an ordinance-officer of the United States Army.
>
> 3. Rolls of all the officers and men to be made in duplicate; one copy to be retained by the commander of the troops, and the other to be given to an officer to be designated by General Sherman. Each officer and man to give his individual obligation in writing not to take up arms against the Government of the United States, until properly released from this obligation.
>
> 4. The side-arms of officers, and their private horses and baggage, to be retained by them.

5. This being done, all the officers and men will be permitted to return to their homes, not to be disturbed by the United States authorities, so long as they observe their obligation and the laws in force where they reside.

Johnston and Sherman both read and signed the document once Schofield had finished, then the general took pen in hand again and wrote out the agreement he had previously reached orally with Johnston under the title "Supplemental Terms":

1. The field transportation to be loaned to the troops for their march to their homes, and for subsequent use in their industrial pursuits. Artillery-horse may be used in field transportation, if necessary.

2. Every brigade or separate body to retain a number of arms equal to one-seventh of its effective strength, which, when the troops reach the capitals of their states will be disposed of as the general commanding the department may direct.

3. Private horses, and other private property of both officers and men, to be retained by them.

4. The commanding general of the Military Division of West Mississippi, Major-General Canby, will be requested to give transportation by water, from Mobile or New Orleans, to the troops from Arkansas and Texas.

5. The obligation of officers and soldiers to be signed by their immediate commanders.

6. Naval forces within the limits of General Johnston's command to be included in the terms of this convention.[17]

With the documents signed, their commanders bid farewell to each other and departed for their respective camps. General Grant again showed his support for Sherman when he reached headquarters in Raleigh by endorsing the terms. The next morning, he began his

---

[17] *Service with the Third,* 173–74.

trip back to Washington. The Confederate army had been surrendered under terms that the government would accept, and he had allowed Sherman to salvage his reputation in the process.

The news of the surrender had a euphoric effect on Sherman's army. At last the war was over. Captain Julian Hinkley expressed his joy and optimism in a letter to his wife, saying, "The angel of Peace has spread his wings over our country once more. The glad tidings were announced to the army last night by General Sherman in general orders..... It was a glorious day for us who have seen the thing through from the beginning to the end. General Sherman also says that he expects 'soon to have the pleasure of conducting this army to its homes...'"[18]

Some others had found reasons to be in no hurry to get home. "I found some of the prettiest girls there that I have seen in the South," wrote one soldier about a trip to nearby Haywood, "I would like to garrison the place."[19]

On 2 May, General Joseph E. Johnston issued his final orders to the army, General Orders No. 22:

> Comrades: In terminating our official relations, I earnestly exhort you to faithfully observe the terms of pacification agreed upon; and to discharge the obligations of good and peaceful citizens, as well as you have performed the duties of thorough soldiers in the field. By such a course, you will best secure the comfort of your families and kindred, and restore tranquillity to our country.
>
> You will return to your homes with the admiration of our people, won by the courage and noble devotion you have displayed in the long war. I shall always remember with pride the loyal support and generous confidence you have given me.

---

[18] Untitled circular, 20 April 1865, Heartt and Wilson Family Papers, Southern Historical Collection, University of North Carolina, Chapel Hill NC.

[19] Charles S. Brown to Mother and Etta, 18 April 1865, Charles S. Brown Papers, Perkins Library, Duke University, Durham NC.

> I now part with you with deep regret—and bid you farewell with feelings of cordial friendship; and with earnest wishes that you may have hereafter all prosperity and happiness to be found in the world.

Not all of Johnston's officers shared his view that the war was hopeless and the time had come to lay down their arms. General Wade Hampton was strongly opposed to the action and was determined to fight on. "I shall fight as long as my Government remains in existence," he wrote, "when that ceases to live I shall seek some other country, for I shall never take the 'oath of allegiance.'" True to his word, Hampton, along with most of the cavalry, took their leave of Johnston's army on 26 April. The officers and men of the cavalry had been called to Hampton's side by means of the following circular, distributed by the general:

> All officers and men of the Cavalry Corps of the Army of Northern Virginia who have escaped capture, and are not now on parole, are earnestly called upon to join me at once, mounted or dismounted, and strike another blow for the defense of their country. And now particularly should the men of my North Carolina Brigade assemble, and prove that the valor which has triumphed upon a hundred fields is undiminished, and that blows as heavy as those of yore can again be struck. Our cause is not desperate, if our men will rally around and cling to the old battle flags that so often have led them to victory.[20]

In contrast to the surrender of Lee's army at Appomattox, there was to be no formal ceremony involved in the disbandment of Johnston's troops. Instead of marching to an assigned place to turn in their arms to an observing line of Federal infantry, the Confederates

---

[20] *The War of the Rebellion: A Compilation of the Official Records of the Union and Confederate Armies* (Washington, DC: Government Printing Office, 1895) ser. 1, vol. 47, pt. 3, 322.

were to gather the weapons themselves and then turn them over to Federal authorities in Greensboro, where Captain Jasper Myers of the Ordinance Department waited to receive them.[21]

The men assembled by regiments and by brigades, and at the command of their officers, simply stacked their muskets wherever they happened to be camped at the time. One member of the 18th Tennessee remembered: "The brigade moved slowly and sadly out into an open field where the officers sheathed their swords and the men silently stacked their trusty guns. Then the unarmed command moved out of sight."[22]

Some of the men could not bear to think that the end had come. Soldiers clustered around their flags and wept openly at having to turn over the glorious banners. In many instances, small swaths of fabric were cut as souvenirs, and there were instances where the flags were taken by a member of the regiment to be secreted away. Such was the case in the 1st South Carolina Artillery. When the muskets were stacked, the regimental flag was removed from its staff and the empty staff placed upon the stacks. The flag, a symbol of their sacrifice, and the dreams of a now defeated nation would not be surrendered.[23]

Johnston had directed that four-fifths of the muskets were to be collected; the other fifth was to be retained by the troops for their own protection on the march home. According to the supplemental terms of the surrender forwarded by General Schofield, the number to be retained by the Confederates was only to be one seventh. However, the error was discovered by Captain Myers in Greensboro when the weapons were turned in, and was quickly rectified by Confederate command.

With the weapons collected, the army was ordered to Salisbury, where they received from the Federal forces ten day's rations per

---

[21] John Barrien Lindsley, *The Military Annals of Tennessee: Confederate, First Series, Embracing a Review of Military Operations with Regimental and Memorial Rolls Compiled form Original and Official Sources* (Nashville: J. M. Lindsley, 1886) 360.

[22] Johnson and Buel, *Battles and Leaders*, 4:768.

[23] Charles Inglesby, *Historical Sketch of the First South Carolina Artillery* (Charleston: n.p., n.d.) 20–22. Duke University Pamphlet Collection.

man. Johnston organized the army into three groups based upon the geographic destination of the units, and on 5 May the army broke up forever when the columns marched from Salisbury. Two of the columns headed south, one traveling on the road via Chester and Newberry, South Carolina, and the other going by way of Spartansburg and Abbeville. The third column, composed of men from Tennessee and other more western states, marched by way of Morganton and Asheville to Strawberry Plains in east Tennessee. North Carolina troops generally did not take part in the march. In most instances, they left Salisbury individually or in small groups for home. Including his own army, and those troops under his immediate department command, Johnston surrendered a total of 31,243 men, or almost 4,000 more than Lee surrendered at Appomattox.[24]

The march home was to be the last time these soldiers would share the experience of army life and it was a stirring one: "When the Tennesseans had passed beyond Salisbury, they halted and formed line as if in review, when General Cheatham came down the line, shaking the hands of every soldier, not one missed, while great big tears rolled down his cheeks."[25]

---

[24] Gen. William T. Sherman, *Memoirs of W. T. Sherman by Himself*, 2 vols. (New York: Charles L. Webster & Co., 1891) 2:346–48.

[25] William Worsham, *Old Nineteenth Tennessee Regiment, C.S.A.* (Knoxville: Paragon Printing Co., 1902) 177.

CONCLUSION

As Johnston and his army were preparing to stack arms and begin their march home, Sherman and most of his army was preparing for their journey home as well. Being the victors, however, the Union troops could look forward to a very different reception than the Confederates were to receive. Before they departed North Carolina, the Union troops availed themselves of one final opportunity to burn and destroy. General Slocum observed a large group of soldiers gathered around a cart they had set fire to, and sent a staff officer to ascertain the meaning of the action. When the officer returned, he informed Slocum that one of the soldiers had directed him to "Tell General Slocum that cart is loaded with New York papers for sale to the soldiers. These papers are filled with the vilest abuse of General Sherman. We have followed General Sherman through a score of battles and through nearly two thousand miles of the enemy's country, and we do not intend to allow these vile slanders against him to be circulated among his men." Slocum stated that this was the last property he saw destroyed by Sherman's men during the war and that he "witnessed the scene with keener satisfaction than I had felt over the destruction of any property since the day we left Atlanta."[1] Sherman's army traveled through Virginia, where they had the opportunity to see firsthand some of the sites where the fighting had taken place there. Around Richmond, one Union officer noted: "The works about the city wear a formidable aspect but considering nature,

---

[1] Robert Underwood Johnson and Clarence Clough Buel, *Battles and Leaders of the Civil War*, 4 vols. (New York: The Century Company, 1884–1888) 4:757.

Sherman penetrated many as strong positions in Georgia."[2] Another officer wrote about Richmond: "We had all hoped we would be sharer's in the glory of the fall of the Rebel Capital & Strong hold [sic] but it is much better as it is for the western army can boast of enough victories without this one and the bitter feeling among eastern troops against western ones would have been increased if we had been participants in their glory of taking Richmond."[3]

The march through North Carolina and Virginia was not made with the easy gait of a triumphant army returning home for the accolades of their people and government; rather, it more closely resembled a forced march on the eve of a critical engagement. Corps commanders had placed bets on whose men could reach Richmond faster, and the troops were driven in May heat for distances of 25–30 miles a day for no other reason than to win the wager. Sherman's army experienced some of the worst straggling it saw during the war as thousands of soldiers succumbed to the heat and exertion and fell out of the ranks. Several hundred men became ill and dozens who had survived all the perils of battle died of heat exhaustion. One Union sergeant spoke for the army when he said, "We have never made a much harder march and some of our Generals deserve to have their necks broke for such Tom foolery [sic] after the war."[4] At last, Washington was reached and the army went into camp preparatory for the Grand Review of the armies and the formal mustering out of the troops. Many of the resentments held by the eastern and western armies for each other came to the surface as easterners derisively commented on the shabby, unmilitary appearance of the westerners, and Sherman's troops answered with jokes about the "paper collar soldiers" from the east who were more interested in how they looked then how they fought. Several fistfights broke out between the commands and it was decided that the armies be camped separately to avoid any large-scale altercations.

---

[2] Joseph T. Glatthaar, *The March to the Sea and Beyond: Sherman's Troops in the Savannah and Carolina Campaigns* (New York: New York University Press, 1986) 180.

[3] Ibid., 179.

[4] John D. Inskeep Diary, 6 May 1865, Ohio Historical Society, Columbus OH.

The animosity between the members of the two armies was unwittingly fueled by the thousands of spectators who flocked to the city to see their victorious troops. The Army of the Potomac, operating as it did in the area around the capital, had lost its novelty by reason that it had been seen many times before by the spectators. Sherman's army, on the other hand, was a new sight, and the people clamored to get a look at the soldiers who had made all those celebrated marches they had read about in the newspapers.

There were no longer any feelings of resentment toward Sherman or his army held by the Northern populace, however. Gone was the outrage that had been whipped up by Stanton and Speed's accusations of disloyalty toward the general. Sherman had secured the surrender of the remaining Confederate army of any consequence in the South, and in doing so, had restored himself to public favor. But Sherman was not so quick to forget the incident himself. He felt his reputation had been wronged through the actions of his superiors and was not about to simply forgive and forget. The general was very cold in his relations with Secretary Stanton, General Halleck, and President Johnson, and went so far as to publicly snub each of them during the Washington Review. It was an injustice that would fire his resentment for years to come and would cause him to have hard feelings toward these three gentlemen until his death.

The campaign through the Carolinas had been a success, despite all of the mistakes and missed opportunities on Sherman's part. Rarely in the annals of military history has a campaign conducted with such mediocrity been crowned with such everlasting glory. Sherman exhibited an uncharateristic laxity in regard to holding on to his army in the march through the Carolinas. It is possible that, since leaving Atlanta, he had become overly confident that the Confederates were powerless to field any army that could confront him. However, that does not explain his lack of caution upon hearing that Johnston was concentrating in his front after the Confederates had already shown a willingness to fight at Kinston and Averasboro. To keep his army separated as it was, in the face of possible danger, shows that he had been fully lulled into a sense of false security, though it is hard to determine how this could be when one considers that Sherman himself had expressed the view that the Confederates were liable to put up a fight once he heard that Johnston had been reinstated to command.

Prior to Bentonville, Sherman's confidence seems to have pervaded the thinking of his officer corps, save that of General Jeff Davis. Davis appears to be the only high-ranking officer on the scene who was anxious about the Confederate intentions prior to the battle. Through his overconfidence, Sherman allowed his army to be surprised while it was separated, and narrowly escaped what would have been a crushing defeat, to his own reputation if not to the war effort, at this late date in the war.

Once his army was concentrated on the field of battle, Sherman showed a reluctance to commit to any large-scale fighting. He went from denouncing the existence of any appreciable numbers of Confederates in his front to grossly overestimating their number in the course of one day. This flip-flopping does not necessarily reflect badly on Sherman himself, but it shows a definite lack of work on the part of his staff. Sherman was not in the possession of any reliable information concerning the size or makeup of Johnston's army through the entire campaign in the Carolinas. He was essentially operating blind. Lack of Confederate resistance during the campaign before Averasboro had seemed to substantiate the inaccurate reports he was receiving as to Confederates military capability in the region, so the general cannot be held wholly responsible for his lack of knowledge.

In his tactical operations on the battlefield, Sherman's actions were motivated partially from this lack of definite information, but they were also further reinforcement of what had come to symbolize a Sherman campaign. The general had shown a tendency through his campaigns not to commit his troops to a massive blow, but rather to fight his battles while using only parts of his command, relying on position and maneuver more than on brute force. This tendency, as much as his inflated estimation of the Confederate force, caused him to refrain from delivering the knockout blow at Bentonville.

Last, after expressing a fear that Johnston's army would either link up with Lee or escape to the South, bringing on a long and exhausting chase, Sherman failed to keep a close hold on the Confederates. By marching on to Goldsboro after the battle, he gave Johnston a 20-mile head start on his army. Confederate cavalry was in constant contact with the Union army throughout the campaign and kept Johnston fully informed of the Federal movements. Because of this, Johnston could start his retreat at the same time the Federals moved, and he would be able to increase his advantage through the delaying tactics of his cavalry, as was evidenced by the fact that he had increased the distance between his army and the Federals to over 80 miles at the time of the surrender. If Johnston had not believed that prolonging the war was neither responsible nor humane, he could have escaped his pursuers altogether and put off the final decision for weeks or possibly months.

For Johnston's part, the campaign was essentially the best that could be made of a bad situation. Put in command of an army that did not exist, as such, at the time, he did a commendable job of making that force a reality. Still, the numerical disparity between his army and that of the enemy forced him to limit its use accordingly. Though removed from army command the previous year by President Davis on the accusation that he preferred maneuvering to fighting, he proved his critics wrong when he fell upon Sherman's separated wing. On the battlefield, his control of his army was superior to Sherman's and victory was denied him because of the one error in judgment he made on 19 April: diverting McLaws's troops from the assaulting force to support Bragg. Even with this reduction to his striking power, he might have succeeded in driving the Federals from the field, had it not been for the determined and heroic stand made by General Morgan and his division, who bought time for the XX Corps to come up, get in line, and prepare to accept the Confederate charge. To Morgan and his men goes the credit for saving the day and the battle, and for keeping Sherman's reputation intact.

Johnston seems to have been better served in regard to intelligence than was Sherman. Generals Hampton and Wheeler provided him with accurate information in a timely manner, so that Johnston appears to have been able to more quickly react to situations than could Sherman. The fault in this is not Sherman's, but rather his cavalry chief's, Judson Kilpatrick. During the campaign, Kilpatrick was simply out performed by Hampton and Wheeler.

General Johnston had been criticized for remaining on the field after the first day's fighting when Sherman's whole army was up. Critics state that it was useless exposure of his army in the face of overwhelming odds and could have served no possible advantage for the Confederates. Indeed, it could have brought about the entrapment of his army. In defense of Johnston, the two men had fought against one another on numerous occasions in the past and Johnston was quite familiar with Sherman's tendencies. Johnston was counting on Sherman to act as he had always done and to not commit his entire army in a frontal attack against prepared works. If Sherman did assault with part of his army, then Johnston might still have been able to accomplish his desired goal of crippling a part of the Federal army by repulsing that attacking force. In his book *Bentonville: The Final Battle of Sherman & Johnston*, historian Nathaniel Cheirs Hughes, Jr., asserts that Johnston's aggressive nature at Bentonville confounded Sherman by being contrary to what that general had come to expect from the Confederate leader. He suggests that Johnston had come to know Sherman and his tendencies better that Sherman had come to know Johnston, a supposition that seems to be entirely correct.

During the retreat from Bentonville, Johnston kept his army in hand admirably. Much has been made about the number of desertions from the Confederate ranks during the withdrawal, but the fact is that they were not as high as the number of desertions that occurred in the army after Missionary Ridge. Also, many of the men who did desert during this time did so not to escape further military service, but rather to extend it by not being captured and paroled. Johnston's major problem with the desertions was not so much the number of men who were leaving the ranks as it was how thin the ranks were initially. With regiments numbering only thirty to forty men, a few deserters could create gaping holes, and Johnston needed every man. Also, some of the deserters had taken to robbing the citizens in the surrounding area, and these bands of roving bandits served to further magnify the problem.

Regarding Johnston's lack of manpower, there were several sources of additional men that could have made the difference and turned the tide in favor of the Confederates at Bentonville. First, there were the state troops of Georgia and South Carolina that were refused Johnston and his army by Governors Brown and McGrath respectively. Second, there was the force that General Beauregard had amassed under his personal command, amounting to between 6,000 to 8,000 men. While Beauregard did need a substantial number of the men in his command to guard strategic points along the remaining line of supply, the number he retained was more than sufficient for the job, and some could have been forwarded to Johnston. It is probable that Johnston did not press for these troops out of deference to the man he was replacing in department command. Governors Brown and McGrath, however, had no such reasons to withhold any men from Johnston's army. The Confederate military had already evacuated those states and the remaining portion of the war was to be fought in North Carolina. The only event at that juncture that would have restored Confederate authority to all or parts of those states was a Southern victory on the battlefield, and by virtue of a strict adherence to states rights, these two governors were depriving Johnston of the means necessary to accomplish it.

Though it was witness to some of the hardest fighting to take place during the Civil War, Bentonville has been all but forgotten by historians of the era. This tendency held true even among people who had lived through the war. In a letter dated 25 December 1894, General Dabney Maury stated, "Hardee, Carter Stevenson, Hampton and Butler and McDonald, who were there and in many another hard fought fight, Have told me that Bentonville was the handsomest Battle they ever saw—and so little interest did it arouse then, that no less a Soldier than Gen. Hunton lately asked me what Battle was Bentonville."[5]

To the soldiers of Slocum's wing and to the Confederates involved, it was indeed a battle, as attested to by the more than 10

[5] Gen. Dabney Maury to "My Dear Major," 25 December 1894, John Warwick Daniel Papers, Perkins Library, Duke University, Durham NC.

percent casualty rates among the Confederates. In terms of importance, this battle was every bit as important to the Union war effort as the victory at Five Forks and was equally significant in bringing the war to a close. Had the left wing been defeated there, the Confederacy's options would have expanded noticeably. Johnston, temporarily unencumbered by Sherman, could have cooperated with Lee's army, as had been his wish all along, and though there is little question that the North would still have achieved final victory, the war would have continued.

Lee has received a great deal of credit, and deservedly so, for surrendering in the name of humanity and putting an end to the fighting. But Lee was surrounded and was left with few options other than sacrificing his men or disbanding them to fight as guerrillas. This was not the case with Johnston. He had put a distance of four hard days march between himself and his pursuer and was in a position to elude the Federals altogether and escape back into South Carolina and Georgia. While in no way detracting from the humane example set by General Lee in ending the fighting of his army on terms that would help to heal the wounds of war, Johnston showed even more foresight in this matter. If he had adhered strictly to the wishes of President Davis, he would only have prolonged the inevitable, and in the process would have fueled the sentiments of those in the North who wished to punish the South after the war.

Sherman and Johnston had formed a strong mutual admiration for each other, forged through the fire of battle, which continued after the war until the time of their respective deaths. In fact, General Johnston would become a victim of this admiration and respect when he died from pneumonia, which he contracted while attending the funeral of his old adversary. As Sherman's casket passed by on that cold and blustery day, Johnston removed his hat in salute. When friends pleaded with him to put his hat back on, the old general replied that if he were in the casket and Sherman was paying his respects, Sherman would have taken his hat off.

Sherman has been regarded by many historians to be the most able strategist of the war, and his campaigns have become a standard part of any analysis of the war. He emerged as one of the greatest military heroes in the North and remains today one of the most recognized figures in American military history. Johnston became one of the leading figures of the Confederacy's Lost Cause in the romantic histories written after the war. He was one of the most beloved generals of the South, rivaling among his own army the devotion shown to Robert E. Lee by the Army of Northern Virginia. But there was more than just admiration. Johnston was also the equal in ability of any army commander, prompting Dabney Maury to declare: "I really consider Joe Johnston the greatest General of them all."[6]

[6] Ibid.

APPENDIX

THE OPPOSING ARMIES

THE UNION ARMY

Major General William T. Sherman

The Left Wing: Major General Henry W. Slocum

Fourteenth Corps: Brigadier General Jefferson C. Davis

1st Division: Brigadier General William P. Carlin

1st Brigade: Colonel Harrison C. Hobart—104th Illinois, 42nd Indiana, 88th Indiana, 33rd Ohio, 94th Ohio, 21st Wisconsin

2nd Brigade: Colonel George P. Buell—13th Michigan, 21st Michigan, 69th Ohio

3rd Brigade: Lt. Colonel David Miles—38th Indiana, 21st Ohio, 74th Ohio, 79th Pennsylvania

2nd Division: Brigadier General James D. Morgan

1st Brigade: Brigadier General William Vandever—16th Illinois, 60th Illinois, 10th Michigan, 14th Michigan, 17th New York

2nd Brigade: Lieutenant-Colonel John S. Pierce—34th Illinois, 78th Illinois, 98th Ohio, 108th Ohio, 113th Ohio, 121st Ohio

3rd Brigade: Colonel Benjamin D. Fearing—85th Illinois, 86th Illinois, 110th Illinois, 125th Illinois, 37th Indiana (1 company) 52nd Ohio

Provost Guard: 110th Illinois

3rd Division: Brigadier General Absalom Baird

1st Brigade: Colonel Morton C. Hunter—82nd Indiana, 23rd Missouri (4 companies), 11th Ohio, 17th Ohio, 31st Ohio, 89th Ohio, 92nd Ohio

2nd Brigade: Lieutenant Colonel Thomas Doan—75th Indiana, 87th Indiana, 101st Indiana, 2nd Minnesota, 105th Ohio

3rd Brigade: Colonel George P. Este—74th Indiana, 18th Kentucky, 14th Ohio, 38th Ohio

Artillery: Major Charles Houghtaling—Battery C, 1st Illinios; Battery I, 2nd Illinois; 19th Indiana; 5th Wisconsin

20th Corps: Brigadier General Alphesus S. Williams

1st Division: Brigadie-General Nathaniel J. Jackson

1st Brigade: Colonel James L. Selfridge—5th Connecticut, 123rd New York, 141st New York, 46th Pennsylvania

2nd Brigade: Colonel William Hawley—2nd Massachusetts, 13th New Jersey, 107th New York, 150th New York, 3rd Wisconsin

3rd Brigade: Brigadier General James S. Robinson—82nd Illinois, 101st Illinois, 143rd New York, 61st Ohio, 82nd Ohio, 31st Wisconsin

2nd Division: Brigadier General John W. Geary

1st Brigade: Colonel Arlo Pardee, Jr.—5th Ohio, 29th Ohio, 66th Ohio, 28th Pennsylvania, 147th Pennsylvania

2nd Brigade: Colonel George W. Mindil—33rd New Jersey, 119th New York, 134th New York, 154th New York, 73rd Pennsylvania, 109th Pennsylvania

3rd Brigade: Colonel Henry A. Barnum—60th New York, 102nd New York, 137th New York, 29th Pennsylvania, 111th Pennsylvania

3rd Division: Brigadier General William T. Ward

1st Brigade: Colonel Henry Case—102nd Illinois, 105th Illinois, 129th Illinois, 70th Indiana, 79th Ohio

2nd Brigade: Colonel Daniel Dustin—33rd Indiana, 85th Indiana, 19th Michigan, 22nd Wisconsin

3rd Brigade: Colonel William Cogswell—20th Connecticut, 33rd Massachusetts, 136th New York, 55th Ohio, 73rd Ohio, 26th Wisconsin

Artillery: Major John A. Reynolds—Battery I, 1st New York; Battery M, 1st New York; Battery C, 1st Ohio

Right Wing: Major General Oliver O. Howard

15th Corps: Major General John A. Logan

1st Division: Brigadier General Charles R. Woods

1st Brigade: Colonel William B. Woods—12th Indiana, 26th Iowa, 27th Missouri, 31st Missouri, 32nd Missouri, 76th Ohio

2nd Brigade: Colonel Robert F. Catterson—26th Illinois, 40th Illinois, 103rd Illinois, 97th Indiana, 100th Indiana, 6th Iowa, 46th Ohio

3rd Brigade: Colonel George A. Stone— 4th Iowa, 9th Iowa, 25th Iowa, 30th Iowa, 31st Iowa

2nd Division: Major General William B. Hazen

1st Brigade: Colonel Theodore Jones—55th Illinois, 116th Illinois, 127th Illinois, 6th Missouri, 30th Ohio, 57th Ohio

2nd Brigade: Colonel Wells S. Jones—111th Illinois, 83rd Indiana, 37th Ohio, 47th Ohio, 53rd Ohio, 54th Ohio

3rd Brigade: Brigadier General John M. Oliver—48th Illinois, 90th Illinois, 99th Indiana, 15th Michigan, 70th Ohio

3rd Division: Brigadier General John E. Smith

1st Brigade: Brigadier General William T. Clark—63rd Illinois, 93rd Illinois, 48th Indiana, 59th Indiana, 4th Minnesota, 18th Wisconsin

2nd Brigade: Colonel Clark R. Wever—56th Illinois, 10th Iowa, 17th Iowa (1 company), 26th Missouri (2 companies), 80th Ohio

4th Division: Brigadier General John M. Corse

1st Brigade: Brigadier General Elliot W. Rice—52nd Illinois, 66th Indiana, 2nd Iowa, 7th Iowa

2nd Brigade: Colonel Robert N. Adams—12th Illinois, 66th Illinois, 81st Ohio

3rd Brigade: Colonel Frederick J. Hurlbut—7th Illinois, 50th Illinois, 57th Illinois, 39th Iowa

Unassigned: 110th USCT, 29th Missouri

Artillery: Lieutenant Colonel William H. Ross—Battery H, 1st Illinois; Battery B, 1st Michigan; Battery H, 1st Missouri; 12th Wisconsin

Escort: 15th Illinois Cavalry, 4th Ohio Cavalry

17th Corps: Major General Frank P. Blair, Jr.

1st Division: Major General Joseph A. Mower

1st Brigade: Brigadier General John W. Fuller—64th Illinois, 18th Missouri, 27th Ohio, 39th Ohio

2nd Brigade: Brigadier General John W. Sprague—35th New Jersey, 43rd Ohio, 63rd Ohio, 25th Wisconsin

3rd Brigade: Colonel John Tillson—10th Illinois, 25th Indiana, 32nd Indiana

3rd Division: Brigadier General Mortimer Leggett

1st Brigade: Brigadier General Manning Force—20th Illinois, 30th Illinois, 31st Illinois, 45th Illinois, 12th Wisconsin, 16th Wisconsin

2nd Brigade: Brigadier General Robert K. Scott—20th Ohio, 68th Ohio, 78th Ohio, 17th Wisconsin

4th Division: Brigadier General Giles Smith

1st Brigade: Brigadier General Benjamin F. Potts—14th and 15th Illinois Battalion, 53rd Illinois, 23rd Indiana, 53rd Indiana, 32nd Ohio

3rd Brigade: Brigadier General William W. Belknap—32nd Illinois, 11th Iowa, 15th Iowa, 16th Iowa

Artillery: Major Frederick Welker—Battery C, 1st Michigan; 1st Minnesota, 15th Ohio

Unassigned: 9th Illinois

10th Corps: Major General Alfred H. Terry

1st Division: Brigadier General Henry W. Birge

3rd Brigade: Colonel Nicholas W. Day—24th Iowa, 38th Massachusetts, 128th New York, 156th New York, 175th New York, 176th New York

2nd Division: Brigadier General Adelbert Ames

1st Brigade: Colonel Rufus Daggett—3rd New York, 112th New York, 117th New York, 142nd New York

2nd Brigade: Colonel John S. Littell—47th New York, 48th New York, 76th Pennsylvania, 97th Pennsylvania, 203rd Pennsylvania

3rd Brigade: Colonel G. F. Granger—13th Indiana, 9th Maine, 4th New Hampshire, 115th New York, 169th New York

3rd Division: Brigadier General Charles J. Paine

1st Brigade: Colonel Devin Bates—1st USCT, 30th USCT, 107th USCT

2nd Brigade: Colonel Samuel A. Duncan—4th USCT, 5th USCT, 39th USCT

3rd Brigade: Colonel Albert M. Blackman—6th USCT, 27th USCT, 37th USCT

Artillery: 22nd Illinois, 16th New York, 3rd US

23rd Corps: Major General John M. Schofield (commander of Army of the Ohio after 2 April), Major General Jacob D. Cox

1st Division: Brigadier General Thomas H. Ruger

1st Brigade: Colonel Isaac N. Stiles—120th Indiana, 124th Indiana, 128th Indiana, 180th Iowa

2nd Brigade: Colonel John C. McQuiston—123rd Indiana, 129th Indiana, 130th Indiana, 28th Michigan

3rd Brigade: Colonel Minor T. Thomas—25th Massachusetts, 8th Minnesota, 174th Ohio, 178th Ohio

2nd Division: Brigadier General Joseph A. Cooper

1st Brigade: Colonel Orlando H. Moore—26th Kentucky, 25th Michigan, 132nd New York, 52nd Pennsylvania, 6th Tennessee

2nd Brigade: Colonel John Mehringer—107th Illinois, 80th Indiana, 23rd Michigan, 111th Ohio, 118th Ohio

3rd Brigade: Colonel Silas A. Strickland—91st Indiana, 50th Ohio, 181st Ohio, 183rd Ohio

3rd Division: Brigadier General Samuel P. Carter

1st Brigade: Colonel Oscar W. Sterl—12th Kentucky, 16th Kentucky, 100th Ohio, 104th Ohio, 8th Tennessee

2nd Brigade: Colonel John S. Casement—65th Illinois, 65th Indiana, 9th New Jersey, 103rd Ohio, 177th Ohio

3rd Brigade: Colonel Thomas J. Henderson—112th Illinois, 63rd Indiana, 140th Indiana, 17th Massachusetts

Artillery: Lieutenant Colonel Terance J. Kennedy—22nd Indiana, 16th New York, 3rd US Battery F, 1st Michigan, 15th Indiana, 19th Ohio, 23rd Indiana, 3rd New York

Cavalry: Brigadier General Judson Kilpatrick

1st Brigade: Colonel Thomas J. Jordan—3rd Indiana Battalion, 8th Indiana, 2nd Kentucky, 3rd Kentucky, 9th Pennsylvania

2nd Brigade: Colonel Smith D. Atkins—92nd Illinois, 9th Michigan, 9th Ohio, 10th Ohio, McLaughlin's Ohio Squadron

3rd Brigade: Colonel Thomas T. Heath—1st Alabama, 5th Kentucky, 5th Ohio, 13th Pennsylvania

THE CONFEDERATE ARMY

General Joseph E. Johnston (as reorganized on 9 April)

Hardee's Corp: Lieutenant General William J. Hardee

Brown's Division: Major General John C. Brown

Smith's Brigade: Brigadier General James A. Smith—1st Florida (consolidated 1st, 3rd, 4th, 6th and 7th Infantry and 1st Cavalry), 1st Georgia (consolidated 1st, 57th, and 63rd), 54th Georgia (consolidated 37th and 54th, and 4th Battalion)

Govan's Brigade: Brigadier General D. C. Govan—1st Arkansas (consolidated 1st, 2nd, 5th, 6th, 7th, 8th, 13th, 15th, 19th, 24th Arkansas, and 3rd Confederate), 1st Texas (consolidated 6th, 7th, 10th and 15th Infantry and 17th, 18th, 24th, and 25th Cavalry)

Hoke's Division: Major General Robert F. Hoke

Clingman's Brigade: Brigadier General Thomas L. Clingman—8th North Carolina, 31st North Carolina, 36th North Carolina, 40th North Carolina, 51st North Carolina, 61st North Carolina

Colquitt's Brigade: Brigadier General Alfred Colquitt—6th Georgia, 19th Georgia, 23rd Georgia, 27th Georgia, 28th Georgia

Hagood's Brigade: Brigadier General Johnson Hagood—11th South Carolina, 21st South Carolina, 25th South Carolina, 27th South Carolina, 7th South Carolina Battalion

Kirkland's Brigade: Brigadier General W. W. Kirkland—17th North Carolina, 42nd North Carolina, 50th North Carolina, 66th North Carolina

1st Brigade Junior Reserves: Brigadier General L. S. Baker—1st North Carolina, 2nd North Carolina, 3rd North Carolina, 1st North Carolina Battalion

Cheatham's Division: Major General Benjamin F. Cheatham

Palmer's Brigade: Brigadier General Joseph B. Palmer—1st Tennessee (consolidated 1st, 6th, 8th, 9th, 16th, 27th, 28th, 34th, and 24th Battalion), 2nd Tennessee (consolidated 11th, 12th, 13th, 29th, 47th, 50th, 51st, 52nd, and 154th), 3rd Tennessee (consolidated 4th, 5th, 19th, 24th, 31st, 33rd, 35th, 38th, and 154th), 4th Tennessee (consolidated 2nd, 3rd, 10th, 15th, 18th, 20th, 26th, 30th, 32nd, 37th, 45th, and 23rd Battalion)

Gist's Brigade: Colonel W. G. Foster—46th Georgia, 65th Georgia, 2nd Georgia Battalion, 8th Georgia Battalion, 16th South Carolina, 24th South Carolina

Artillery: Major B. C. Manly—Bridges' Louisiana Battery, Atkin's North Carolina Battery, Walter's South Carolina Battery, Zimmerman's South Carolina Battery, Tucker's Virginia Battery

Stewart's Corps: Lieutenant-General Alexander P. Stewart

Loring's Division: Major General William W. Loring

Featherston's Brigade: Brigadier General W. S. Featheston—1st Arkansas (consolidated 1st and 2nd Mounted Rifles and 4th, 9th, 25th), 3rd Mississippi (consolidated 3rd, 31st, and 40th), 22nd Mississippi (consolidated 1st, 22nd, 33rd, and 1st Battalion), 37th Mississippi Battalion

Lowery's Brigade: Brigadier General Robert Lowery—29th Alabama, 12th Louisiana, 14th Mississippi (consolidated 5th, 14th and 43rd), 15th Mississippi (consolidated 6th, 15th, 20th and 23rd)

Shelley's Brigade: Brigadier General C. M. Shelley—1st Alabama (consolidated 16th, 33rd, and 45th), 17th Alabama, 27th Alabama (consolidated 27th, 35th, 49th, 55th, and 57th)

Walthall's (McLaws's) Division: Major General E. C. Walthall

Harrison's Brigade: Colonel George P. Harrsion, Jr.—1st Georgia (regulars), 5th Georgia, 5th Georgia Reserves, 32nd Georgia, 47th Georgia, Bonaud's Battalion

Conner's Brigade: Brigadier General John D. Kennedy—2nd South Carolina (consolidated 2nd, 20th, and Blanchard's Reserves), 3rd South Carolina (consolidated 3rd, 8th and 3rd Battalion), 7th South Carolina (consolidated 7th and 15th)

Artillery: Major A. Bunett Rhett—Anderson's Georgia Battery, Brooks' Georgia Battery, LeGardeur's Louisiana Battery, Parker's South Carolina Battery, Stuart's South Carolina Battery, Wheaton's Georgia Battery

Lee's Corps: Lieutenant General Stephen D. Lee

Hill's Division: Major General Daniel H. Hill

Sharp's Brigade: Brigadier General J. H. Sharp—24th Alabama (consolidated 24th, 28th, and 34th), 8th Mississippi Battalion (consolidated 5th, 8th, 32nd, and 3rd Battalion) 9th Mississippi (consolidated 7th, 9th, 10th, 41st, 44th, and 9th Battalion), 19th South Carolina (consolidated 10th and 19th)

Brantly's Brigade: Brigadier General W. F. Brantly—22nd Alabama (consolidated 22nd, 25th, 39th, and 50th), 37th Alabama (consolidated 37th, 42nd, 54th), 24th Mississippi (consolidated 24th, 27th, 29th, 30th, and 34th), 58th North Carolina (consolidated 58th and 60th)

Stevenson's Division: Major General Carter L. Stevenson

Henderson's Brigade: Brigadier General R. J. Henderson—1st Georgia Battalion (consolidated 1st Georgia Confederate, 1st Battalion, 25th, 29th, 30th, and 66th), 39th Georgia (consolidated 34th, 39th, and 56th), 40th Georgia Battalion (consolidated 40th, 41st, and 43rd), 42nd Georgia (consolidated 36th, 42nd, and 34th)

Pettus' Brigade: Brigadier General E. W. Pettus—19th Alabama, 20th Alabama, 23rd Alabama, 54th Virginia Battalion

Artilley: Kanapaux's South Carolina Battery

Cavalry: Lieutenant General Wade Hampton

Wheeler's Corps: Lieutenant General Joseph Wheeler

Butler's Division: Major General M. C. Butler

1st Alabama, 3rd Alabama, 51st Alabama, 2nd Georgia, 3rd Georgia, 4th Georgia, 5th Georgia, 6th Georgia, 12th Georgia, 1st Tennessee, 2nd Tennessee, 4th Tennessee, 5th Tennessee, 8th Tennessee, 9th Tennessee Battalion, 3rd Confederate, 8th Confederate, 10th Confederate, 1st Kentucky, 3rd Kentucky, 9th Kentucky, 3rd Arkansas, 8th Texas, 11th Texas, Allison's Squadron

Logan's Brigade: Brigadier General T. M. Logan—1st South Carolina, 4th South Carolina, 5th South Carolina, 6th South Carolina, 19th South Carolina Battalion, Phillips's Georgia Legion, Jeff Davis's Legion, Cobb's Georgia Legion, 10th Georgia

Artilley: Hart's South Carolina Battery, Earle's South Carolina Battery

Unassigned: Kelly's South Carolina Battery, Swett's Mississippi Battery, Abell's Floirda Battery, 10th North Carolina Battalion (company 1), 3rd North Carolina Artillery Battalion, 13th North Carolina Artillery Battalion, Pioneer Regiment, Naval Brigade

BIBLIOGRAPHY

Manuscripts

Adelbert M. Bly Papers. State Historical Society of Wisconsin, Madison, Wisconsin.

Albert Quincy Porter Papers. Library of Congress, Washington, DC.

Augustine Thomas Smythe Papers. Southern Historical Collection, University of North Carolina, Chapel Hill, North Carolina.

C. C. Platter Diary. University Archives, University of Georgia, Athens, Georgia.

Charles Berry, Sr., Papers. Iowa State Historical Society, Iowa City, Iowa.

Charles S. Brown Papers. Perkins Library, Duke University, Durham, North Carolina.

Charles S. Dickinson Diary. Charles H. Dickinson Papers. State Historical Society of Wisconsin, Madison, Wisconsin.

Conrad Cramer Papers. Greensboro Historical Museum, Greensboro, North Carolina.

Daniel Miles Tedder Diary. Daniel Miles Tedder Papers. Southern Historical Collection, University of North Carolina, Chapel Hill, North Carolina.

Ezra Button Diary. John B. Tripp Papers. State Historical Society of Wisconsin, Madison, Wisconsin.

Frank L. Ferguson papers. Military History Institute, US Army, Carlisle Barracks, Pennsylvania.

General Lafayette McLaws Papers. Southern Historical Collection, University of North Carolina, Chapel Hill, North Carolina.

Gibson County Civil War Papers. Indiana Historical Society, Indianapolis, Indiana.

Griffith Family Papers. Iowa State Historical Museum and Archives, Des Moines, Iowa.

Heartt and Wilson Family Papers. Southern Historical Collection, University of North Carolina, Chapel Hill, North Carolina.

James A. Congleton Papers. Library of Congress, Washington, DC.

James Burkhalter Diary. Illinois State Historical Society, Spingfield, Illinois.

James T. Reeve Papers. State Historical Society of Wisconsin, Madison, Wisconsin.

John Batchelor Diary. Illinois State Historical Society, Spingfield, Illinois.

John D. Inskeep Papers. Ohio Historical Society, Columbus, Ohio.

John E. Risedorph Diary. Minnesota Historical Society, St. Paul, Minnesota.

John W. Daniel Papers. Perkins Library, Duke University, Durham, North Carolina.

John Wesley Daniels Diary. Bentley Historical Library, University of Michigan, Ann Arbor, Michigan.

L. T. Hunt Papers. Ohio Historical Society, Columbus, Ohio.

Levi Nelson Green Diary. Minnesota Historical Society, St. Paul, Minnesota.

Robert Bruce Hoadley Papers. Perkins Library, Duke University, Durham, North Carolina.

R. P. Howell Papers. Southern Historical Collection, University of North Carolina, Chapel Hill, North Carolina.

S. S. Farewell Papers. Iowa State Historical Society, Iowa City, Iowa.

Thomas Smythe Letters. Southern Historical Collection, University of North Carolina, Chapel Hill, North Carolina.

W. C. Johnson Diary. Library of Congress, Washington, DC.

W. McK. Heath Diary. Ohio Historical Society, Columbus, Ohio.

William C. Robinson Papers. Illinois State Historical Society, Spingfield, Illinois.

William T. Humphrey Papers. Chicago Public Library, Chicago, Illinois.

Primary Sources

Anderson, Mary Ann, editor. *The Civil War Diary of Allen Morgan Geer: Twentieth Regiment/Illinois Volunteers*. New York: Cosmos Press, 1977.

Aten, Henry J. *History of the 85th Illinois Volunteers*. Hiawatha IL: Regimental Association, 1901.

Bauer, Jack K. *Soldiering: The Civil War Diary of Rice C. Bull, 123rd New York Volunteer Infantry*. San Rafael CA: Presidio Press, 1977.

Belknap, C. E. *Bentonville: "What a Bummer Knows About It."* Volume 12. Washington, DC: The Military Order of the Loyal Legion of the United States, District of Columbia, 1887.

Bell, John T. *Tramps and Triumphs of the Second Iowa Infantry*. Omaha NE: Gibson, Miller, and Richardson, 1886.

Bennett, L. G. and Haigh, W. M. *History of the Thirty-Sixth Regiment Illinois Volunteers, During the War of the Rebellion*. Aurora IL: Knickerbocker & Hodder, Printers and Binders, 1876.

Bradley, G. B. *The Star Corps; or Notes of an Army Chaplain During Sherman's March to the Sea*. Milwaukee: Jermain & Brightman, 1865.

Boyle, John Richard. *Soldiers True: The Story of the One Hundred and Eleventh Regiment Pennsylvania Veteran Volunteers*. New York Eaton & Sons, 1903.

Brooks, A. L. and Hugh T. Lefler. *The Papers of Walter Clark*. Chapel Hill: University of North Carolina Press, 1948.

Brown, Alonzo L. *History of the Fourth Regiment of Minnesota Infantry Volunteer*. St. Paul: The Pioneer Press, 1892.

Brown, Norman D. *One of Cleburne's Command: The Civil War Reminiscences and Diary of Capt. Samuel T. Foster, Granbury's Texas Brigade CSA*. Austin: University of Texas Press, 1980.

Calkins, William. *The History of the One Hundred and Fourth Regiment of Illinois Volunteer Infantry*. Chicago: Donohue & Henneberry, 1895.

Canfield, S. S. *History of the 21st Regiment Ohio Volunteer Infantry*. Toledo: Vrooman, Anderson & Bateman, 1893.

Capers, Walter Branham. *The Soldier-Bishop: Ellison Capers*. New York, 1912.

Carlin, General William P. *The Battle of Bentonville*. Volume 3. Cincinnati: Military Order of the Loyal Legion of the United States, Ohio; Robert Clark and Company, 1884.

Chamberlain, W. H. *History of the Eighty-First Regiment, Ohio Infantry Volunteers,* Cincinnati Gazette Steam Printing House, 1865.

Clark, Walter. *Histories of the Several Regiments and Battalions from North Carolina in the Great War, 1861-1865*. 5 volumes. Raleigh, 1901.

Clark, Walter A. *Under the Stars and Bars*. Augusta GA: Chronicle Printing Company, 1960.

Cluett, William. *History of the 57th Regiment Volunteer Infantry*. Princeton: Lesee Republican Job Department, 1886.

Collins, George. *Memoirs of the 149th Regiment New York Volunteer Infantry*. St. Louis: Nixon-Jones Printing Company, 1893.

Committee. *Ninety-Second Illinois Volunteer*. Freeport IL: Journal Steam Publishing House and Bookbindery, 1875.

Committee. *The Story of the Fifty-Fifth Regiment Illinois Volunteer Infantry*. Clinton MA: W. J. Coulter, Clinton, 1887.

Cox, General Jacob Dolson. *Military Reminiscences of the Civil War*. New York: Charles Scribner's Sons, 1900.

Croom, Wendell. *The War History of Company C Sixth Georgia Regiment*. Fort Valley: Survivors of the Company, 1879.

Dean, Benjamin. *Recollections of the 26th Missouri Infantry,* Southwest Missourian Office, Lamar, 1892.

Develling, C. T. *History of the Seventeenth Regiment*. Zanesville OH: E. R. Sullivan, 1889.

Dickert, D. Augustus. *History of Kershaw's Brigade*. Dayton OH: Morningside Bookshop, 1976.

Dougall, Captain Allan H. *Bentonville*. Indianapolis: The Military Order of the Loyal Legion of the United States, Indiana, 1898.

Eddy, T. M. *The Patriotism of Illinois. A Record of the Civil and Military History of the State in the War for the Union*. Chicago: Clarke & Company Publishers, 1866.

Evans, General Clement A. *Confederate Military History*. 12 volumes. New York: Thomas Yoseloff, 1962.

Fleharty, S. F. *Our Regiment: A History of the 102nd Illinois Infantry Volunteers*. Chicago: Brewster & Hanscom, 1865.

Fletcher, William. *Rebel Private: Front and Rear*. Austin: University of Texas Press, 1954.

Floyd, David. *History of the Seventy-Fifth Regiment Indiana Infantry Volunteers*. Philadelphia, 1893.

Gage, M. D. *From Vicksburg to Raleigh, or a Complete History of the Twelfth Regiment Indiana Volunteer Infantry*. Chicago: Clark & Company, 1865.

Garrett, Jill. *Confederate Diary of Robert D. Smith*. Columbia SC: United Daughters of the Confederacy, 1975.

Grant, U. S. *Personal Memoirs*. 2 volumes. New York: Charles L. Webster & Company, 1885.

Grecian, J. *History of the Eighty-Third Regiment, Indiana Volunteer Infantry*. Cincinnati: John F. Uhlhorn, 1865.

Grigsby, Melvin. *The Smoked Yank*. Sioux Falls SD: Bell Publishing Company, 1888.

Grunert, William, *History of the One Hundred and Twenty-Ninth Regiment Illinois Volunteer Infantry*. Winchester: R. B. Dedman, 1866.

Hagood, General Johnson. *Memoirs of the War of the Succession*. Columbia SC, 1910.

Hays, E. Z. *History of the Thirty-Second Regiment Ohio Volunteer Infantry*. Columbus OH: Cott & Evans, 1896.

Hinkley, Julian. *Service With the Third Wisconsin Infantry*. Madison: Wisconsin History Committee, 1912.

Holmes, J. Taylor. *52nd O.V.I. Then and Now*. Columbus OH: Berlin Print, 1989.

Horrall, S. F. *History of the Forty-Second Indiana Volunteer Infantry*. Chicago: self published, 1892.

Howard, General O. O. *Autobiography of Oliver Otis Howard*. 2 volumes. New York: The Baker & Taylor Company, 1908.

Howe, M. A. DeWolfe. *Marching with Sherman: Passages from the Letters and Campaign Diaries of HENRY HITCHCOCK Major and Assistant Adjutant General of Volunteers November 1864-May 1865*. New Haven: Yale University Press, 1927.

Hubert, Charles. *History of the Fiftieth Regiment Illinois Volunteer Infantry*. Kansas City: Western Veteran Publishing Company, 1894.

Inglesby, Charles. *Historical Sketch of the First South Carolina Artillery*. Charleston: n.p., n.d. Duke University Pamphlet Collection.

Jackson, David P. *The Colonels Diary: Journals Kept before and during the Civil War by the Late Colonel Oscar L. Jackson of New Castle, Pennsylvania, Sometimes Commander of the 63rd Regiment O.V.I.* Sharon PA: self published, 1922.

Johnston, General Joseph E. *Narrative of Military Operations Directed During the Late War Between the States by Joseph E. Johnston, General, C.S.A.* New York: D.Appleton and Company, 1874.

Jones, John B. *A Rebel War Clerk's Diary*. Volume 2. Philadelphia: J. B. Lippincott & Company, 1866.

Kinnear, J. R. *History of the Eighty-Sixth Regiment Illinois Volunteer Infantry*, Chicago: Tribune Company's Book and Job Printing Office, 1866.

Lucas, D. R. *History of the 99th Indiana Infantry*. Lafayette IN: Rossert, Spring, 1985.

Marcy, Major Henry C. *Sherman's Campaign in the Carolinas*. Boston: The Military Order of the Loyal Legion of the United States, Massachusetts, 1900.

Marshall, R. V. *An Historical Sketch of the Twenty-Second Regiment Indiana Volunteers*. Madison: Courier Company, 1877.

Marvin, Edwin E. *The Fifth Regiment Connecticut Volunteers*. Hartford CT: Wiley Waterman & Eaton, 1889.

McCain, General Warren. *A Soldiers' Diary or the History of Company L Third Indiana Cavalry*. Indianapolis: Warren A. Patton, 1885.

McAdams, F. M. *Every-Day Soldier Life*. Columbus: Chas. M. Cott & Company, 1884.

McClurg, Alexander C. *The Last Chance of the Confederacy*. Chicago: The Military Order of the Loyal Legion of the United States, Illinois; A. C. McClurg and Company, 1891.

Merrill, Samuel. *The Seventieth Indiana Volunteer Infantry*. Indianapolis: The Bowen-Merrill Company, 1900.

Morse, Loren. *Civil War Diaries of Bliss Morse*. Boston: Pittcraft, 1964.

Nichols, Major George Ward. *The Story of the Great March, From the Diary of a Staff Officer*. New York: Harper & Bros. Publishers, 1865.

Ninety-Second Illinois Volunteers. Freeport IL: Journal Steam and Bookbindery, 1875.

Orendorff, H. H. *Reminiscences of the Civil War From Diaries of Members of the 103rd Illinois Volunteer Infantry*. Chicago: Press of J. F. Leaming & Company, 1904.

Osborn, Hartwell. *Trials and Triumphs: The Record of the Fifty-Fifth Ohio Volunteer Infantry*. Chicago: A. C. McClurg & Company, 1904.

Osborn, Thomas. *The Fiery Trail: A Union Officer's Account of Sherman's Last Campaigns*. Knoxville: University of Tennessee Press, 1986.

Owens, Ira. *Greene County Soldiers in the Late War, Being a History of the Seventy Fourth O.V.I.* Dayton OH: Christian Publishing House Print, 1884.

Payne, Edwin. *History of the Thirty-Fourth Regiment of Illinois Volunteer Infantry*. Clinton IA: Allen Publishing Company, 1903.

Pepper, George. *Personal Recollections of Sherman's Campaigns in Georgia and the Carolinas*. Zanesville OH: High Dunne, 1866.

Perry, Henry. *History of the Thirty-Eighth Regiment Indiana Volunteer Infantry*. Palo Alto CA: F. A. Stuart, 1906.

Pinney, Nelson A. *History of the One Hundred and Fourth Ohio Volunteer Infantry During the War of the Rebellion from 1862-1866*. Akron OH: Werner and Loman, 1866.

Porter, General Horace. *Campaigning With Grant*. New York: The Century Company, 1897.

Quint, Alonzo. *The Record of the Second Massachusetts Infantry*. Boston: James P. Walker, 1867.

Remington, Cyrus. *A Record of Battery I, First N.Y. Light Artillery Volumes*. Buffalo: Press of the Courier Company, 1891.

Ricks, Augustus J. *Carrying The News Of Lee's Surrender to the Army of the Ohio*. Cincinnati: The Military Order of the Loyal Legion of the United States, Ohio; Robert Clarke & Company, 1888.

Ridley, R. L. *Battles and Sketches of the Army of Tennessee*. Mexico MO: Missouri Publishing Company, 1906.

Rogers, Robert. *The 125th Regiment Illinois Volunteer Infantry*. Champaign IL: Gazette Steam Print, 1882.

Rood, H. H. *History of Company A Thirteenth Iowa Veteran Infantry*. Cedar Rapids MI: Daily Republican, 1889.

Rood, H. W. *Story of the Service of Company E, and the Twelfth Wisconsin Regiment, Veteran Volunteer Infantry*. Milwaukee: Swain & Tate Company, 1893.

SeCheverell, J. Hamp, *Journal History of the Twenty-Ninth Ohio Veteran Volunteers 1861-1865*. Cleveland: n.p., 1883.

Sherlock, E. J. *Memorabilia of the Marches and Battles in which the One Hundredth Regiment of Indiana Infantry Took an Active Part*. Kansas City: Gerard-Woody Printing Company, 1896.

Sherman, General William T. *Memoirs of W. T. Sherman By Himself*. 2 volumes. New York: Charles L. Webster & Company, 1891.

Smith, Charles. *The History of Fuller's Ohio Brigade*. Cleveland: A. J. Watt, 1909.

Spencer, Cornelia. *The Last Ninety Days of the War in North Carolina*. New York: Watchman Publishing Company, 1866.

Stevenson, Thomas. *History of the 78th Regiment O.V.I.* Zanesville OH: Hugh Donne, 1865.

Stewart, Nixon. *Dan McCook's Regiment. 52nd O.V.I.* Alliance: self published, 1900.

Storrs, John. *The Twentieth Connecticut*. Ansonia CT: Press of the Naugatuck Valley Sentinel, 1886.

Sutherland, Daniel E. *Reminiscences of a Private: William E. Bevens of the First Arkansas Infantry, C.S.A.* Fayetteville: University of Arkansas Press, 1992.

Taylor, John. *Sixteenth South Carolina Regiment, C.S.A, From Greenville County, S.C.* self published, 1963.

Temple, Wayne C. *The Civil War Letters of Henry C. Bear: A Soldier in the 116th Illinois Volunteer Infantry*. Harrogate: Lincoln Memorial University Press, 1961.

The War of the Rebellion: A Compilation f the Official Records of the Union and Confederate Armies. 128 volumes. Washington, DC: Government Printing Office, 1880-1901.

Toombs, Samuel. *Reminiscences of the War, Comprising a Detailed Account of the Experiences of the Thirteenth Regiment New Jersey Volunteers*. Orange NJ: Journal Office, 1878.

Tourgee, Albion W. *The Story of a Thousand; Being a History of the Service of the 105th Ohio Volunteer Infantry in the War for the Union from August 21, 1862 to June 6, 1865*. Buffalo: S. McGerald & Son, 1896.

Trimble, Harvey. *History of the Ninety-Third Regiment Illinois Volunteer Infantry*. Chicago: The Blakely Printing Company, 1898.

Underwood, Adin. *The Three Years' Service of the Thirty-Third Mass. Infantry Regiment, 1862-1865*. Boston: A. Williams & Company, 1881.

Williamson, Charles. *Reminiscences of a Boy's Service with the 76th Ohio*. Menasha OH: George Banta Publishing Company, 1908.

Winther, Oscar Osburn. *With Sherman to the Sea: The Civil War Letters Diaries & Reminiscences of Theodore Upson*. Baton Rouge: Louisiana State University Press, 1943.

Worsham, William J. *Old Nineteenth Tennessee Regiment, C.S.A.* Knoxville: Paragon Printing Company, 1902.

Wright, Henry. *History of the Sixth Iowa Infantry*. Iowa City: State Historical Society of Iowa, 1923.

Newspapers, Magazines, and Periodicals

Anderson, Mrs. John H. "North Carolina Boy Soldiers at the Battle of Bentonville." *Confederate Veteran Magazine* 35/3 (1927): 174–76.

———. "What Sherman Did to Fayetteville." *Confederate Veteran Magazine* 32/2 (1924): 138–40.

Buford, M. M. "Surrender of Johnston's Army." *Confederate Veteran Magazine* 28/3 (1920): 170–71.

Davis, M. J. "Eighth Texas Cavalry at Bentonville." *Confederate Veteran Magazine* 23/3 (1915): 184.

"Died in the Last Ditch." *Confederate Veteran Magazine* 2/3 (1894): 200.

Ford, A. P. "The Last Battles of Hardee's Corps." *The Southern Bivouac* 8 (August 1885): 141.

Fuller, D. F. "Battles at Averasboro, N.C." *Confederate Veteran Magazine* 5/3 (1897): 151–52.

"Gen. Joseph Wheeler's Farewell to his Men." *Confederate Veteran Magazine* 1/1 (1893): 62.

Halsey, Ashley, Jr. "The Last Duel in the Confederacy." *Civil War Times Illustrated* 1/7 (November 1962): 6–8, 31.

Harcourt, A. P. "Terry's Texas Rangers." *The Southern Bivouac* 11 (November 1882): 96–97.

Holman, J. A. "Concerning the Battle at Bentonville." *Confederate Veteran Magazine* 6/3 (1899): 153–54.

Holmes, James G. "The Artillery at Bentonville." *Confederate Veteran Magazine* 3/2 (1895): 103.

Lambert, R. A. "In the Battle of Bentonville." *Confederate Veteran Magazine* 37/3 (1929): 221–23.

Lawrence, R. DeT. "On the Retreat from Charleston." *Confederate Veteran Magazine* 29/2 (1931): 90.

McGuin, J. P. "Greek Meeting Greek." *The Southern Bivouac* 8 (August 1884): 549–50.

Miller, G. K. Untitled article. *Confederate Veteran Magazine* 3/2 (1895): 71.

Morris, W. H. "The Other Side at Fayetteville, N.C." *Confederate Veteran Magazine* 20/2 (1912): 83–84.

Ravenell, Samuel W. Untitled article. *Confederate Veteran Magazine* 47/1 (1939): 124.

Ridley, B. L. "Last Battles of the War." *Confederate Veteran Magazine* 3/1 (1895): 20, 70–71.

Sanders, Robert W. "The Battle of Averasboro, N.C." *Confederate Veteran Magazine* 34/4 (1926): 215–16, 299–300.

Smith, Jessie S. "On the Battlefield of Averasboro, N.C." *Confederate Veteran Magazine* 34/1 (1926): 48–50.

Thompson, Charles Willis. "The Golden Anniversary of Peace within the Union." *New York Times*, 4 April 1915, 1.

Vance, Senator Zebulon. "Last Days of the War, North Carolina." *Confederate Veteran Magazine* 6/3 (1898): 211–13.

Watson, B. F. "In the Battle of Bentonville." *Confederate Veteran Magazine* 37/2 (1929): 95.

Wood, A. "The Last Shots by Gen. Johnston's Army." *Confederate Veteran Magazine* 16/6 (1908): 585.

Secondary Sources

Adamson, A. P. *Brief History of the Thirtieth Georgia Regiment.* Jonesboro GA: Freedom Hill Press, Inc., 1987.

Anders, Leslie. *The Eighteenth Missouri*. Indianapolis: The Bobbs-Merrill Company, 1968.

Andrews, W. H. *Footprints of a Regiment: A Recollection of the 1st GA. Regulars 1861-1865*. Atlanta GA: Longstreet Press, 1992.

Barnard, Harry Vollie. *Tattered Volunteers: The Twenty-Seventh Alabama Infantry Regiment, C.S.A.* Northport NY: Hemitage Press, 1965.

Barrett, John Gilchrist. *North Carolina as a Civil War Battleground.* Raleigh: North Carolina Department of Cultural Resources, 1980.

Barrett, John G. *Sherman's March Through the Carolinas*. Chapel Hill: University of North Carolina Press, 1956.

———. *The Civil War in North Carolina*. Chapel Hill: University of North Carolina Press, 1963.

Blassingame, Wyatt. *William Tecumseh Sherman: Defender of the Union*. Englewood Cliffs NJ: Prentice-Hall, Inc., 1970.

Bowman, John S. *The Civil War Almanac*. New York: Gallery Books, 1983.

Boyd, James P. *The Life of General William T. Sherman*. New York: Publishers' Union, 1891.

Bradley, Mark L. *Last Stand in the Carolinas: The Battle of Bentonville*. Campbell CA: Savas Publishing Company, 1996.

Brown, Thaddeus C. S., Samuel J. Murphy, and William G. Putney. *Behind the Guns: The History of Battery I 2nd Regiment, Illinois Light Artillery*. Carbondale: Southern Illinois University Press, 1965.

Canfield, Cass. *The Iron Will of Jefferson Davis*. New York: Fairfax Press, 1978.

Commager, Henry Steele. *The Blue and The Gray*. New York: Fairfax Press, 1982.

Connelly, Thomas Lawrence. *Autumn of Glory: The Army of Tennessee, 1862-1865*. Baton Rouge: Louisiana State University Press, 1971.

Daniel, Larry J. *Cannoneers in Gray: The Field Artillery of the Army of Tennessee, 1861-1865*. Tuscaloosa: University of Alabama Press, 1984.

Davis, William C. *Battle at Bull Run: A History of the First Major Campaign of the Civil War*. Baton Rouge: Louisiana State University Press, 1977.

Dunkelman, Mark H. and Michael J. Winey. *The Hardtack Regiment: An Illustrated History of the 154th Regiment, New York State Infantry Volunteers*. Rutherford NJ: Fairleigh Dickinson University Press, 1981.

Edwards, William B. *Civil War Guns*. Secaucus NJ: Castle Books, 1962.

Eisenciml, Otto and Ralph Newman. *The American Iliad*. Indianapolis: The Bobbs-Merrill Company, 1947.

Faust, Patricia L. *Historical Times Illustrated Encyclopedia of the Civil War*. New York: Harper Perennial, 1986.

Foote, Shelby. *The Civil War: A Narrative*. New York: Random House, 1958.

Gibson, John M. *Those 163 Days: A Southern Account of Sherman's March From Atlanta to Raleigh*. New York: Bramhall House, 1961.

Glatthaar, Joseph T. *The March to the Sea and Beyond: Sherman's Troops in the Savannah and Carolinas Campaigns*. New York: New York University Press, 1986.

Hallock, Judith Lee. *Braxton Bragg and Confederate Defeat*. Volume 2. Tuscaloosa: University of Alabama Press, 1991.

Hattaway, Herman. *General Stephen D. Lee*. Jackson: University Press of Mississippi, 1976.

Headley, J. T. *The Great Rebellion*. Washington, DC: The National Tribune, 1866.

Hendricks, Howard O. "Imperiled City: The Movement of the Union and Confederate Armies Toward Greensboro in the Closing Days of the Civil War in North Carolina." Master's thesis, University of North Carolina, Greensboro, 1987. Manuscript section, library of The University of North Carolina at Greensboro.

Hicken, Victor. *Illinois in the Civil War*. Urbana: University of Illinois Press, 1966.

Holland, J. G. *The Life of Abraham Lincoln*. Springfield: Gurdon Bill, 1866.

Hughes, Nathaniel Cheairs, Jr. *General William J. Hardee: Old Reliable*. Baton Rouge: Louisiana State University Press, 1965.

———. *Bentonville: The Final Battle of Sherman & Johnston*. Chapel Hill: University of North Carolina Press, 1996.

Johnson, Robert Underwood and Clarence Clough Buel. *Battles and Leaders of the Civil War*. 4 volumes. New York: The Century Company, 1884–1888.

Leeper, Lieutenant Colonel Wesley Thurman. *Rebels Valiant: Second Arkansas Mounted Rifles (Dismounted)*. Little Rock: Pioneer Press, 1964.

Lindsley, John Barrien. *The Military Annals of Tennessee: Confederate First Series, Embracing a Review of Military Operations with Regimental and Memorial Rolls Compiled from Original and Official Sources*. Nashville: J. M. Lindsley, 1886.

Losson, Christopher. *Tennessee's Forgotten Warriors: Frank Cheatham and His Confederate Division*. Knoxville: University of Tennessee Press, 1989.

Luvaas, Jay. *The Battle Bentonville March 19-20-21, 1865*. Smithfield NC: Bentonville United Daughters of the Confederacy, n.d.

McFeely, William S. *Grant: A Biography*. New York: W. W. Norton & Company, 1982.

New York Monuments Commission. *In Memoriam: Henry Warner Slocum 1826-1894*. Albany: J. B. Lyon Company Printers, 1904.

The Photographic History of the Civil War. Secaucus: The Blue & Grey Press, 1987.

Roman, Alfred. *The Military Operations of General Beauregard in the War Between the States 1861-1865 Including a Brief Sketch and Narrative of Service in the War with Mexico*. New York: Harper and Brattens, 1884.

Rowell, John W. *Yankee Cavalrymen: Through the Civil War with the Ninth Pennsylvania Cavalry*. Knoxville: University of Tennessee Press, 1971.

Seitz, Don C. *Braxton Bragg: General of the Confederacy*. Columbia: The State Company, 1924.

Symonds, Craig L. *Joseph E. Johnston: A Civil War Biography*. New York: W. W. Norton & Company, 1992.

Tenney, W. J. *The Military and Naval History of the Rebellion in the United States with Biographical Sketches of Deceased Officers*. New York: D. Appleton & Company, 1867.

Warner, Ezra J. *Generals in Blue: Lives of the Union Commanders*. Baton Rouge: Louisiana State University Press, 1960.

———. *Generals in Grey: Lives of the Confederate Commanders.* Baton Rouge: Louisiana State University Press, 1959.

Wharton, Don. *Smithfield As Seen by Sherman's Soldiers*. Smithfield NC: Smithfield Herald Publishing Company, 1977.

Wheeler, Richard. *Sherman's March: An Eyewitness History of The Cruel Campaign the helped end a Crueler War*. New York: Thomas Y. Crowell, Publishers, 1978.

Woodward, W. E. *Meet General Grant*. New York: Liveright Publishing Corporation, 1928.

Yearns, W. Buck and Barrett, John G. *North Carolina Civil War Documentary*. Chapel Hill: University of North Carolina Press, 1980.

INDEX